the arts–education interface:
a mutual learning triangle?

John Harland
Pippa Lord
Alison Stott
Kay Kinder
Emily Lamont
Mary Ashworth

Published in June 2005 by the
National Foundation for Educational Research
The Mere, Upton Park
Slough, Berkshire SL1 2DQ

Designed by Stuart Gordon at NFER
Figures by Patricia Lewis
Cover photograph courtesy of Kate Dyer

Contents

Foreword

It gives me great pleasure to introduce *The Arts-Education Interface: a mutual learning triangle?* As a member of the then Arts Council of England, I enjoyed working with the Education and Training department at the Arts Council on the early development of the arts-education interface (AEI). It is therefore richly satisfying to see the results of this innovative programme of action research.

Although the AEI built on many years of experience of artists working in schools, it represented a steep change in arts education. First, it was designed from the outset to be a research programme. It had a clear hypothesis to test: that different outcomes would be achieved by different models of arts intervention in schools. Second, it was tailored to a specific context – two Education Action Zones (EAZs) – in two contrasting areas of England. Third, the Arts Council worked in a new way, by employing coordinators in each of the zones to broker relationships between schools on the one hand and artists and arts organisations on the other.

Brokerage has been further developed in the Arts Council's Creative Partnerships programme. But in this important national programme, creative directors do more than just broker relationships between schools and artists. Creative Partnerships (CPs) are jointly planned by schools, CP staff and artists – a partnership at many different levels.

There are significant learning points in the report for those working in arts education and for those using the arts to help teaching and learning become more creative. My hope is that the results of the research will be of value to practitioners and help shape practice in schools.

I would like warmly to thank John Harland and his team at the National Foundation for Educational Research for their hard work in managing a complex and ambitious research programme resulting in a report which makes a significant contribution to our knowledge and understanding of arts education. Thanks are due, too, to those Arts Council staff who have worked so hard to make the AEI a success. Last, but certainly not least, I would like to thank the teachers and pupils of the participating schools, the artists, LEA and EAZ staff, all of whom contributed to the constructive outcomes of the initiative. When it started, the subject of arts and education was already important. In the meantime, it has become very, very important.

Sir Christopher Frayling, Chair, Arts Council England

Acknowledgements

First and foremost, we are indebted to all the pupils, teachers, artists, Local Education Authority and Education Action Zone personnel who gave us their valuable time throughout the demanding fieldwork phase of the research. The study would not have been possible without them.

We would also like to acknowledge the vital contribution of the Arts Council England, who funded and managed the programme and its research. We would particularly like to thank John Conlon, national coordinator of the Arts and Education Interface (AEI) at the Arts Council, for his insightful advice and support throughout. We are especially grateful to Sara Rickard and Ruth Treharne, the two regional Arts Council coordinators, for their enthusiasm and commitment in the liaison work with artists, schools and ourselves. Our thanks are also extended to Helen Clare, Kerry Furneaux, Ann Bridgwood and Karen Dust of the Arts Council.

We would like to acknowledge the valuable contributions made by our former colleagues, Satpal Kaur and Paul Doherty, in conducting some of the fieldwork. We would also like to thank Satpal for the formidable task of coordinating the data processing, as well as Bethan Evans for her initial analytical work. We are also grateful to Caroline Gulliver for her help with the preliminary coding of the data. We would also like to thank Stuart Gordon and the staff of CMIS for their work on the book and its launch, and Hilary McElderry, Sally Wilson, Ann Black and Julie Thompson for their secretarial support throughout the project.

Executive summary

Introduction, aims and methods

In 2001, the then Arts Council of England[i] and Regional Arts Boards launched the Arts and Education Interface (AEI) initiative. Its aim was to explore the relationship between the arts and education through a programme of arts-based interventions organised within the Education Action Zones (EAZs) of Bristol and Corby. The Arts Council commissioned the National Foundation for Educational Research (NFER) to study these interventions[ii].

The aims of the research were:

- to examine the outcomes of different interventions on pupils and young people, teachers, schools, artists and arts organisations
- to explore the factors that affect the range and quality of those effects
- to draw out any general lessons for developing effective practices.

The study researched 15 interventions, which took place during the academic years 2001/02 and 2002/03. The sample included a cross-section of schooling phases, different educational sectors and a range of artforms. Partnerships between the arts and education communities were initiated by locally based AEI Arts Council coordinators. The research followed the progress of five one-off interventions, four multiple artform series interventions and three developmental single artform interventions – all of which had a focus on the pupils' or young people's learning. The remaining three interventions concentrated on the professional development of teachers.

For each intervention, the fieldwork comprised the collection of data in three phases:

- baseline (prior to the intervention taking place)
- intervention and immediate impact (during or immediately after)
- follow-up (longer-term).

Data was collected through a range of techniques, including one-to-one interviews, questionnaires and observations. Pupils, teachers, headteachers, artists, arts organisation directors and EAZ and Arts Council staff were interviewed. In total, 690 interviews were conducted.

The outcomes of arts interventions

Outcomes for pupils and young people

Eleven broad categories of effects for pupils and young people were identified. The most frequently and strongly reported of these were:

- affective outcomes such as enjoyment, pride and a sense of achievement

- artform knowledge, appreciation, skills and techniques

- personal development, especially self-esteem and self-confidence

- social development, particularly teamwork and awareness of others.

There were mid-ranking levels of impact on developments in creativity, changes in attitudes towards the arts and transfer beyond the arts. The effects nominated least frequently and with limited intensity were knowledge and skills beyond the arts, social and cultural knowledge, thinking skills and communication and expressive skills.

In general, there was a fairly high degree of correspondence between aims and outcomes. Where aimed for, outcomes were more strongly achieved than where they were not aimed for and some of the least commonly cited aims reflected the lowest profile pupil outcomes: social and cultural knowledge, thinking skills and general communication and expressive skills. However, there were higher profile outcomes in the broad category 'personal development' than had been aimed for (particularly for self-confidence and self-esteem), whereas there was a lower profile for creativity compared with other types of outcome than had been aimed for. Outcomes such as improvements in attitudes towards and behaviour in the artform, transfers to life in school and to self-esteem were the most likely types of outcome to be achieved even where they were not aimed for. On the other hand, knowledge and skills beyond the artform and outcomes related to social and cultural knowledge were unlikely to be achieved unless they were a specific aim.

Each of the artforms displayed distinctive configurations of outcomes for pupils. Comparatively, the visual arts engendered developments in creativity, aesthetic judgement making and interpretative skills more highly than any other artform. Dance was relatively strong on teamwork and physical wellbeing outcomes. Drama displayed the greatest potential for generating a wide array of effects, as well as for 'strong' impacts. Whilst music produced the narrowest range of effects, it was the only artform to stimulate impacts comparatively strongly in the realms of social and cultural knowledge.

Gains in artform appreciation and confidence in their own artform ability were more prevalent among secondary school pupils than their primary counterparts, whilst primary schools monopolised knowledge, skills and appreciation beyond the arts as an outcome. Compared with the effects of arts education in the normal in-school secondary arts curriculum (Harland *et al.*, 2000), AEI arts interventions in secondary schools were more likely to deliver artform appreciation and high levels of enjoyment, but less likely to achieve expressive skills.

One-off interventions resulted in a narrower range of reported effects than those where pupils experienced multiple phases. Examples of developmental or sustained learning, continuity or progression seldom occurred. Only a limited number of 'outcome routes' were identified and these were more likely to be found in the developmental or multiple-phase interventions that were conceived as sequential.

The pre- and post-questionnaire results showed a slight decline in many secondary pupils' perceptions about their learning in the arts and about themselves in relation to school. In terms of attitudes towards the arts, the most notable change in a negative direction occurred for the item, 'I really enjoy ... I really dislike [the artform] at school'. The downward trend in perceptions of 'self' was evident in many of the items. Pupils in one particular phase (occurring at the start of their secondary school careers) became less favourable in their attitudes on all 16 of the questionnaire items about self (e.g. self-esteem, understanding themselves, self-image at school, ability and in relations with others). Although these results may signal a sobering backcloth of declining levels of positive self-esteem for many pupils, the high impact of the arts interventions (according to the interviewees' testimony) on exactly these qualities of personal development takes on new significance and meaning. This, taken together with the above finding on incremental learning, may point to the need for longer-term strategies that sustain and develop learning outcomes, as well as particular qualities such as self-esteem.

Outcomes for teachers, schools and host institutions

The most frequently nominated outcomes for teachers and schools across the range of interventions (pupil-focused and teacher-focused) were:

- enhanced knowledge and skills, particularly artform knowledge and skills in managing arts interventions

- impacts on classroom practices, particularly modelling on the artists

- institutional and strategic outcomes, chiefly in multi-phase interventions where sequential links were planned for.

Other outcomes for teachers comprised motivational and attitudinal (e.g. enthusiasm to recreate artists' practices); affective outcomes (e.g. enjoyment and confidence, although this could also be undermined) and new awareness (e.g. seeing pupils or the artform in a new light).

In addition, for teachers involved in teacher-focused interventions, material and provisionary outcomes, on which they could draw following the interventions, were prevalent. Despite this, for all types of intervention, the extent to which teachers were able to make significant and sustained changes to their practice remained an open question.

Outcomes for artists and arts organisations

Generally, effects on artists were less frequent and appeared less substantial than those on pupils and teachers. The most frequently mentioned outcomes for artists were:

- new awareness and value shifts (e.g. changes in perceptions and values concerning alternative teaching or classroom management styles)

- affective outcomes (e.g. sense of achievement, satisfaction and enjoyment, although some relayed disappointments and frustrations)

- enhanced knowledge and skills, in particular understanding different pupils' capabilities.

However, many of the effects cited by artists appeared to be of an immediate or short-term nature, or quite minor in scope. In particular, it seemed that for experienced arts educators there was limited capacity for gaining outcomes which were distinctive from those already acquired from their previous work. However, there was evidence that longer interventions had allowed artists to reflect on their practices and refine them in a sustained and incremental manner.

Outcomes overall

A second-level analysis, drawing together the outcomes for pupils, teachers and artists (previously considered separately) and involving a criterion-based rating by the researchers, was undertaken. This involved the rating of each phase in the 15 interventions into high, medium or low outcomes for effects on pupils, teachers and artists. According to the overall ratings:

- very few interventions achieved high impact across the board for all participants
- most commonly, there was a higher impact for pupils than for teachers, who in turn generally received a higher impact rating than artists
- the highest effects ratings for teachers were not necessarily in those focused on providing professional development for teachers.

Factors that affect the outcomes of arts interventions

Factors that affect outcomes for pupils

From a framework of 20 broad factors perceived to affect pupil outcomes, the highest profile factors emerged as:

- artist's pedagogy
- type of content
- manageability
- emphasis on the end product
- pupil factors
- relevance
- artist–pupil relationship
- continuity and progression.

Other factors deemed to impart an important influence on pupil outcomes included enjoyability, group size, group composition and issues relating to timing or duration.

However, when researchers used a second-level analysis to examine the interventions which appeared to be the most successful in terms of pupil outcomes (i.e. impact ratings denoting breadth, depth, corroboration and triangulation of sources and aims achieved), four features were consistently apparent in the effective interventions. According to this second-level researcher analysis[iii], features that were commonly associated with high effect ratings included:

- type of intervention
- the nature and extent of planning
- artist–teacher relationship
- the amount and spread of time.

In other words, the highest impact ratings were to be found in multiple phase interventions rather than one-offs, in those emphasising collaboration and joint planning between teachers and artists prior to interventions, in those with positive artist–teacher relationships and in those afforded larger amounts of time (rather than smaller amounts), with continuity and progression built in and where the distribution of time achieved fitness for purpose[iv] With regards to the nature and extent of planning in particular, the teachers and artists themselves had rarely cited this as having an impact on pupil outcomes.

From interviewees' perceptions, certain factors emerged as exerting a strong influence on pupil outcomes across all artforms (primarily, artist's pedagogy and type of content), though some variations were apparent. References to pupil outcomes were more intense in primary than in secondary or out-of-school settings, though artist's pedagogy remained most important across all three. The main factors were fairly uniform across the different types of intervention, with artist's pedagogy, type of content and pupil factors showing up consistently.

An analysis of associations between perceived factors and specific pupil outcomes revealed several salient findings. Pupils rated type of content as the main factor associated with seven different pupil outcome categories and artist's pedagogy with nine. The contribution of artist's pedagogy to developments in creativity, personal development and affective outcomes were noted similarly by teachers and artists. The role of the end product was rated highly by artists and teachers as key to affective outcomes and personal development. Pupils, teachers and artists all attributed a high rating to group composition determining social development.

Factors that affect outcomes for teachers and artists

From 14 broad categories of factors those with the highest profile overall were:

- the nature and extent of planning
- the artist–teacher relationship
- the role of the teacher during the intervention.

An analysis of the specific associations between factors and outcomes for teachers and artists revealed that content dominates teacher effects. What the intervention consisted of was felt to exert most influence on a range of outcomes, including motivation, affective outcomes, new awareness and value shifts, knowledge and skills and, ultimately, changes in teachers' practice. In contrast, it was pupil factors that were felt to be most influential for the artist. Opportunities for reflection were also key to artists' development of future practice.

Implications for policy and practice

Arguably, in recent years, the most influential document on arts education policy has been the Robinson Report (1999) report, which, to a certain extent, re-packaged 'arts education' as 'creative and cultural education'[v.] However, the sheer breadth and quality of pupil outcomes from arts interventions portrayed in Chapter 2 pose the question of whether aligning arts education initiatives too closely with the aims of creative and cultural education may be limiting and unsympathetic to the strengths and capacities of arts interventions. The results of the research clearly show that (a) the processes of arts education interventions provide more than creative and cultural outcomes and (b) that these two outcome types were not among the most frequently or strongly reported forms of impact of arts interventions. This would suggest that if policies on arts interventions are informed too heavily on an interpretation of the Robinson Report as emphasising the inter-changeability of arts education with creative and cultural education, there is a risk that many other powerful and, arguably, on the basis of this evidence, more immediately attainable effects associated with arts interventions could be eclipsed. Consequently, the research does not substantiate an interpretation of the Robinson Report that suggests that it is the elements of creative and cultural development which are especially important and instrumental in arts education as mediated through arts interventions. Other dimensions would seem to be as important, if not more important.

For many pupils and young people, a new world of arts knowledge and skills was opened up through their encounter with professional artists. In a national and international policy context that frequently accentuates instrumental justifications for arts education and arts-education partnerships, the importance of learning the knowledge, skills and discipline associated with particular artforms should not go unnoticed. These may well constitute the foundation stones upon which all other learning outcomes need to be built. This would counsel against 'quick fix' solutions which assume that instrumental effects can be achieved without first establishing some solid foundations in artform knowledge and skills.

The high ranking of affective outcomes and the fact that so many young people found their involvement with AEI thoroughly engaging, stimulating and fulfilling, underlines the substantial contribution that arts interventions can make to meeting the Government's vision of ensuring that learning is an enjoyable experience. However, it is arguable that over-reliance on the capacity of arts interventions to achieve enjoyment and other affective outcomes may detract attention from the planning for other additional learning goals. Concerted efforts may be needed to avoid this happening.

The array of outcomes in the personal domain suggest an important contribution for arts interventions in what many would see as the most fundamental aspect of young people's education: their emotional health. This evidence offers endorsement to the investment by government departments, Arts Council England and various charitable foundations in the arts as a means of engaging issues of social exclusion and suggests that the role of arts education in the social inclusion agenda may benefit from even greater attention.

There is good evidence that interventions also supported impacts on young people's social development, including increased awareness and recognition that there is an equivalent centre of self in other people. The findings regarding the limited extensions to social and cultural knowledge raised the question of whether arts interventions, perhaps like normal arts education in schools, tend to accentuate form, skills and processes rather than content and meaning, in contrast to the adult world of arts which is redolent with social, moral and cultural issues.

The analysis of the relationship between outcomes and aims indicated that the limitations in the range of effects achieved may be the result of bounded ambitions rather than shortcomings in the design and implementation of arts interventions. However, with particular relevance to the Creative Partnership programme, it was significant that developing creativity was one notable exception in this regard: the design and delivery of AEI interventions did not generate this outcome to the level it was aimed for.

The evidence also suggests that more attention should be paid to the issue of how highly engaging interventions will impact upon pupils' attitudes to the artform in the school. Arts interventions are likely to affect the way that pupils see and feel about their exposure to teachers' normal practice and curriculum provision. If an intervention is to avoid provoking critical reactions to the normal school diet, it would seem unwise for teachers not to get fully involved in designing, planning, helping execute, sustaining and learning from the intervention and the artist's input.

A major contribution of the AEI research is that it brings a sound evidence-based methodology to bear upon the identification of features associated with successful or, more aptly, effective arts-education interventions. The AEI research endorsed a number of features highlighted in previous studies: joint planning and shared aims in Sharp and Dust (1997) and clear objectives, extended contact (though shorter term interventions could be effective in their own terms) and responsiveness to the needs of the pupils ('relevance' in our terminology) in Turner (1999). In so far as these factors have been identified by at least two studies, their significance for policy and practice is noteworthy.

The majority of the most frequently and strongly identified characteristics of effective interventions were not highlighted by previous research. These comprised:

- artist's pedagogy
- type of content
- manageability

- emphasis on the end product

- pupil factors

- artist–pupil relationship

- continuity and progression.

The central nature of these factors is very different to those prioritised in earlier studies. While the latter have tended to concentrate on organisational and managerial dimensions, the findings of the current study have accentuated features associated with the coalface reality of teaching and learning interactions – those adjoining the classroom or workshop experience. In short, the study prompts the question: are policies surrounding interventions at the arts-education interface as close to the point of learning as this research suggests they should be?

How schools, other host institutions and brokers can access artists with the identified qualities is an issue that needs to be further addressed. If the artist's pedagogy is a critical factor, what information is available to schools and other sites about individual or organisational capacities in this respect?

This links to the issue of training and professional development for artists, teachers and others in the management, design and execution of arts interventions: what forms of provision can best develop these professionals' awareness, knowledge and values surrounding the identified factors?

Planning in high-rated outcome interventions embraced more than logistical matters, important though they were. In these cases, planning was about engaging in and committing to a collaborative process regarding the appropriate aims, design, content, context and pedagogies for the intervention, thus arriving at a creative and constructive 'chemistry' between artist and teacher – and like all relationships, the good ones have to be worked at.

AEI occasionally revealed a lack of investment by some teachers and schools in getting hold of an intervention and driving it forward and especially in devising programmes of work that could facilitate longer-term incremental learning. Artists' lack of investment in the educational as opposed to the artistic dimensions of interventions was also apparent. Those viewing arts interventions as a low investment, an easy opportunity to provide a pleasant but essentially temporary diversion for young people will reap dividends (or lack of them) accordingly.

We would like to reiterate the value of one general and overarching characteristic of effective practice alluded to earlier: the Mutual Learning Triangle (MLT). This underlines the substantial benefits to be gained by ensuring that all three of the main participant groups: (i) pupils/young people/learners; (ii) teachers/schools or other host agents and (iii) artists/arts organisations are fully engaged in and learn from the arts intervention and its legacy. The MLT offers the potential to add considerable value to bilateral learning approaches. The evidence from AEI frequently testified to the adverse consequences of omitting one side of the triangle. We would not want to go as far as recommending that the triangles should always be equilateral ones, but, on the basis of the evidence discussed here, we would suggest that something approaching equivalence in MLTs would, in the majority of cases, raise the odds appreciably in favour of arts interventions generating successful outcomes.

Notes

i   In April 2002, the Arts Council of England and the ten Regional Arts Boards joined together to form a single development organisation for the arts. This new body is called Arts Council England.

ii   The interpretations of the evidence set out in the report are those of the authors and not necessarily those of the sponsors or members of the Steering Group.

iii The second-level analysis entailed the researchers recording descriptive data on the key factors and processes – what actually happened before, during and after the interventions (e.g. their aims, degree of planning, curriculum content) for each of the phases. The researchers then surveyed the extent to which noted processes and features regularly appeared against phases with high, medium or low outcomes.

iv   This notion of a time spread with 'fitness for purpose' takes account of the context of the particular activities, the school and the pupils involved. So, for example, every morning for one week might be fit for the purpose of working with children with special needs; but two one-hour sessions two weeks apart might be inappropriate for producing a banner, where pupils didn't have time to finish their work because within each hour, time was needed to set up and put away and where they would have preferred a two-hour block.

v   'By creative education we mean forms of education that develop young people's capacities for original ideas and action; by cultural education we mean forms of education that enable them to engage positively with the growing complexity and diversity of social values and ways of life.' (Robinson Report, 1999 p. 6)

1 Researching the arts and education interface

In 2001, the then Arts Council of England[i] and the Regional Arts Boards (RABs) launched the Arts and Education Interface (AEI) initiative. Its aim was to explore the relationship between the arts and education through a programme of arts-based interventions organised within the Education Action Zones (EAZs) of Bristol and Corby. To this end, the Arts Council commissioned the National Foundation for Educational Research (NFER) to study the impact of exposure to a range of these interventions on the learning, intellectual, emotional and social development of young people. The 15 interventions took place during the academic years 2001–02 and 2002–03. This report sets out the findings of NFER's research into the AEI interventions.

This first chapter traces the evolution of the AEI initiative, noting specific changes in the national and regional contexts that occurred during its lifetime. It outlines some factual details of the 15 interventions and their respective settings and describes the evaluation's aims and methodology. It also presents some working definitions of terms used in the report and, in conclusion, explains the structure of the chapters that make up the report.

1.1 The evolution of AEI

The initiative was conceived in the late 1990s as a response to the lack of rigorous empirical evidence on which to base policies relating to arts interventions and education. The paucity of studies concerned with the effects on young people of participating in the arts was widely acknowledged and in particular longitudinal evaluations in the field were rare. Accordingly, the AEI initiative was designed to inform policy-making and professional practice by extending the existing body of relevant research.

In response to the Policy Action Team 10 Report (PAT 10) produced by the Department for Culture, Media and Sport (DCMS, 1999), it was agreed that issues surrounding social inclusion would be included within the research brief, alongside other areas for investigation, such as personal and institutional development. In order to complement studies previously carried out by Arts

Council staff, it was decided to concentrate the research on young people aged between three and 18.

While planning progressed at the Arts Council, the EAZs were submitting proposals for the second round of funding and some of these emphasised the role of the arts in community development. Following a proposal from the EAZ's advisory service, it was decided to locate the research within two or three selected EAZs. The Arts Council drew up a shortlist of EAZs whose bids regarded the arts as fundamental to their application.

The EAZs of Bristol and Corby were selected because they represented two contrasting examples of the interface between arts organisations and both formal and informal education. Bristol is a large city with a well-developed arts infrastructure, where it was anticipated that 'external' arts interventions would be provided by a range of arts organisations. Corby, by contrast, is a medium-sized new town; where arts opportunities are comparatively limited and it was anticipated that arts interventions would be generated internally, within and between educational sites within the EAZ.

Bristol EAZ serves an area of 'significant deprivation' (Bristol Education Action Zone, 2001) in the city centre with high rates of crime, drug-related problems and unemployment (30 per cent of Bristol's total unemployment is to be found here). Forty-six per cent of the population live in flats, many of which are high rise. Transience is seen as a major problem and there are large numbers of pupils with English as an additional language in some schools. The zone contains 22 schools, including nine of the 13 schools with the highest free school meals (FSM) entitlement in Bristol. The proportion of pupils in the EAZ from black and minority ethnic groups is high (50 per cent at primary and 55 per cent at secondary level) and while this diversity 'brings cultural richness to the area', there is 'a huge gap in attainment' between white pupils in the EAZ and pupils from ethnic minority groups. However, levels of attainment for all ethnic groups for the year 2000 were 'well below the national averages' at all key stages.

In its bid for the second round of funding (*Challenge for Corby*, 1999), Corby EAZ identified 12 'key factors of need'. These included high and constant rates of unemployment, youth unemployment and employee turnover and 'a grave mismatch' between skills available and jobs on offer. Average incomes were 'significantly' below the national average; the crime rate was considerably higher than the national average and debt was seen as a major problem. The number of pupils with FSM in the majority of schools was also considerably higher than the national average.

In 1999, according to the same document, Corby had the eighth worst level of adult literacy problems in the country (21 per cent of the population as opposed to 15 per cent nationally) and the third worst level of numeracy problems (43 per cent of the population, 33 per cent nationally). Although, at key stages 1 and 2, Zone schools were achieving 'broadly in line' with national averages, there was 'a significant dip' in performance for the beginning of key stage 3 and throughout key stage 4. Moreover, at age 16, the staying-on rate was more than 20 per cent below the national average. The incidence of Special Educational Needs (SEN) was more than twice the national average and there were high levels of school refusal and truancy, particularly in key stages 3 and 4. Out of schools provision was 'patchy' and the EAZ had only one youth club.

Both EAZs were seen to present opportunities for relating arts education practice to the immediate context of educational sites. In line with all EAZs, schools in Bristol and Corby were free to suspend or relax the national curriculum, in order to raise levels of achievement and to meet key learning objectives, in particular the numeracy and literacy attainment targets. Both EAZs had indicated that any changes in the curriculum would be seen to benefit the arts.

Under the guidance of a centrally-based Arts Council AEI national coordinator, two local AEI Arts Council coordinators, working from local EAZ offices, initiated appropriate partnerships between the arts, education, community and business sectors. The Arts Council provided funding and/or additional resources to arts organisations participating in the initiative and covered (if needed) any supply costs incurred by schools when staff were involved in interviews for the research. In addition to facilitating the interventions studied through the national research programme, the coordinators were also engaged in implementing other activities and strands contained within the wider AEI programme. This included:

- teachers attending a conference and observing practice in the USA
- teachers' participation in action research projects for post-graduate degrees
- networking and coordination meetings and forums
- supporting the wider programme of EAZ initiatives
- organising projects and events for pupils and young people in schools and organisations not involved in the AEI research reported here.

While a small number of pupils, teachers and schools involved in the researched elements also participated in some of the wider activities (not researched), the majority of participants in the researched projects did not.

1.2 Changing contexts

Before turning to the study itself, this section outlines factors in the national and regional contexts that have impinged on the initiative and its research.

First, the introduction of Creative Partnerships (CP) in September 2002 affected the working context of the AEI and its evaluation. A four-year government initiative funded by the DCMS, CP aims to foster effective, sustainable partnerships between schools and the widest possible range of cultural and creative professionals, in order to deliver high quality cultural and creative opportunities for young people to develop their learning, both across and beyond the formal curriculum. To varying degrees, members of the AEI management and coordination team became involved in the CP programme.

Second, administrative developments both for the Arts Council and for the EAZs continued throughout the lifetime of the project. During 2001–02, the Arts Council undertook a major restructuring exercise. There were various structural developments in the EAZs and both Zones were successful in achieving funding as a Youth Music Action Zone (YMAZ).

Third, during 2002, following the requirements of the Protection of Children Act (GB. Statutes, 1999), the DfES introduced changes to the disclosure service which directly affected artists working in schools. Consequently, from May 2002, any artist employed by the Arts Council was required to obtain a certificate of enhanced disclosure. Following Steering Group discussions, it was decided that the Arts Council's AEI coordinators in each of the two EAZs would advise artists to apply to the LEA as the appropriate registered body. The coordinators transferred the funds for the payment of artists from AEI to the EAZs. Subsequent changes to the disclosure policy introduced rapidly by the DfES in August 2002 (in response to the tragic events at Soham) caused widespread delay in the completion of disclosure procedures. The repercussions for schools, in terms of availability of teaching staff for the first weeks of September, caused some to delay the start of the new academic year and in Corby the interventions were at a standstill until artists could obtain their enhanced disclosure certificates. This delay was a contributory factor in reducing the time for at least two of the interventions designed to include a period of development over the academic year.

Reference must also be made to the Arts Council's 'celebrations', which marked the end of the AEI initiative. These events took place in Corby and Bristol in early July 2003. Organised by the EAZs, the local AEI coordinators and the Arts Council celebrations coordinator, the celebrations provided opportunities for the young people who participated in AEI to showcase their work alongside the work of professional artists. In response to concern that awareness of the forthcoming celebrations might influence the nature of the interventions involved, it was decided that researchers should introduce the concept of 'celebrations' and their possible effects into their interview schedules.

Having outlined the dynamic nature of the overall context of the AEI programme, a depiction of the research and its methods, along with brief details of each of the 15 interventions, are offered.

1.3 The study and its interventions

1.3.1 Aims

The overall aim of the research was to extend evidence-based knowledge of the impact of arts interventions in education and of the characteristics of effective practices. The three specific objectives were as follows:

(i) To evidence, identify, compare and examine the effects of different interventions, in particular their impact on learners, but also their outcomes for teachers, schools, local communities, artists and arts organisations

(ii) To explore and compare the different reasons, factors and processes that affect the range and quality of effects achieved or not achieved by the various interventions

(iii) To draw out any general lessons from these analyses for developing effective practices that are appropriate to the contexts in which they operate.

1.3.2 The interventions

In the light of an NFER paper which suggested some broad types of intervention that might be included in the study, Arts Council coordinators negotiated a range of initiatives in the two EAZs that broadly corresponded to the proposals. It was originally intended that 14 interventions, seven in each of the participating EAZs would be investigated. These would comprise:

- four one-off, relatively 'short-term' interventions, each involving a specific arts organisation, for a particular group of young people in a single educational site (e.g. ranging from a single session of half a day to sessions of two hours a day for two weeks)

- five 'series' type interventions, in which the same group of young people experience a series of activities or projects across a range of artforms over a period of a time

- five sustained 'developmental' interventions, aimed at supporting incremental learning in a specific artform with the same groups over an extended period of time.

The sample offered a cross-section of schooling phases (e.g. nursery, secondary), different educational sectors (e.g. a special school, informal out-of-school settings) and a diverse range of artforms. At the outset, all but two of the interventions were primarily concerned with working directly with children or young people. The remaining two concentrated specifically on the development of teachers and their practice. During the course of the study, because one school was unable to sustain its teacher-development intervention into a second year, an additional intervention of this type was added to the research, giving a total of 15 interventions.

As fieldwork proceeded, two of the three original 'types' of intervention where artists worked directly with pupils were re-defined. In practice, an intervention design did not always appeal to the schools involved; in some cases, it was found too difficult to organise. For example, as a result of staffing and organisational problems in one school, an intended developmental intervention in art eventually comprised a single phase and was thus re-classified as short-term. The developmental types proved especially hard to mount. The interventions which actually occurred were characterised as follows:

- one-off (five interventions)

- series: multiple artforms (four interventions of between two and six phases each)

- developmental: single artform (three interventions: two in drama with three phases each and one in music with five phases).

On further examination, it seemed that not all developmental interventions were viewed as a cohesive programme where each phase built on the last with the intention of incremental learning. The intervention planned as developmental in music, for example, actually involved five distinct experiences of music. The way the experiences were ordered in sequence was not deemed to be important by the music teacher involved and they were not planned with developmental outcomes in mind. It is also worth noting that the length of individual phases of interventions varied considerably, from an hour-long performance, to a four-day residency, to a full term of weekly sessions.

Similarly, the 'series' interventions were not always mounted according to the original intention or definition described above. For example, they did not always involve the same group of pupils throughout the constituent phases and some did not always have the same teachers (e.g. one 'series' intervention focused on different young people in every phase; another had different teachers in most phases and sometimes different pupils).

For readers who would like more background information about the types of intervention and artforms studied, brief anonymised details of the 15 AEI research interventions and their constituent phases are set out in Appendix 1. Details of the intervention's EAZ location, educational host sites, client groups, artists, learning content, timing and duration, type of venue and cost are sum-marised in this appendix. As outlined there, the interventions comprised:

- out-of-school hours gospel singing workshops and performance
- dance workshops and performance in a secondary school
- a visit by nursery aged children to a local gallery-museum
- an in-school theatrical performance for key stage 1 children
- print making workshops in a secondary school
- multi-artform phases (including photography) in a special school
- multi-artform phases (including poetry and live art) in a secondary school
- multi-artform phases (radio, film and turntablism[ii]) in a youth centre
- multi-artform phases (music, visual art, drama) in a primary school
- a drama-based developmental intervention for key stage 1 pupils
- a drama-based (physical theatre) developmental intervention for key stage 4 pupils

- a music-based developmental intervention for key stage 3 pupils

- a dance-based teacher development programme in a primary school

- a Latin American dance teacher development programme in a primary school

- a visual arts-based (digital imagery, ceramics) teacher development programme in a primary school.

1.3.3 Methodology

In order to provide comparisons across these 15 interventions, the research design established a common methodological framework. The design also included an element of flexibility to allow researchers to select the data collection methods and techniques most suited to the contexts and needs of individual cases. Each of the 15 interventions was assigned to a member of the research team who customised the overall research design, according to the specific nature of the artform and timescale involved.

The field research started in July 2001 and continued until July 2003. For each intervention, the fieldwork was carried out in three stages, in order to collect three discrete but interrelated sets of data:

- baseline (information on the participants, the school and the artist/arts organisation before the intervention took place)

- intervention and immediate impact (the content and process of the intervention and views on the experience and its immediate impact from those involved)

- follow-up (perceptions of any longer-term impact of the intervention).

Data was collected through a selection of the following techniques, according to the circumstances of each intervention:

(i) perceptions of learners, teachers, artists, school managers and significant others (e.g. parents) through one-to-one interviews

(ii) perceptions of learners through researcher-administered short questionnaires (only for children over the ages of seven or eight, these questionnaires were customised to suit the particular artform/phase and an example of one is reproduced as Appendix 2)

(iii) observations (with some videoing) of teaching and learning

(iv)   produced work, portfolios, annotated photos of work etc

(v)   existing assessments, schools' baseline assessments, examination and scores in standard assessment tasks, teacher assessments

(vi)   behavioural indicators (e.g. attendance)[iii].

Researchers developed a raft of core interview schedules for different types of participants at the three different stages of data collection (i.e. baseline, intervention and immediate impact and follow up). The core or 'master' schedules were then adapted by researchers to suit the circumstances of each particular intervention. An example of a core schedule is reproduced as Appendix 3, a secondary pupil's follow-up schedule.

The total numbers of interviews completed during the fieldwork with pupils, teachers and artists were as follows:

- Pupils: 376

- Teachers (including nursery staff): 163

- Artists: 126

In addition to fieldwork relating directly to the interventions, data collection also included a series of 'context' interviews with personnel from the Arts Council, the two EAZs, the RABs and the LEAs. These interviews aimed to collect a range of perceptions on the wider context of the interventions in Bristol and Corby, for the period during which they took place. A total of 12 context interviews were completed in Bristol and 13 in Corby, including those with the local arts coordinators. In all a total of 690 interviews were conducted.

To facilitate the analysis of the data collected on the outcomes and the key process and context factors commonly associated with outcomes, we have coded and interpreted the evidence according to three overarching models or typologies – two for the effects (i.e. one for pupil effects and another for the providing professionals, namely teachers and artists) and one for the factors. These have been developed by steering a course between basing them on previously generated typologies, allowing comparison with other studies and adjusting and refining the categories within the typologies to ensure that they accurately reflect the particular AEI data and experience. The pupil effects and the key factors typologies were developed from similar but less refined ones in the *Effects and Effectiveness* (Harland *et al*., 2000) study, while the outcomes for professionals typology was derived from a study of professional development outcomes for teachers (Kinder and Harland, 1991).

The coding of the interview data for both outcomes and key factors was carried out by members of the research team. The researchers coded the data to spread-sheets and included references to either effects or process factors wherever they appeared in the interview data, not just in response to the particular questions concerned. With regard to outcomes, all types of participant were asked in an open-ended item first for their views on effects or what 'they had got out of the project' (e.g. see items 4.1 and 4.2 in Appendix 3). There then followed a series of more focused items which prompted the interviewee to consider whether effects had been experienced in specified domains (e.g. communication skills) – see items 4.3 to 4.17 in Appendix 3. In the analysis and interpretation (e.g. the rating of strength of effects) greater weight was given to responses to the initial open-ended item than to subsequent prompted items (the criteria used to rate the strength of effects is described in Chapter 2, see section 2.2.2). A similar approach was taken to the coding of the key process factors, though in this case relevant responses were even more likely to be volunteered from items through-out the whole schedule. The intervention and immediate impact schedules tended to focus on perceptions of process factors, but examples of items exploring issues to do with the perceived efficacy of the interventions can be seen in section 3 of Appendix 3.

For the AEI study we adopted a similar data collection and analysis methodology to that used in our research into the effects of arts education in secondary schools (Harland *et al.*, 2000). However, we also endeavoured to improve and develop the methodological underpinnings used before. In particular, relative to the earli-er study, the AEI research has extended the methodological rigour in six main ways:

- by developing indicators of the strength as well as frequency of effects and outcomes

- by enhancing the process of triangulating the perceptions of young people, teachers and artists

- by generating analyses of the variation in effects by such background variables as artform, type of intervention and type of educational setting

- by exploring a developmental perspective in understanding outcomes (e.g. outcome routes and 'distances travelled') – this involved looking more closely at where the children and young people are at prior to the intervention (e.g. collecting baseline data on their previous learning in the relevant area, their different needs and paces of learning)

- by examining tighter empirical links between processes and outcomes, thus strengthening the evidence base to the exposition of key features in effective intervention

- by cross-checking the perceptual data from the three main participant groups with a researcher or second-level analysis of the associations between high and low outcome interventions and key process variables (see Chapter 6).

A little more information on this latter point, the second-level analysis, may be helpful. Chapters 4 and 5 report teachers', artists' and pupils' perceptions of what factors and processes appeared to them to have impacted on outcomes, Chapter 6 describes the results of a more 'objective' researcher-oriented analysis of these factors. To do this, the researchers looked for consistent patterns and associations between the outputs of two contributory analyses. The first of these involved the rating of each phase in the 15 interventions into high, medium or low outcomes for effects on pupils, teachers and artists. This method of analysis and the criteria used to rate the phases are described in section 6.2. The second-level analysis entailed the researchers recording descriptive data on the key factors and processes – what actually happened before, during and after the interventions (e.g. their aims, degree of planning, curriculum content) for each of the phases. A description of this analytical process is described in section 6.3. The researchers then surveyed the extent to which noted processes and features regularly appeared against phases with high, medium or low outcome (again see section 6.3 for a description of this process and its added value).

As an output of these various analyses, the results presented throughout the report are based on two broad kinds of evidence: (i) the perceptions of key partic-ipants and (ii) the findings of the researcher-led second-level analysis. To avoid confusion, unless otherwise stated, results derived from the perceptual data are set out in Chapters 3, 4 and 5, whereas those from the researcher-led second-level analysis are described in Chapter 6.

The use of these two broad types of data may give rise to questions about their relative status and validity: which carries more weight? Clearly, a finding that is corroborated by both types is well substantiated. However, in cases where a find-ing is supported by one data type but not the other, we do not suggest that either source should be given primacy. Rather than giving more weight to findings from one of the two data sources, it is more appropriate to ask why the particular finding may not be evident in both types. In most cases, this centres on inquiring why participants may or may not have perceived certain processes, factors or outcomes to be important.

1.3.4 Setting up the interventions

Protocols were negotiated during the early stages of the research covering communication and the flow of information between those involved at all stages of the interventions. Most importantly, the protocols stressed the neutrality and detachment of the AEI coordinators' role and the corresponding importance of encouraging schools and artists to negotiate with one another directly in terms of overall design and day-to-day planning. In practice, however, specific circumstances made a stance of minimum coordinator involvement and brokerage difficult to achieve.

The two Arts Council coordinators forged initial links with managers in schools and other organisations. In most cases, following subsequent discussion with headteachers and artform teachers, the coordinators then contacted an artist or arts organisation deemed appropriate to meet the needs expressed and investigated their interest and availability. Once this had been established, the coordinator arranged a meeting to introduce the intervention partners.

In some schools, at this point, the Arts Council coordinator was able to leave the artist and the school to make the arrangements for the intervention. In others, however, where communication within a school was more difficult, for example, the coordinator continued to liaise with both partners until all arrangements appeared to be completed, in order to ensure that both were kept fully informed of developments. Throughout the process of setting up the intervention, the coordinator briefed the researcher concerned.

Fourteen educational sites were originally selected according to the research criteria. In the event, two of these withdrew during the first year of the research and a third requested to have their involvement substantially reduced for the second year. Three alternative sites agreed to take part in the project and the data collection plans for the type of intervention in question were adapted to take changes in duration into account.

1.4 Definitions

Various terms of reference recur throughout the report. In the interests of clarity, specific definitions are given below.

- Intervention – this applies to the intervention in its entirety, which was negotiated by the arts coordinator with the staff at the educational site, whether 'one-off', 'series' or 'developmental'. It includes any collaboration between the artist or arts organisation and teacher in advance, all the work carried out by the artist (possibly in conjunction with teachers) with the young people, including any performance or final display and any subsequent related activities undertaken by the teacher.

- One-off interventions involve a self-contained period of activity between the artist and the educational setting. This might be a single event, or it might involve a number of workshop sessions in a single 'phase' (see below), which might or might not lead to a final performance or display.

- Series interventions involved more than one discrete phase, with each phase concentrating on a different artform (e.g. a series intervention might include drama, dance, music and poetry phases, one each term and each phase might involve more than one 'session' – see below).

- Developmental interventions involved more than one phase, all concentrating on the same artform over an extended period of time.

- Phases refer to discrete programmes of work which make up the longer series or developmental interventions (e.g. one developmental intervention in drama consisted of six phases broadly one per term; each phase might contain one or more sessions and might be provided by different artists).

- Sessions refer to specific encounters between the artist (possibly with teachers) and the young people at a specific time (e.g. one of the weekly activities during the poetry phase of a series intervention).

- The terms site and setting include schools, nursery schools and youth centres.

1.5 About the report

The report is divided into a further six chapters[iv]:

- Chapter 2 examines the impact of the AEI interventions on pupils and young people and explores the relationships between pupil outcomes and aims, art-forms, types of setting and types of intervention.

- Chapter 3 considers the evidence on the impact of the AEI interventions on teachers, schools, artists and arts organisations.

- Chapter 4 analyses the range and frequency of process factors perceived to have contributed to the outcomes for pupils identified in Chapter 2.

- Chapter 5 examines the range and frequency of process factors perceived to have contributed to the outcomes for teachers and artists identified in Chapter 3.

- Chapter 6 assesses the overall impact of each of the 15 interventions and investigates whether the most successful ones display similar design and delivery traits.

- Chapter 7 concludes the report by drawing out some general lessons from these analyses for developing effective practices.

Throughout the ensuing chapters, our overriding purpose is to relay a discipline of analysis, grounded in the social science tradition that may, at first, appear far from the norm in the worlds of arts and arts education reportage.

Our brief was to investigate the AEI by applying this discipline to the 15 rich and varied examples of arts opportunities for young people that the AEI initiative overall has unquestionably afforded. The report eschews narrative, celebration and extended exemplars. Neither does it in any way attempt to be a 'handbook' or 'how-to guide'. Instead, the report attempts a rigorous and systematic examination of the 'DNA' of arts interventions: depicting or 'deconstructing' first their effects on pupils, teacher and artists and then the factors or elements that made those outcomes happen. We hope the opportunity granted to us to marry contemporary arts activity and social science qualitative analysis will provide new insights which policy-makers and practitioners will find a useful addition to their thinking.

Notes

i In April 2002, the Arts Council of England and the 10 Regional Arts Boards joined together to form a single development organisation for the arts. This new body is called Arts Council England. For ease of reference, the new name is used throughout the rest of the report.

ii The term 'turntablism' was first coined in 1995 by DJ Babu (Beat Junkies) and describes a sub-genre of pop music which emerged from Hip-Hop. Turntablists use the phonograph turntables and techniques such as scratching and beat juggling to create new musical compositions, rather than simply playing existing music.

iii The researchers reviewed all the assessments, behavioural, attainment and attendance data collected, but could find no convincing or even tentative patterns to report. However, some such data did help teachers to back up what they were saying about individual pupils. For example, in the music-secondary intervention, there were one or two pupils whom the teacher felt had matured over the two years (not necessarily because of AEI) and whose music performance assessment results had improved because they seemed to be more confident about themselves (not necessarily about music).

iv The interpretations of the evidence set out in the report are those of the authors and not necessarily those of the sponsors or members of the Steering Group.

2 Outcomes for pupils and young people

2.1 About this chapter

Chapters 2 and 3 focus on one of the foremost aims of the study, namely to identify and compare the effects of AEI interventions on a range of participants. This chapter covers the outcomes for pupils and young people, while the following one considers the outcomes for teachers, schools and other host institutions, as well as those for artists and arts organisations.

2.1.1 Overview

The frequency, strength and nature of outcomes for pupils and young people (2.2)

A model of potential effects of arts interventions on young people is presented. The variation with which these modelled effects were actually nominated by teachers, artists and the young people themselves is then outlined, focusing on how often [frequency] and with what degree of emphasis [strength] these effects were mentioned. Illustrations and first-hand accounts of high- and low-ranking pupil effects are relayed, with accompanying policy and practice implications outlined.

Outcomes and aims (2.3)

This section explores whether the outcomes achieved were aimed for by teachers and artists. In order to examine this issue, descriptions of the overall aims of the AEI initiative, written aims and the most and least frequent aims of the interventions are offered.

Variations in outcomes by key variables (2.4)

This is followed by a delineation of how effects varied by artform, type of setting, cost, location and type of intervention.

Outcome routes and developmental learning (2.5)

The penultimate section in this chapter presents a discussion of how and whether developmental learning occurred for pupils experiencing arts interventions.

The chapter concludes with a summary of the main findings (2.6).

2.2 The frequency, strength and nature of outcomes for pupils and young people

2.2.1 Mapping the potential effects of arts interventions on young people

As a way of beginning the analysis of the impacts that arts interventions may have on young people, we propose a heuristic model of outcomes. By that, we mean a conceptual framework that embraces all the main potential outcomes of arts interventions for pupils regardless of whether or not they were actually achieved in the AEI initiative. By comparing this model against the data collected, it becomes possible to examine which effects were evident in the projects studied and which were not.

In developing such a model, AEI is probably the first study in the UK to map out systematically the range of possible pupil effects from several interventions led by artists and teachers (and other professionals) working in partnership and across different artforms. Sharp and Dust (1997) identified several of these outcomes, but their focus was on 'benefits' rather than effects and these were not organised into a coherent framework, nor examined in relation to process variables. Similarly, in a study of seven artist-based projects, Turner (1999) reported a number of 'gains' for pupils, but these were not claimed to be comprehensive or structured into a formal schema. Harland *et al.* (2000) offered a range of effects from arts education in secondary schools, but did not examine outcomes specifically associated with programmes involving artists. Consequently, it is hoped that the model described here can build on these earlier studies and provide a framework that will aid future research and evaluations, as well as inform artists and teachers in their planning and reviewing of similar interventions.

The model takes into account the findings from the AEI interventions, as well as the outcome categories from previous research (e.g. Harland *et al.*, 2000; Sharp and Dust, 1997). Attempts have been made to define categories in a way which reflects the language and terminologies used by pupils, teachers and artists, though in some cases these varied considerably across the three main participant groups. Terminology from other research (e.g. Winner and Hetland, 2000) was also used where it was felt to provide a particularly appropriate nomenclature.

Notwithstanding these attempts, several of the outcome categories are not expressed in terms that many of the participants, especially pupils, would use. The reason for this is that we wanted each category to encompass what all types of interviewee (teachers, artists, pupils etc) reported. In other words, to facilitate comparison and corroboration across participant types, we wanted a single coding frame in which to code up all interviewees' responses, but within that we clearly have sub-codes with different discourses and languages from different respondents. Furthermore, we found that typologies based on categories closer to participants' vocabularies tended to be too extensive to permit the forms of analysis rendered possible by typologies pitched at higher levels of abstraction, though inevitably at the cost of increased insensitivity to the linguistic nuances of particular interviewees. To go some way to compensate for this, the chapter includes descriptive accounts of the outcome categories in the terms adopted by participants (these are presented as quoted comments in italics). It should be stressed that our interviews always offered opportunities for open-ended responses before we probed around specific topics (e.g. around the area of creativity we probed concepts like imagination, ability to experiment, take risks, innovate, to make things, to create things and to have ideas).

Outlined below, the model contains 11 broad outcome categories (I–XI) and 33 sub-categories (A, B, C etc).

I Affective outcomes

The first broad category is made up of three sub-types of effect:

A. Immediate enjoyment and therapeutic effects

Examples of enjoyment may include references to 'fun' and experiencing a 'thrill'. This sub-category could also include relaxation or cathartic outcomes, as well as any descriptions of activities being 'therapeutic' in the short term.

B. Sense of achievement, satisfaction and happiness

This sub-type captures more deep-seated manifestations of pupils' affective responses e.g. 'pride' in their achievements, coupled with an inner sense of fulfilment. It also includes references to longer-term 'therapeutic' outcomes.

C. Sense of physical wellbeing

Included here are references to physical wellbeing, health and fitness and increased body awareness – 'how bodies work' or 'using their bodies in different ways'.

II Artform knowledge, appreciation and skills

This broad grouping contains five sub-types of effect:

A. Artform knowledge

This covers impacts on pupils' understanding of the elements of the artform (such as colour and rhythm), associated definitions, artform processes and the historical or cultural context of the genre of the artist/art.

B. Artform appreciation

This encompasses pupils' appreciation of a broader repertoire of styles within the artform and the professional arts world, including what it is like to be an artist and what their role entails. It also embraces pupils valuing or appreciating the products or performances within the artform more.

C. Artform skills and techniques

This embraces references to skills and techniques for using and manipulating the tools and materials in the artform (including skills in display and performance). It also includes 'artform discipline' and appropriate behaviours.

D. Interpretative Skills

This includes pupils' enhanced ability to 'read' and decode artform processes and products and to develop the critical skills to do so – in essence to become 'artform literate' and a critical listener/viewer.

E. Ability to make aesthetic judgements

This signifies pupils' enhanced capacity to value and care for others' work and their ability to make evaluative/critical judgements about the quality of works of art, based on such criteria as aesthetic merit.

III Social and cultural knowledge

This broad category contained three effect sub-types:

A. Social and moral issues

This could encompass increased awareness of issues such as equal opportunities, racism and disability, as well as bullying, conflict and issues relating to drugs and alcohol.

B. Environment and surroundings

This sub-type describes pupils' greater awareness of their environmental, visual and social surroundings and may include making greater sense of the world about them and their place within it.

C. Cultures, traditions and cultural diversity

Included here are references to enhanced awareness of people's cultures and traditions (including arts and non-arts related), enrichments to one's own sense of cultural identity and greater multicultural awareness.

IV Knowledge, skills and appreciation beyond the arts

Pupils' knowledge and appreciation in areas of learning beyond the arts can also be addressed and extended – for example, where the content of the intervention is directly related to other curriculum areas such as science, history or literature. By selecting other foci, skills like reading and sensory awareness (e.g. a sense of touch) can also be developed.

V Thinking skills

Two sub-categories are included:

A. Cognitive capacities, concentration, focus and clarity

The sub-category emphasises effects on mind and thought in the moment. In the longer term, these skills can manifest themselves as improved memory, enhanced flexibility of thought, or nonverbal reasoning skills.

B. Problem-solving skills

This describes pupils' problem-solving, not just in the moment, but finding strategies for getting from 'a' to 'b'. It includes independent thinking skills and thinking skills within a group.

VI Developments in creativity

Developments in the realm of creativity include, at a basic level, using and 'practising' given themes and ideas, or at a more enhanced level capacities for original thought, imagination and exploration, including 'trying out' and incorporating others' ideas with your own. At a more advanced level, impacts in this category were associated with higher levels of risk-taking.

VII Communication and expressive skills

This broad category is made up of two outcome sub-types:

A. Artistic communication and expressive skills

This encompasses pupils becoming more able to express themselves through the arts. It can also include pupils' increased recognition of the arts as providing media for self expression and their feeling 'free' to use them.

B. Generic communication skills

This can be viewed as the more transferable of the two types, including: the use of language (both spoken and written); the expansion of vocabulary; improvements in verbal skills, speaking and listening and pupils' ability or confidence in expressing their ideas, values or opinions.

VIII Personal development

Effects relating to pupils' personal development include a range of attitudes, attributes and skills, resonating with Gardner's (1993) description of intra-personal intelligences. These are categorised here into five sub-types:

A. Sense of self and identity

This sub-type refers primarily to pupils developing an awareness of their own identities and increased understanding of their own personalities or emotions, including awareness of themselves as members of a class/group.

B. Self-esteem

Enhancements here could involve pupils feeling 'better about themselves', a sense of 'pride' in themselves, feeling less concerned or worried about what others may think of them and feeling 'empowered'.

C. Self-confidence

Increases in self-confidence could include: pupils' feeling more able to speak out or contribute their ideas, feeling more confident in their general abilities and overcoming shyness or embarrassment.

D. Artform confidence

Artform confidence included pupils' enhanced belief in their abilities in the artform and feeling more confident whilst performing, or more willing to perform in front of an audience.

E. Sense of maturity

This comprises the skills and attributes contributing to pupils' growing maturity. It includes: becoming more motivated and organised, taking responsibility and recognising the benefits of working hard and learning.

IX Social development

Social development, which approximates Gardner's concept of inter-personal intelligences, is classified into three sub-types of effect:

A. Working with others and teamwork

This essentially describes pupils' developing better working relationships – with other pupils, teachers or artists and learning the social skills of working together in an effective way.

B. Social relationships

This includes making new friends and developing social (as opposed to working) relationships with a teacher or artist. It also includes pupils' ability to expand their social circle – feeling more confident engaging with new people.

C. Social awareness of others

This sub-type comprises increased empathy for others and their situations, enhanced tolerance or sensitivity and the breaking down of social barriers between people.

X Changes in attitudes towards and involvement in the artform

This category is made up of five sub-types:

A. Attitudes to learning the artform

This covers pupils' desire to repeat intervention experiences or do more of the artform. Changes in pupils' enthusiasm for the artform within regular schooling and the importance attached to learning it are also included.

B. Positive image of artform ability

This comprises pupils' sense of 'being better' at the artform overall, particularly within regular school lessons, with possible improvements in 'hard indicators' such as grades.

C. Attendance and behaviour during artform activities

This category includes all references (either in perceptions or 'hard indicators') to changes in pupils' attendance and behaviour during intervention sessions, or in artform lessons following the intervention.

D. Participation in the artform beyond school

This covers pupils' increasing (or desiring to increase) their participation in the artform – either informally at home, or through attendance at extra-curricular clubs. For those already participating in the artform, increased motivation is also included.

E. Attitudes towards careers in the artform

At a basic level, this includes pupils being more aware of the possibilities for careers within the artform. At a deeper level, pupils may have experienced a desire to pursue a career in the artform and have actually taken steps towards that goal.

XI Transfer beyond the artform

This final category contains outcomes transferring beyond the arts, to three arenas in particular:

A. Life in school

Reports of attitudes, skills and intelligences transferring directly to other areas of learning, specific subjects and school in general are classified here. Also included are changes in general attainment, attendance, behaviour and subject-choice.

B. Current life outside school

This encompasses effects on pupils' everyday lives beyond school, including work and extra-curricular activities (not related to the artform) and home life. Transfers to other artforms in which pupils were involved (or began to participate) are included.

C. Future life and work

Transfers to pupils' future lives include effects viewed as important for 'adult life', applicable to the world of work in general, or to careers and future leisure activities within arenas other than those of the artform of the intervention.

The above ordering of the broad categories is deliberate in that it is intended to signal the extent to which the broad outcomes may have the transferability to develop from the immediate effects associated with the learning moment into outcomes that are applied in wider arenas. As illustrated in Figure 2.1, the initial and most immediate effects appear at the top of the model, while those requiring greater degrees or distance of transfer appear at the bottom. Using Moga *et al.*'s (2000) metaphors, the initial outcomes would seem to suggest 'near transfer' or a 'narrow bridge', while the latter ones would appear to denote 'far transfer' or a 'wide bridge'.

Figure 2.1   Pupil effects model

I   Affective outcomes

II   Artform knowledge, appreciation and skills

III   Social and cultural knowledge

IV   Knowledge, skills and appreciation beyond the arts

V   Thinking skills

VI   Developments in creativity

VII   Communication and expressive skills

VIII Personal development

IX   Social development

X   Changes in attitudes towards and involvement in the artform

XI   Transfer beyond the artform

2.2.2 Frequency and nature of pupil effects in the AEI

Equipped with this model, we can now examine which of the outcome types were and were not evident in the data collected from the AEI interventions. Which were the most and least prevalent? Which were the strongest and weakest? What were the salient features of the effects achieved?

To address these questions, this section considers the frequency with which each outcome type was reported in 32 phases of the AEI interventions (the remaining phases were primarily concerned with teacher development and as such are discussed in Chapter 3). These 32 phases or projects provide a rich seam from which to extract general lessons about the outcomes achieved (or not achieved, as the case may be) by artist-education partnerships. Although in a statistical sense, they cannot be taken as representative, as they were restricted to only two geographical areas, they can be seen as quite 'typical' examples of artist-education interventions and bear close resemblance to other projects reported in recent literature (e.g. Downing, 1996; Oddie and Allen, 1998; Tambling and Harland, 1998; Turner, 1999; Doherty and Harland, 2001; Castle *et al.*, 2002; Downing *et al.*, 2002; Godfrey, 2002; Ings, 2002; Pringle, 2002).

As an indication of the general 'breadth' of an outcome across the initiative as a whole, the number of phases in which each outcome was evidenced is reported. In addition, a 'strength' classification for each outcome is considered – a researcher rating was made which took into account whether the effect was experienced by only some, most or all of the pupils taking part and whether the level of impact reported by each was slight or extensive. This rating was based on evidence collected through a series of interviews with pupils, young people, teachers and artists (for an example of the outcome items asked in the interviews, see Appendix 3, section 4). The criteria used to make the rating comprised: the number of interviewees in the group concerned registering the effect; the emphasis placed on the expression of the effect (e.g. in the language used to describe it); the number of times it was mentioned in an interview; whether the response was from an open or prompted item and whether interviewees felt an outcome was achieved by few, some or many pupils. The examination of both the 'breadth' across the initiative and relative 'strength' of each outcome marks an advancement on Harland *et al.* (2000), where the frequencies of outcomes were compared solely on the basis of the number of times each was cited, with no distinction between references to substantial effects and those of a more limited nature.

Frequencies of broad outcomes

As a starting point, we report the number of phases where interviewees identified an effect within each of the 11 broad outcome categories.

Five of the 11 broad categories were cited as resulting in all 32 phases. These five were:

- affective outcomes

- artform knowledge, appreciation and skills

- personal development

- changes in attitudes towards involvement in the artform

- transfer beyond the artform.

All but two effects were evident in 28 or more phases. These two were: knowledge, skills and appreciation beyond the arts (registered in only seven out of 32 phases) and social and cultural knowledge (18 out of 32 phases).

However, this does not take into account the relative strength of the effects within each outcome category. Figure 2.2 provides an indication of the emphasis placed on each category, based on the maximum strength rating determined for the different types of interviewees (e.g. if most pupils interviewed described having made considerable gains in an outcome category, this was classified as a 'considerable effect for most/all' in that category, even if teachers and artists did not concur).

Figure 2.2   Strength of different effects

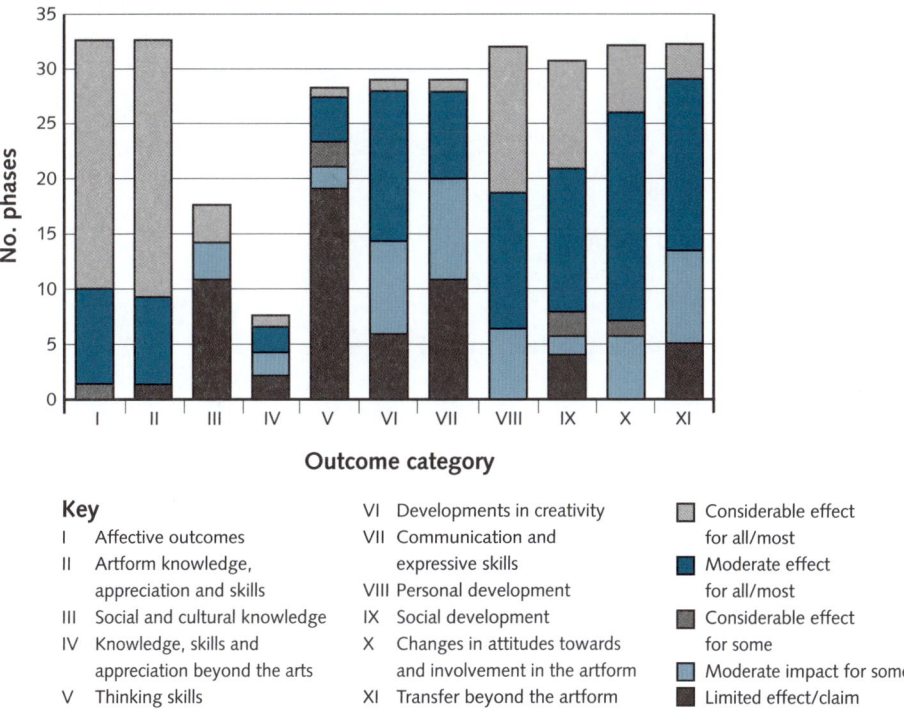

Outcome category

Key

I	Affective outcomes	VI	Developments in creativity
II	Artform knowledge, appreciation and skills	VII	Communication and expressive skills
III	Social and cultural knowledge	VIII	Personal development
IV	Knowledge, skills and appreciation beyond the arts	IX	Social development
V	Thinking skills	X	Changes in attitudes towards and involvement in the artform
		XI	Transfer beyond the artform

- ▨ Considerable effect for all/most
- ▨ Moderate effect for all/most
- ▨ Considerable effect for some
- ▨ Moderate impact for some
- ▨ Limited effect/claim

Affective outcomes and artform knowledge, appreciation and skills were the categories where interviewees from the highest number of phases described an impact (often considerable) on most or all of the participants. These could be deemed to be the outcomes where interviewees perceived the 'strongest' impact as a result of AEI. These top categories were followed by personal development and social development.

Although developments in creativity, communication and expressive skills and thinking skills were referenced in the vast majority of phases, these broad categories were amongst those with the highest numbers of phases recording limited impact (or where effects were 'claimed' with little substantiation). The categories with the greatest number of phases with limited impact were thinking skills (19 phases), social and cultural knowledge (11 phases), communication and expressive skills (11 phases) and developments in creativity (6 phases). These categories also recorded the least number of phases of 'considerable effect for most'.

Frequencies of sub-types of effect

To enlarge the picture gained from the frequencies of the broad categories of outcome, it is instructive to consider the frequencies and strength with which each of the different sub-types was reported. Ranking all of the different sub-types according to the number of phases where a considerable impact for most/all participants was reported gives a top five comprising:

- immediate enjoyment and therapeutic effects
- artform knowledge
- artform skills and techniques
- artform appreciation
- sense of achievement, satisfaction and happiness.

The results for all the different sub-types are presented in Figure 2.3.

A composite view of frequencies and strength

Combining the results for the frequencies of broad and sub-type categories, as well as those for the breadth and strength of outcomes, a composite view of the effects with the highest and lowest profiles can now be offered.

The effects with the highest profile (i.e. frequency combined with strength) in AEI were:

- affective outcomes, especially immediate enjoyment and therapeutic effects and sense of achievement, satisfaction and happiness – within this broad category, sense of physical wellbeing was an outcome reported as resulting from the least phases and often at a more moderate level of impact.
- artform knowledge, appreciation and skills – within this broad category the ability to make aesthetic judgements and artform interpretative skills were less frequently reported and with more limited impact
- personal development, notably self-esteem and self-confidence, with sense of self and identity the least prevalent
- social development, particularly working with others and teamwork and social awareness of others.

Figure 2.3   Breadth and strength of sub-type effects

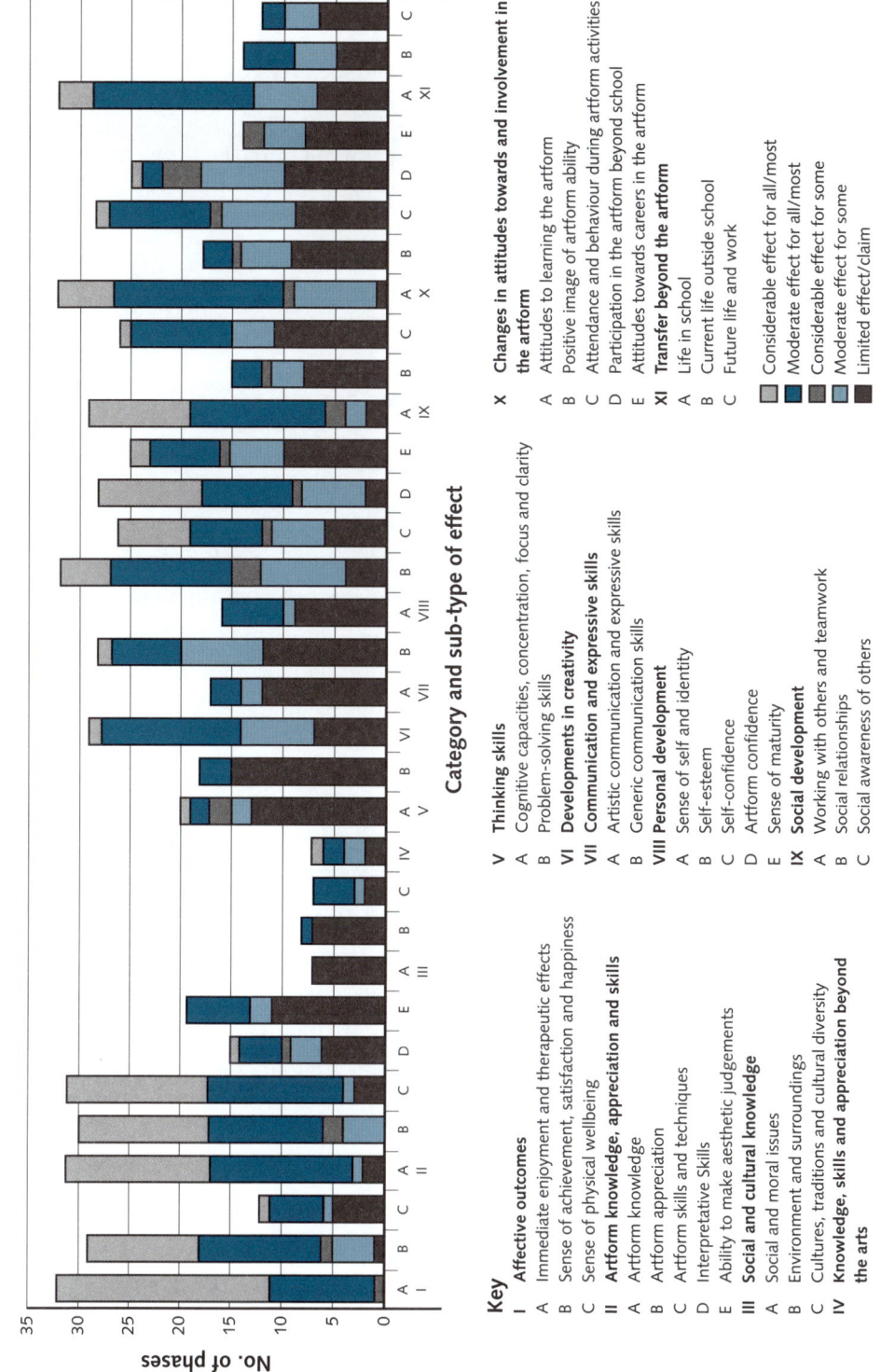

Category and sub-type of effect

Key

I   Affective outcomes
A   Immediate enjoyment and therapeutic effects
B   Sense of achievement, satisfaction and happiness
C   Sense of physical wellbeing

II   Artform knowledge, appreciation and skills
A   Artform knowledge
B   Artform appreciation
C   Artform skills and techniques
D   Interpretative Skills
E   Ability to make aesthetic judgements

III   Social and cultural knowledge
A   Social and moral issues
B   Environment and surroundings
C   Cultures, traditions and cultural diversity

IV   Knowledge, skills and appreciation beyond the arts

V   Thinking skills
A   Cognitive capacities, concentration, focus and clarity
B   Problem-solving skills

VI   Developments in creativity

VII   Communication and expressive skills
A   Artistic communication and expressive skills
B   Generic communication skills

VIII   Personal development
A   Sense of self and identity
B   Self-esteem
C   Self-confidence
D   Artform confidence
E   Sense of maturity

IX   Social development
A   Working with others and teamwork
B   Social relationships
C   Social awareness of others

X   Changes in attitudes towards and involvement in the artform
A   Attitudes to learning the artform
B   Positive image of artform ability
C   Attendance and behaviour during artform activities
D   Participation in the artform beyond school
E   Attitudes towards careers in the artform

XI   Transfer beyond the artform
A   Life in school
B   Current life outside school
C   Future life and work

- Considerable effect for all/most
- Moderate effect for all/most
- Considerable effect for some
- Moderate effect for some
- Limited effect/claim

The effects with the lowest profile in AEI were:

- knowledge, skills and appreciation beyond the arts

- social and cultural knowledge, with social and moral issues constituting the sub-effect receiving the most ratings for limited impact

- thinking skills – both sub-types were heavily associated with limited impact

- communication and expressive skills, in which, interestingly, fewer phases were noted to result in artistic expressive skills than those related to general communication skills.

Salient features of the high profile outcomes

Affective outcomes

This first broad category, which included the sub-types immediate enjoyment and therapeutic effects, sense of achievement, satisfaction and happiness and sense of physical wellbeing, was the most frequently referenced outcome, consistently nominated and rated highly by all interviewees across the AEI. However, perhaps not surprisingly, physical wellbeing was less evident than the other sub-types, noted mainly in dance and physical drama interventions.

Often constituting the most immediate and direct effect of arts activities, examples of enjoyment were particularly evident, including references to 'fun', 'excitement', getting a 'buzz' or 'adrenalin rush' and experiencing a 'thrill' or 'delight'. At its most fulsome, one artist described the outcome of an AEI as pupils becoming 'dizzy with the experience'. Accounts of relaxation or cathartic outcomes also emerged: interviewees variously noting that an intervention produced 'a feel-good factor', reduction of stress ('letting off steam', 'chilling out', 'feeling calmer') and a sense of escapism in the moment (experiencing 'magic', 'awe and wonder'). Descriptions of activities being 'therapeutic' in the short term were also collected.

The sub-type sense of achievement, satisfaction and happiness, capturing a more deep-seated manifestation of pupils' affective response to interventions, was also prevalent. Here, it was pupils' 'pride' in their achievements, coupled with the inner sense of satisfaction or fulfilment that resulted ('feeling pleased with themselves' 'being chuffed to bits') which were frequently specified. 'Happiness' references intimated the capacity of interventions to alter pupils' mood over and above enjoyment or relaxation during the activity – carried into the next lesson, or as part of their general personality. References to longer-term 'therapeutic' outcomes were also garnered.

Accounts categorised under sense of physical wellbeing included references to health and fitness, increased body awareness ('how bodies work', using their bodies in different ways) and better body control.

It is perhaps in no way surprising that affective outcomes from the AEI initiative should dominate the discourse of pupils, teachers and artists and it is indeed worth noting again both the frequency and also the intensity of the descriptors in many instances. Such a flowering of positive emotion may intimate what sets the experience of arts interventions apart from the 'normal' curriculum diet for many pupils. Certainly, it can be said that arts interventions achieve and confirm the government's 'enjoyment is the birthright of every child' commitment. The evidence clearly underlines the substantial contribution that arts interventions can make to meeting the Government's vision of ensuring that learning is an enjoyable experience (DfES, 2003).

A question mark might be posed about the sustainability of affective outcomes and how far they are used to generate learning outcomes beyond the (albeit powerful) sense of enjoyment and fulfilment in the immediate aftermath of the experience[i]. There may well be an ever-present risk that turns one of the great strengths of arts interventions into a major weakness: arguably, over-reliance on the capacity of arts interventions to achieve enjoyment and other affective outcomes may detract attention away from the planning for other additional learning goals.

Artform knowledge, appreciation and skills

This broad grouping actually contained five types of effect, three of which, artform knowledge, artform appreciation and artform skills and techniques again showed much prevalence across the AEI, with a high rating for intensity.

Examples of increased artform knowledge included pupils' better understanding of: the elements or building blocks of the artform (such as 'depth, colour and form' in art, 'structures rhythm and harmony' in music; 'routines' and 'space' in dance), as well as associated definitions and terminology (such as 'character' in drama, 'stabs, jingles and beds' in radio and 'shade' and 'diagonals' in photography). In addition, there were references to greater technical understanding of artform processes (such as firing clay, composing) and the historical, contemporary and/or cultural context of the genre or artist/arts organisation ('where it came from' or 'we learnt a lot about different musics and cultures').

Closely associated, but slightly less referenced than artform knowledge was increased artform appreciation. There were many accounts of pupils' appreciation of: a broader repertoire of styles within the artform (having their 'eyes opened', 'art is not just painting', 'music's more than just playing an instrument') and sometimes pupils' 'amazement' at such discoveries was particularly striking. New awareness of the professional arts world, including 'what it is like to be an artist' and what their role entailed also emerged in some instances.

Developments in artform skills and techniques were also highly evident across the AEI. Some skills could be artform specific (such as using cutting tools in art, learning to sing better in music), but others were more generic (such as physical coordination and control or use of the voice). It is noteworthy that, as well as pupils' existing artform skills being developed or extended, there were examples of completely new skills learnt (e.g. using a mixing desk in turntablism or, as was noted for one drama intervention: 'it's given the [pupils] a whole set of ways of working'. In addition, there were accounts of pupils acquiring 'artform discipline' (such as 'I learnt to be an audience', take instructions, or watch the conductor).

The two further artform outcome-types were also evident though less prevalent. Interpretative skills, that is becoming 'artform literate' and a critical listener/viewer was noted, albeit considerably less frequently. Examples included the ability to 'read between the lines' in drama, interpret meanings and emotions in poetry and 'listen deeper' in music, or use one's 'internal ear'. Finally, an increased ability to make aesthetic judgements was referenced in about half of the phases. The enhanced capacity to value and care for others' work based on the virtues of effort and intrinsic artistic merit (e.g. 'everyone can have a go' and 'no-one can say that's rubbish') surfaced among older pupils, as well as their ability to make evaluative judgements about the quality of works of art based on such criteria as aesthetic merit.

The sheer range and depth of artform related outcomes is surely another notable finding about arts interventions and their impact on young people. For many pupils and young people, a new world of arts meanings and skills appears to have opened up from their encounter with professional artists. In a national and international policy context that frequently accentuates instrumental justifications for arts education and arts-education partnerships, the importance of learning the knowledge, skills and discipline associated with particular artforms should not go unnoticed. These may well constitute the foundation stones upon which all other learning outcomes need to be built. The question might be posed, however, as to how far teachers and artists were able to capitalise on this vibrant initiation and development in the artforms.

Personal development

This third high-ranking outcome included advances in self-esteem, self-confidence and artform confidence, as well as the somewhat less frequently noted sense of maturity and identity.

Self-esteem surfaced particularly in the discourse of teachers and artists, though pupils also noted feeling 'good' or 'better about myself, proud' or 'special' as a result of AEI involvement. This was often linked to the fulfilment accruing from the recognised quality and success of the interventions' products or performances. As one artist picturesquely noted, the pupils were 'smug and smiley' from the acclaim received. Increased self-confidence also was often referenced: pupils generally 'coming out of their shell, having a go, speaking up more', as well as artform confidence, often from 'realising capabilities' or 'recognising' the acquisition of new skills.

While sense of maturity was a less universal effect within interventions, there were a number of references to behaviours and attitudes modulated because of involvement in the AEI (e.g. more 'commitment, motivation, discipline' 'greater responsibility...self control...independent working', or even, as one primary pupil put it, 'learning you can't always get what you want'. Self-identity outcomes were least nominated, but accounts of pupils 'understanding more about themselves' and having a sense of self ('I know myself better...you can understand more of what you want to be') did emerge in both primary and secondary age groups.

This array of outcomes in the personal domain is again significant. Such positive impacts suggest an important contribution for arts interventions in what many would see as the most fundamental aspect of young people's education: their emotional health. This evidence offers endorsement to the investment by government departments, Arts Council England and various charitable foundations in the arts as a means of engaging issues of social exclusion and suggests that the role of arts education in the social inclusion agenda may benefit from even greater attention. Those professionals and sponsors who support the disengaged or disaffected (or seek to prevent such attitudes emerging) may perhaps see enormous potential in using arts to address the lack of self-esteem which often underpins these young people's anti-social activities and anti-learning stances.

Social development

The three sub-types of this outcome covered increased ability to work with others and teamwork, the capacity to develop new social relationships and enhanced awareness – empathy or sensitivity to others.

The most common and strongest outcome reported from the AEIs was the ability to work with others. There were numerous references to better 'collaboration', 'cooperation' and 'teamwork' between pupils (also noted as 'sharing', 'trusting', 'supporting' and 'helping each other'), as well as a new group cohesion, 'a sense of pulling together'. In some instances (notably among them, a special school), the capacity to form new and productive working relations with adults and teachers was cited. The capability for new social friendships was less frequently noted as an outcome. However, some interviewees did suggest primary pupils were 'better able to deal with new people coming in' or 'got to know each other quicker' and it was sometimes said that secondary pupils had 'formed close friendships', were more 'confident to make new friends' or 'found mixing with new people easier' ... 'socialised more'. The enhanced social awareness or empathy outcome also emerged, though not so universally intense for all participating pupils. Comments like 'learning to be a good friend', being able to 'give each other praise', be 'more aware of others' feelings' or '[the intervention] made me think of everybody else' were testament to this sub-type of social development emerging among some primary pupils. From their secondary peers, it was more the discourse of respect for others, better understanding of each other, tolerance and learning people are different which surfaced.

A version of Gardner's 'interpersonal intelligence' was very apparent for certain pupils experiencing an AEI. Statements from artists, teachers and particularly pupils themselves suggest perhaps a moving towards what the great Victorian novelist George Eliot called the recognition that there is 'an equivalent centre of self' in other people. The individual, familial and societal benefits of such developments in our young people are no doubt self-evident and it may be that the potential of arts interventions through artist-based partnerships in this arena requires more prominence and acclaim. Equally, for wider impact, further and sustained opportunities to work and learn in this way may also be required, given that so much of young people's in-school learning and assessment is heavily focused on solo individual performance. In advancing the skills of teamwork, arts interventions would seem to offer a powerful curriculum strategy for developing the social skills much required in the workplace.

Salient features of the low profile outcomes

Knowledge, skills and appreciation beyond the arts

This category, with its focus on achieving learning directly related to other curriculum areas, was not only the least referenced overall, but also emerged as an outcome exclusively associated with interventions in primary schools.

Adults and pupils in seven primary AEI phases variously noted 'learning to identify materials', 'that objects are fragile', 'learning the shape of the rainbow', 'about books', 'shapes and sizes' or 'a few more words'. All such statements (usually accompanied by the word 'learn') related directly to specific themes or subject matter that made up the content of a particular phase and it was notable that all types of interviewee were able to identify how the intervention reinforced or introduced concepts from a wider discourse than the arts.

The complete absence of references to this outcome for secondary pupils is perhaps unsurprising. The primary school tradition of a 'topic work' approach (or cross-curriculum learning) has few parallels in the pedagogy of key stage 3 and 4. Does it remain the case that as long as subject boundaries are maintained and protected in the secondary curriculum, this potential for embracing the content of one subject area in the curriculum experience of another will have little resonance with either pupils or teachers? The finding also suggests that the much-publicised debate in recent years about so-called transfer effects (e.g. Eisner, 1998; Winner and Hetland, 2000) may have been something of an esoteric irrelevance, since in practice, at least in this country, there may be (in addition to the organisational obstacles in secondary schools) signs of a reluctance or lack of confidence to 'use' the arts to develop other areas of the curriculum. This interpretation gains further significance when it is considered that the AEI interventions all took place in EAZs where there were strong aspirations and pressures to improve, for example, literacy and numeracy levels. In the light of this, it remains, from a policy perspective, an intriguing question as to why more of the interventions or phases were not channelled in these directions.

Social and cultural knowledge

Three sub-types here all revolved around pupils' greater awareness, in relation to: social and moral issues (IIIA); their environmental and social surroundings (IIIB) and their own and other cultures and traditions (IIIC). As already noted, these were among the least referenced effects, with the limited number of explicit comments by pupils themselves particularly evident.

Awareness of social and moral issues was nominated by a handful of artists and teachers: usually in relation to specific AEI content (e.g. apartheid because of gospel singing, the ethics of hunting animals, the dilemmas of a particular character in a play). Similar low level and largely adult testaments surfaced for new environmental awareness: there were references to an expansion of pupils' own geographical horizons ('made them feel there is a world out there that's accessible to them', 'giving them a wider experience of the world' by a visit to a nearby town); or increased awareness of their current surroundings (e.g. pupils' being 'more interested in classroom displays' than before; or 'seeing the world in a different light'). More pupil voices did attest to impact in the third sub-type, relating to enhanced cultural and multi-cultural awareness, where non-Western artforms were the focus of the intervention. Comments like 'I learnt about different cultures' … 'religions' or 'languages' did surface, but not with any intensity, while adult comment referred to 'increased cultural awareness of race' or 'greater awareness of cultures and philosophies and comparison with Western life-styles'. Finally, it is worth noting that overall, not only were references here numerically small, some comments from adults seemed generalised and often largely aspirational in tone: accompanied by words like 'could', 'might be' and 'hope so'.

The relative lack of effects in this domain must give pause for thought. It suggests that social and cultural awareness outcomes may need to be explicitly planned for – or at least articulated – in order for them to resonate with more than a minority of pupils. The re-casting of arts education as 'creative and cultural education' in the Robinson Report (1999), along with its advocacy of artist partnerships, make the limited contribution to social and cultural education of the arts interventions studied here all the more pertinent. Given that, as with most outcomes, the degree of awareness of social and moral issues as an outcome was likely to be a reflection of the content and aims of the interventions, the finding also poses the vexed question of whether arts interventions tend to accentuate form and skills rather than content and meaning, in contrast to the adult world of arts which are often so redolent with social, moral and cultural issues. Recent research from the NFER suggests that artists may not be alone in choosing to accentuate form and skills in the curriculum content: Downing and Watson (2004) found that secondary school visual art teachers focused heavily on skills and techniques rather than the social or moral content of art. However, it is also important to ask whether AEI's distinctive contribution in other effect domains would be compromised by such a focus on the social, moral and cultural content of the arts? Does it suggest there remains a challenge for artists and teachers to find ways of maximising arts interventions' potential for engaging important social and cultural messages without diluting its unique pedagogy?

Thinking skills

With two sub-types, relating to cognitive capacities like concentration and focus, as well as problem-solving skills, this outcome was another example of an effect with limited reference across the AEI as a whole.

Improved concentration was nominated by a small number of pupils, reiterating that exact term ('at the time I could concentrate better than normal', 'it benefited my concentration'), while some artists and teachers, in addition, tended to introduce the notion of 'focus'. A better 'memory/memorising skill' was also on occasion referenced by adult interviewees. Very occasionally, this sub-type of thinking skill was deemed by a pupil to transfer to other learning situations ('if I can concentrate as hard as I can now on how to do drumming ... then I could try that in another lesson'). Problem-solving skills were only sometimes referenced ('thinking around a problem', 'learning to solve problems', 'realising there are different ways of working things out') and evident particularly in certain artists' discourse, as was decision-making skills. Again, here was an outcome arena very much more rarely nominated by pupils themselves and only from two secondary school phases (typical comments here were 'you solve problems and think ahead' and 'I think around things in different ways').

Analysis showed a lack of corroboration between artist and the teachers regarding this category and notably, it was artists who were more often citing the potential gains in problem-solving and decision-making skills inherent in the AEI. Perhaps they uniquely recognise the cerebral rigour, risk and resolution associated with any art creation. However, the low existence or recognition of thinking skill outcomes surely suggests that greater reflection and articulation between and among artists, teachers and pupils is required.

Communication and expressive skills

Two sub-types made up this category of effect: artistic communication skills covered pupils' increased capacity to express themselves through the arts, as well as recognising arts' potential for this self-expression. Generic communication skills related to general enhanced vocabulary and use of language (written and spoken), as well as confidence to express ideas or opinions.

General expressive skills was the more commonly reported effect, with references to pupils at both primary and secondary ages being 'more forthcoming', 'more confident' to speak; having 'improved language', 'talking in full sentences', 'developing conversational skills' or proffering 'more sophisticated questions and answers'. In more than one intervention, pupils themselves suggested they were 'better at explaining'. In addition, several teachers mentioned 'broadened', 'enriched' or 'increased' vocabulary. Artistic expression emerged less frequently, but a few secondary pupils did make apposite comments here, suggesting they had learnt 'you can use singing like a language to communicate, hand gestures are a tool for expression, communication is not just verbal'. Artists and teachers sometimes noted pupils had been given 'a tool for expression', or, as one artist suggested, a pupil had 'found her own voice through music'.

Artistic expression was neither a common nor considerable effect of the AEI interventions for most pupils and generic communication skills, whilst more frequent, were not cited as a major outcome for much of the pupil sample either. Nevertheless, there was a middle-ranking presence overall. Perhaps such outcomes intimate very important potential benefits from an arts intervention, particularly noteworthy in the domain of basic language skills. Equally, as a facet of arts education that may have been overlooked in recent debates, there may be merit in policy makers and practitioners emphasising or re-focusing on the 'tool of self-expression' function of arts. However, the lack of universal impact might suggest that short-term experiences have inevitable limitations in this arena.

Other outcomes

Developments in creativity

In this mid-ranking category of effect, different levels or degrees of creativity were specified. A very few references were made to what might constitute 'basic' creative development through imitation and adaptation of ideas and themes learnt during the arts interventions, while occasionally pupils said they were 'better at trying things out' or 'were using [AEI] ideas in their own work'. More commonly, interviewees' discourse referred to effects on pupils' 'imagination' ('widened', 'improved', 'sparked') or that they had 'done more imaginative work'. Other interviewees volunteered the term 'creativity', saying it had been 'enhanced' or 'increased' by AEI involvement. It was sometimes stated that pupils' 'used', 'developed' or 'tried out' their 'own ideas' more. Beyond that, it was occasionally noted that some pupils were 'more adventurous, more willing to take risks', 'experiment' or 'try new things'.

Although the results from the questionnaires (see 2.5.1) suggest that developments in creativity were a little more prevalent (at least in certain types of interventions) than the interview data would indicate, the findings reveal that, overall, these various discourses of creativity were not volunteered as a considerable effect for the majority of pupils. Furthermore, when we asked all pupils if they had been able to use their own ideas on the projects, it is worth noting that there were as many references from pupils to not being able to use their own ideas, as there were to being able to use their own ideas. Also, where they were able to use their own ideas, many felt this was adapting what someone else had given them, rather than requiring their originality or being inventive with their own ideas. This provides further evidence that as an outcome, pupils and young people did not describe developments in creativity as strongly as they did some of the other outcomes.

At first this may seem surprising, but it may indicate that progression in creativity after the AEI experience was not planned for. Is this an arts skill-base issue for teachers, a pedagogical issue for artists and even an aptitude one for pupils? Does it highlight the lack of follow-up? Or, in working with professional artists, does the encounter with artform discipline and learning technical skills inevitably supplant pupil creativity in the short term? What are the opportunities for experimentation and skill development after an arts intervention? If gains in creativity by encounters with artists are as elusive as this study suggests, a greater investment in the explicit planning and designing for developments in creativity may be required by all participant groups.

Changes in attitudes towards and involvement in the artform

This multi-faceted effects category revolved around altered views of a particular artform because of experiencing an arts intervention in that genre. It may result in pupils' greater interest in doing more of the artform at school; a more positive view of their ability in that area of arts; improvement in behaviour and/or attendance whilst experiencing the artform activities; a desire to increase participation outside school – or even to pursue a career – in that genre and respectively.

In terms of more interest in a particular artform, typical adult comments were that pupils had 'an improved attitude', 'liked [that genre] more' or the arts intervention had made them more 'positive', 'enthusiastic' or 'inspired'. One artist noted 'a thirst for more'. Pupils explained that they were 'more into' a particular artform, felt the arts intervention had 'made [the artform] in general feel more interesting' or 'were working harder' at it or 'taking it more seriously'. Pupils also particularly voiced their sense of improved ability: from both primary and secondary sub-samples came references to technical improvement (doing the artform 'better'), that their output was 'better quality' or that the arts intervention 'helped with normal lessons'. Improved behaviour was noted by a number of pupils, both within and beyond the intervention ('it helps me be good', 'I listen better in [art] lessons now') and teachers also referred to these arenas of improvement (e.g. 'more on-task behaviour' or the 'class is now more attentive'). Sometimes it was noted that behaviour 'improved over the sessions'. Only in an out-of-school intervention was attendance mentioned ('they all turned up and wanted to learn'). However, pupils' behaviour worsening was also noted as an outcome in some instances. Increased voluntary participation out of school was also evident. A small number of pupils described now 'doing [it]', 'practising' or 'making things' at home, or visiting galleries, theatres more. Some mentioned an intention to attend dance, music or drama clubs or 'buy decks'. Beyond a leisure-time pursuit, a few pupils stated they 'might become' or actually 'wanted to be a' … singer, artist, poet, or DJ etc. Others spoke in terms of 'having more ideas of a possible career' or 'being interested in [the genre] as a career', sometimes with reference to first accessing college courses and work placements.

The potential of an AEI to inspire further involvement and commitment to a particular artform was thus in evidence, though again the discourse of pupils and adults was often aspirational rather than actual. It may be that such progression needs clearer avenues, opportunities or sustained support in order to capitalise on the enthusiasm engendered.

Transfer beyond the artform

This category of effect covered three non-arts arenas where the arts intervention had a general impact: life in school, including pupil attainment, aptitudes and attitudes to learning; current home-life and extra curricular activity or behaviour and aspects of future adult life, such as leisure activity or the world of work.

Most commonly reported was an impact on pupils' school life. An intervention might aid learning generally: there were references[ii] to 'improved ability', 'better Standard Assessment Tests (SATs) results' or as one pupil put it 'I feel clever [now]'. Accounts of pupils' enhanced confidence, self-discipline, enthusiasm or concentration transferring to other subjects also surfaced regularly, as did pupils' more positive attitudes to school and learning. Pupils spoke of 'realising school can help you learn', feeling 'happy', 'proud of' or 'different about' school; as well as recognising that 'school is where you can achieve things'. Occasional references to pupils 'wanting to come to school more' and improved behaviour in school also occurred. In terms of current out-of-school life, several primary school interventions were said to have resulted in 'more talk at home', while secondary pupils described 'trying new things' socially because of increased confidence. Occasionally, a pupil was noted to have improved general behaviour ('getting into fights less'), or as one put it, 'music has changed how I have my manners'. An intervention's legacy for future life was much less evident, but sometimes the acquisition of 'skills valuable for any career' were referred to, along with how useful participation in the intervention would be for a CV, college entrance, a Record of Achievement certificate or just for 'opening doors'. One artist powerfully stated the legacy was 'something to draw on creatively … so that other things exist away from social problems'.

In this way, the varied 'value-added' nature of effects being transferred to other arenas was testified to. The impact on attitudes to school and learning seem particularly noteworthy as a contribution to social inclusion. It may be that the kinds of learning experiences offered by an AEI intervention that can engender this change therefore hold important messages for curriculum designers and practitioners alike.

Negative effects

Up to this point the discussion has centred on the positive effects of the AEI interventions. However, occasionally references were made to negative changes. In most categories, the numbers of such references were very limited. In some categories a negative effect would stretch the bounds of possibility (for example, it would seem improbable, if not impossible, to experience an intervention and come away with a negative effect in category artform knowledge).

Categories where the majority of negative effects were reported comprised:

- immediate enjoyment and therapeutic effects (where pupils did not enjoy the activities)

- sense of physical wellbeing (some pupils found interventions physically tiring and references were made to African drumming hurting pupils' hands)

- attendance and behaviour during artform activities (where pupils had misbehaved more than usual in sessions, or in artform lessons since the intervention)

- attitudes to learning the artform (where pupils now had a more negative attitude towards the artform in general, or specifically during school lessons)

- transfer to life in school (where pupils had a more negative response to school as a whole following the intervention).

Whilst such negative forms of impact were rare for most types of effect, those relating to attitudes to learning the artform were found to be more common among secondary pupils who responded to pre- and post- phase/ intervention questionnaires. As we shall see (2.5.1), the evidence on negative attitudinal effects points to a serious problem, which underlines the importance of proper consideration being given to how the risks of causing detrimental outcomes for pupils can be reduced.

Corroboration between pupils, teachers and artists?

In general and from an overall perspective, there was normally a high level of corroboration between pupils, teachers and artists concerning the broad outcomes. The degrees of corroboration were especially high for the most frequently cited broad effects, such as affective outcomes, artform knowledge, appreciation and skills and personal development. Nevertheless, some interesting exceptions to this trend included:

- artists reported thinking skills more frequently than pupils and teachers

- artists reported social development more often than teachers and pupils

- teachers reported social and cultural knowledge more often than artists and pupils

- pupils reported changes in attitudes towards and involvement in the artform and (to a lesser extent) transfer beyond the artform more often than artists or teachers.

With regard to the latter, it seems likely that because artists often had no post-phase contact with the pupils, their knowledge about later effects was inevitably less informed. Similarly, teachers may also have been less aware of attitude or transfer changes that relate to young people's wider school and out-of-school activities.

Despite this consensus at a broad level, greater variation in the reporting of outcomes by the three participant groups was apparent at both phase level and sub-type effect level. Relevant discrepancies are discussed in some of the later sections. But first we address a key issue concerning the relationship between the outcomes reported above and the aims of the interventions.

In this section, we have reported that certain of the effects of arts interventions were more prevalent than others. A number of possible explanations may be suggested: the most and least frequent outcomes are a product of what aims were associated with the interventions (and any infrequent outcomes were largely unintended effects) or the less frequent outcomes represented aims that were selected but seldom achieved in practice. Clearly, if, from a policy perspective, it is considered desirable to increase the impact of arts interventions in the less frequent outcome areas, it is crucial to know whether these effects were aimed for but not attained through the design and delivery or simply not targeted in the first place. It is to these issues we turn next. To set the question of aims and their relation to outcomes in context, we first describe how the aims of the AEI initiative and the specific interventions were framed.

2.3 Outcomes and aims

2.3.1 Aims of the AEI

The overarching aims of the AEI initiative were set out in a number of Arts Council documents. Together with the research strands, the AEI was conceived as a 'strategic initiative … focused on the arts and education interface and designed to facilitate the development and delivery of creative arts education and document its impact on young people …' (Arts Council background information for researchers). The Arts Council wished to 'explore the relationship between arts activities and the wider learning experience for young people in the formal education system by commissioning a range of research activities over three years ...' (Arts Council documentation). Envisaged areas of investigation included:

- to test the impact of the programmes on young people's personal, cultural, intellectual, social and economic development

- appreciation of culture and cultural diversity

- understanding of equal opportunities and social and political issues

- contribution to social inclusion

- enhancements to professional development

- performance in the curriculum.

After initial consultation with potential participants, the key priorities for Bristol and Corby EAZs were documented. For schools in the Bristol EAZ, these priorities included the professional development of staff and arts coordinators, links between nursery, primary and secondary schools to share good practice; artists in and pupil visits out and sustained work with artists. In addition, raising attainment and providing opportunities for the less able to succeed were identified as key whole-school issues (from Bristol Arts Plan, 2001). In Corby EAZ, five areas for action were identified:

- teaching and learning

- literacy

- the inclusion curriculum, particularly at key stage 4

- retention in post-16

- raising self-esteem and extending horizons through enrichment programmes (from *Challenge for Corby*, 1999).

From its inception to its implementation, there was an evolving of aims for the AEI interventions. In practice, with few requirements to adhere to any nationally or locally prescribed set of aims, teachers, other host professionals and artists had considerable latitude to determine their own goals and activities – though, of course, plans for the interventions needed local and national approval.

2.3.2 Aims of the interventions

During the baseline fieldwork, adult interviewees (teachers, headteachers, youth workers, artists and other arts organisation staff) often held impressionistic views of the aims and expectations of projects – what they hoped might be achieved. In many instances, this seemed due to teachers and artists having not yet fully planned what the projects would entail. Pupils themselves rarely articulated perceptions of aims or expectations of projects; in many instances they were unaware of the ensuing project, or held vague views only.

In other cases at baseline, adult interviewees' views on aims were more global than specific to the phase or intervention in which they were involved. These perceptions were due in part to the nature of the interventions, particularly the series and developmental ones, where data was in a number of cases collected as a baseline for the whole of that AEI and its parts – and thus interviewees more naturally gave an overarching view of the aims. Experienced artists/arts-educators and curriculum leaders in the arts tended also to articulate global aims at baseline, relaying the possibilities for wide-ranging outcomes for young people's lives and for the school or artists' future work. Whilst appearing somewhat nebulous, without yet being rooted in concrete contexts for their own projects, these perceptions were often very general and frequently reflected the overall ethos of the AEI and the acknowledged need to provide evidence to make the case for arts interventions:

> *If the outcomes prove that it is highly beneficial for children to be involved in drama projects then that in turn will give credence to a lot of the work we do.*
> (arts education officer)

> *From our side, we just want to give the young people this most fantastic opportunity and hopefully increase their awareness* [of] *the things that are available to them, in the arts field, something that is going to engage and interest young people and just to hopefully increase their awareness and understanding about it and learn from it and maybe take it on and pursue it. …… Young people do feel that they are limited in what they can do and this is going to open up the horizons for them hopefully and take them on to other things.*
> (Youth Service leader)

From these beginnings, at any given point in time there was a continuum from those who were clearer about the aims of the specific interventions and phases to those who were less so. Thus, further evidence was collated on aims from written documentation at the 'process and immediate impact' stages of the data collection.

Aims in the written documentation

Written documentation on aims (see Table 2.1) was obtained from within five of the 12 pupil focused interventions. More specifically, this pertained to eight of the 32 pupil focused phases. (Other documentation was also obtained for other phases, but did not specifically relate to aims. Note also that written aims may have been produced elsewhere, but not provided for the evaluation.)

Table 2.1   Obtained written documentation on aims

Phase/Intervention	Documentation with aims	Produced by/ written by
Secondary, one-off, art	Development plan	Not known
Out-of-school, series, multi artform	Evaluation report	Youth Service
Secondary, series, multi artform, phase 2	Project plan	Artist
Special, series, multi artform, phase 2	School meeting minutes	School senior management team
Special, series, multi artform, phase 3	Project plan	Artist
Primary, developmental, drama, phase 1, 2 & 3	Project proposal for each phase	Arts organisation in collaboration with school

The written aims obtained were expressed in different ways, according to the purpose of the documentation in which they were presented. For example, some documents were presented in the format of project proposals containing aims, objectives, plans for each session (listing such things as materials required, activities, dates and times), as well as proposed budgets for the projects. Project proposals and plans were generally written by artists and arts organisations (rather than teachers) and it is likely that they were produced for the purposes of gaining funding consent for the projects. Some documentation was produced for purposes of internal evaluation and accountability within an organisation. Other documentation recorded minutes of meetings between various parties (teachers, headteachers, artists and arts council representatives) and described some of the processes by which aims and objectives came about.

Some written aims portrayed specific skills and outcomes that it was hoped pupils and young people would gain (including artistic, technical, personal and social skills). Other written aims focused upon the experience that it was hoped pupils would have, such as the experience of working with an artist, the opportunity to develop themselves as an artist and the experience of working as a team. These experiential process-based aims (rather than outcome-oriented ones) were expressed by artists more than by teachers.

Some aims portrayed a sense of 'fit for purpose'. For example, the aims expressed by an artist working in a special school highlighted a sense of achievement, identity and self-expression, which seemed appropriate to the individual needs of the pupils at the school.

In an intervention where artists and teachers worked extremely closely and collaboratively, the aims covered the content of the work, other curriculum areas and linkages with current work being done in the school, outcome measures and evaluation procedures. Although actually documented by the artists, close collaboration led to the most detailed exposition of aims.

2.3.3 The most and least common aims depicted

Given the varying nature of interviewees' responses regarding aims and expectations at baseline (before the start of projects), perceptions of aims have also been examined in the 'process and immediate impact' interviews. Projects were underway at this stage and in some cases the final session with the artist had just taken place. Although the question was asked at the start of the interview, one caveat of this exploration is that these aims were discussed retrospectively with regard to the projects taking place. The following discussion portrays (in the way that they were voiced) the most and least common aims depicted by teachers and artists in the pupil-focused interventions. Pupils' views have not been included in this discussion; prior to interventions, pupils themselves rarely articulated aims or expectations and during or after interventions, when asked about aims, pupils tended to restrict themselves to what they had actually done and learned.

The most common aims

The most commonly cited aims related to the pupils and young people, rather than to the teachers and artists or their organisations. They were voiced in terms of the types of experience that were expected and outcomes that might be achieved. The types of outcomes aimed for were generally those that would not be measured by 'hard' indicators (e.g. it was rare, if ever, for aims to be stated in terms of hard measures such as percentage increases in attendance or attainment).

The most commonly cited aim was to develop pupils' skills and techniques in the artform. This was aimed for in the majority of phases (22) and by both the teacher and artist in nine of these phases. For example, in a primary drama phase, the teacher hoped that the artists would '…give some sort of introduction to how drama is performed, some of the techniques used'; in a music intervention the teacher also hoped that the pupils would 'learn some new technical terms about rhythm and so on … a bit of expression'. In another primary intervention, the teacher aimed for '…the children to have an appreciation of what sculpture actually is and know how to go about planning and designing a sculpture'. Similarly, the artist in this phase was aiming for the children to gain '… experience of working with the willow and making models from paper and making models with clay'.

The second most common aim was to encourage a greater appreciation of the artform. Again, teachers and artists tended to concur over this aim. In some phases it was hoped that the pupils would possess a broader repertoire of styles within the professional arts world:

> …to give them experience of live art and to see how two subjects such as art and drama can actually merge. It was to show them something different really, to challenge their expectations and broaden their outlook about what art is and what drama is.
> (teacher, secondary arts intervention)

It was also hoped that pupils would value or appreciate the products of the artform more:

> When they see a piece of work at the Tate Modern or something similar, they will understand because they have some knowledge … will make them more open to it – that some people express themselves in this way.
> (teacher, secondary arts intervention)

In this particular phase, the artist also aimed to encourage an appreciation of the artform:

> … it was to give the children a different kind of take on what art is in terms of performance, to give them a different way of thinking about … to get them to think differently I suppose in terms of what art can be.

This type of appreciation of thinking around art hints at the notion of interpretation and critical skills, although only in a few cases was it fully articulated in this way as an aim. One example came from the artist working with clay and sculpture: '… I think [it's] important for them to get that skill of actually looking closely at things, because that will help them throughout art, whatever they are looking at.' Teachers and artist also aimed to satisfy this aim of enhanced appreciation by allowing pupils to see what it is like to be an artist and what their role entails: ' … to give them experience of working with an artist or professional'.

Increasing artform knowledge was also an important aim, featuring in 16 phases:

> *The aims really were to make an impact on the children in terms of developing their own knowledge and understanding in that curriculum area, which was historical mostly.*
> (teacher, primary cultural visit)

Aiming for development in creativity was fairly prevalent, featuring in 14 phases. For example, a youth worker from an out-of-school intervention hoped that the young people involved would 'explore their creativity'; a teacher in a secondary arts intervention aimed for the pupils 'to create images, to create art' and an artist in a primary arts intervention commented: '… that is really what I wanted them to get out of it, because I think that you learn a lot about your own creativity by having those range of things that you can do'. Developing pupils' imagination was also fundamental in some interventions.

Within the broad area of personal development, artform confidence was the key aim (interestingly, more so than self-confidence and self-esteem). This was more often aimed for by the artist, than the teacher. In fact, artists aimed for this in three times as many phases as the teachers. For example, the artist in one secondary intervention commented:

> *my first aim was to present* [the artform] *as something that is doable, something that is manageable, something that you can actually try and comprehend, it's not as obscure and meaningless as some students might assume. So it was to demystify this idea of being grand and written by people who are in their ivory towers and in a class of their own.*

In a secondary dance intervention the artist aimed to '… make a piece and to construct a piece that they feel confident in performing' and in a secondary drama intervention the artists hoped the pupils would seize '...the opportunity to turn into performers and to turn into confident people as well as confident performers'.

Both teachers and artists aimed to create enjoyable experiences with therapeutic effects. For example, an artist hoped that the children would 'have a go ... to make a nice sound and have fun, probably both at the same time' (primary music); similarly, the teacher hoped the pupils would 'gain enjoyment'. Another teacher commented 'my objective was for the children to have a good theatre experience and enjoy it' (primary drama). Finally, an artist aimed to '...get them excited about it, make them look forward to it' (secondary drama).

The least common aims

Of the cited aims, the following were articulated in relation to specific phases in only a few cases each: artistic communication and expressive skills, a sense of self and identity, changes in attitudes towards a career in the artform, transfer beyond the artform to current life outside school and to future life and work, an ability to make aesthetic judgements, an awareness of cultures, traditions and ethnic diversity and cognitive capacities, concentration, focus and clarity.

Other cited aims

Other cited aims included skills for team working, increased self-confidence and self-esteem, understanding and empathy with others and benefits to other areas of learning (particularly in terms of the personal and social skills gained). In addition, a performance or product and the experience of the project as an entity were cited as aims.

2.3.4 Aims mapped to outcomes

Having described the general features of the aims associated with the interventions, we can now explore how these aims of interventions map to the outcomes achieved. To do this, the aims, as described by interviewees and presented above were classified according to pupil outcome categories set out in section 2.2.

Were aims achieved?

In almost all cases, every pupil-related aim in every phase was achieved to some extent – according to the classifications of outcome employed earlier (bearing in mind strength and frequency of reported effects). However, it is important to bear in mind that we are considering here aims at a point when they have evolved and clarified and in some instances were somewhat or even radically different from those right at the start. In general, written aims were also reflected in the types of outcomes that pupils gained. Overall, however, there was variation in the extent to which aims were achieved (i.e. strength and frequency of outcome) and differences in the way in which aims and outcomes were voiced. Indeed, it is important to note that there were more recorded outcomes in each phase than aims. Many outcomes were not articulated as aims and some represent unintended outcomes.

Aims most and least frequently achieved

Table 2.2 shows the order of the top six most common types of aims and the top six highest profile pupil outcomes as discussed in sections 2.3.3 and 2.2 respectively.

Table 2.2   Common aims, common outcomes

Effect category	The most common types of aims	Effect category	The highest profile outcomes
IIC	Artform skills and techniques	IA&B	Affective outcomes especially immediate enjoyment and therapeutic effects and sense of achievement
IIB	Artform appreciation	IIA	Artform knowledge
IIA	Artform knowledge	IIB	Artform appreciation
VI	Developments in creativity	IIC	Artform skills and techniques
VIIID	Artform confidence	VIIIB, C & D	Personal development – particularly self-esteem, self-confidence and artform confidence
IA	Immediate enjoyment and therapeutic effects	IXA&C	Social development particularly working with others and teamwork and social awareness of others

On the whole, the most common aims reflect the outcomes with the highest profile for pupil effects: artform knowledge, skills and appreciation and some of the affective outcomes. However, there were perhaps higher profile outcomes in the broad category 'personal development' than had been aimed for; whilst there was a lower profile for creativity (compared with other types of outcome) than had been aimed for. The reasonably high profile social development outcomes, whilst not in the top six aims, were the next most commonly cited aims, although interestingly cited more so by artists than by teachers.

When mapped on to the outcome categories, it was evident that whilst some aims were less frequently cited, there were also some types of outcome that were never cited as aims of specific interventions of phases. Indeed, none of the teachers or artists cited an awareness of social and moral issues as specific aims, although they may have been underlying themes in the content.

Table 2.3   Least common aims, least common outcomes

Effect category	The least common types of aims	Effect category	The lowest profile outcomes
IIIA, B & C	Social and cultural knowledge	IV	Knowledge, skills and appreciation beyond the arts
VIIA	Artistic communication and expressive skills	IIIA, B & C	Social and cultural knowledge
VIIIA	A sense of self and identity	VA & B	Thinking skills
XB&E	A positive image of artform ability and attitudes to careers in the artform	VIIA	Artistic communication and expressive skills
XIB&C	Transfer beyond the artform to current life outside school and future life and work		
IIE	Ability to make aesthetic judgements		
VA & B	Thinking skills, particularly cognitive capacities, concentration, focus and clarity		

Some of the least commonly cited aims (see Table 2.3) reflect the outcomes with the lowest profile for pupil effects: social and cultural knowledge, thinking skills and communication and expressive skills. In addition, the profiles of the aims and outcomes in the sub-categories also reflected this. For example, in the aims relating to the broad category 'personal development', a sense of self and identity was the least aimed for and had a low outcome profile. Similarly, although the ability to make aesthetic judgements was from a high profile category (artform knowledge, appreciation and skills), this too was much less frequently reported as an effect. So, in general, where certain outcome categories or sub-categories were not aimed for, these mapped onto the outcomes with the lowest profiles. That is, the lowest profile outcomes may well be as a result of few aims pertaining to those types of effects.

Did aiming for a particular outcome mean that it was achieved with greater strength?

When all of the pupil outcomes in the AEI are considered, those which were described as having a considerable or moderate impact on most or all of the participants were most likely to have been aimed for. The outcomes having a considerable effect for just some participants were only aimed for in eight per cent of the phases where this outcome occurred. Outcomes evident for only a few individual pupils therefore, appear to be unrelated to aims; the outcomes they receive may be more related to individual differences. The outcomes having only a moderate effect on a few participants, or those with a limited effect for the group, were only aimed for in 16 per cent of the phases.

Therefore, if a particular outcome is aimed for, it is likely to be quite strongly achieved.

Which effects are achieved even when they are not aimed for?

Some outcomes are still achieved in arts interventions, even though they are not explicitly aimed for. As presented in Table 2.4, these were fairly high profile outcomes, but also had a high number of phases in which these types of outcomes were not explicitly aimed for.

Improvements in attendance and behaviour were achieved in 25 phases, despite the fact that, in each case, this was not aimed for. This is an extremely positive finding; it appears that art interventions in schools will affect pupils' behaviour and attendance, during the intervention, or in the artform lessons that follow, as an incidental effect in almost all cases. From the same broad category of outcomes, pupils' attitudes to learning the artform were improved in 24 phases, even though this was not aimed for. This covers the pupils' desire to repeat intervention experiences or to do more of the artform, changes in their enthusiasm for the artform in school and a realisation of the importance attached to learning. Therefore, it seems that arts interventions can encourage pupils to attend subsequent artform lessons and also foster a more positive attitude towards learning. Transfer beyond the artform to life in school was also evident in 24 phases, although it was aimed for in only a moderate number of phases.

Table 2.4   Outcomes achieved but not explicitly aimed for

Effect	Effect category	Number of phases in which effect was recorded but not explicitly aimed for
Attendance and behaviour during artform activity	XC	25
Attitudes to learning the artform	XA	24
Transfer beyond the artform to life in school	XIA	24
Self-esteem	VIIIB	23
Generic communication skills	VIIB	20
Participation in the artform beyond school	XD	19
Sense of achievement, satisfaction and happiness	B	19

Which effects seem unlikely to be achieved if they are not aimed for?

Many types of outcomes were achieved in many phases even where not aimed for. However, it also appeared to be the case that certain types of outcome were rarely cited in cases other than those in which they were aims.

Knowledge, skills and appreciation beyond the arts (outcome category) was only achieved in three phases where it was not aimed for. This suggests that it is more likely that pupils' knowledge and appreciation can be enhanced in areas of learning beyond the arts if this is a specific aim. It is unlikely that it will be produced unintentionally. Furthermore, outcomes related to social and cultural knowledge (outcome category) seem also unlikely to be achieved unless they are specifically aimed for. That is, improved awareness of pupils' surroundings and the world around them, awareness of cultures, traditions and cultural diversity and enhanced awareness of social and moral issues are usually only outcomes where aimed for. These outcome types were the two outcomes with the lowest profile overall as a result of AEI interventions. Perhaps the low incidence of these outcomes is a direct consequence of the fact that they were the least aimed for.

The following three outcomes also seemed unlikely to occur unless they were specifically aimed for: greater appreciation of the artform, artform skills and techniques and physical wellbeing. However, they did not feature among the lowest profile outcomes for pupils; rather they featured as subcategories in two of the three highest profile outcomes for pupil effects. Pupils were very unlikely to develop a greater appreciation of the artform, or develop their artform skills and

the arts–education interface: a mutual learning triangle?

techniques unless this was specifically aimed for. This is also an important finding, signalling that some of the most desired outcomes may only be achieved if they are specifically aimed for. Within the broad category of affective outcomes, achieving a sense of physical wellbeing in pupils also had to be aimed for. However, this is unsurprising given that this would be difficult to achieve in outcomes where physical activity did not feature heavily.

2.3.5 Overview on outcomes and aims

The discussion has considered the profile of aims in relation to the profile of outcomes in the 12 AEI pupil-focused interventions. The key findings are:

- most aims of these interventions and phases were pupil related, relaying expectations for the types of experience and outcomes that might be achieved

- in general, the profile of the most and least common aims matched the profile of outcomes – where aimed for, an outcome was more strongly achieved than where not aimed for

- there were perhaps higher profile outcomes in the broad category 'personal development' than had been aimed for (particularly for self-confidence and self-esteem) – whilst there was a lower profile for creativity compared with other types of outcome than had been aimed for

- some of the least commonly cited aims reflected the lowest profile pupil outcomes: social and cultural knowledge, thinking skills and general communication and expressive skills

- outcomes such as improvements in attitudes towards and behaviour in the artform, transfers to life in school and to self-esteem were the most likely types of outcome to be achieved even where they were not aimed for

- knowledge and skills beyond the artform and outcomes related to social and cultural knowledge were unlikely to be achieved unless they were a specific aim.

2.4 Variations in outcomes by key variables

2.4.1 Do different artforms produce different effects?

The four most common artforms in the AEI were visual arts (including photography), dance, drama (including theatre) and music. The effects from these four artform areas, which comprised 27 of the 32 initiative's pupil-related phases, are evidenced and compared here. The remaining five phases, which involved poetry, live art, turntablism, radio and 'materials', have not been included in the analysis for this sub-section. The 27 phases analysed here consisted of ten for drama, nine for music, five for the visual arts and three for dance. Given the small number for the latter, the results for dance should be treated with caution.

We first present the results in two figures, then discuss variations within broad effect categories before describing the outcomes profile for each of the four main artforms. To the best of our knowledge, this is the first time that such a comparative analysis has been undertaken for arts interventions.

Figure 2.4 displays the proportion of phases where (broad category) effects on pupils were evident and indicates the 'strength' of these effects on pupils. Table 2.5 shows the top five sub-type outcomes in each artform based on a ranking of all of the different sub-types according to the number of phases where a considerable impact for most/all participants was reported, followed by a moderate impact for most/all participants.

Variations within effect categories

All phases in all artforms evidenced effects in affective outcomes, with high percentages of phases showing 'considerable impact for most pupils', though relatively a little less so for music phases. Within this broad category, immediate enjoyment and therapeutic effects was the top sub-type outcome for dance, drama and music (second for visual arts) and IB (sense of achievement, satisfaction and happiness) also figured in the top five sub-type effects for visual arts and music. Sense of physical wellbeing was chiefly associated with dance.

All phases in all artforms evidenced effects in artform knowledge, appreciation and skills, with high percentages of phases showing 'considerable impact for most pupils' in all artforms – all phases in the visual arts registered this considerable impact. Artform skills and techniques was the top sub-type effect for the visual arts and the second highest for dance and music – interestingly, it did not appear in the top five for drama. Artform knowledge was frequently nominated in visual arts, drama and music, though in dance it was more likely to be artform appreciation. Interpretative skills and ability to make aesthetic judgements did not feature strongly as an outcome for any of the artforms, though it was more likely to occur in the visual arts than any other artform.

Figure 2.4 Proportions of phases where each broad type of effect was evident and their strength, by artform

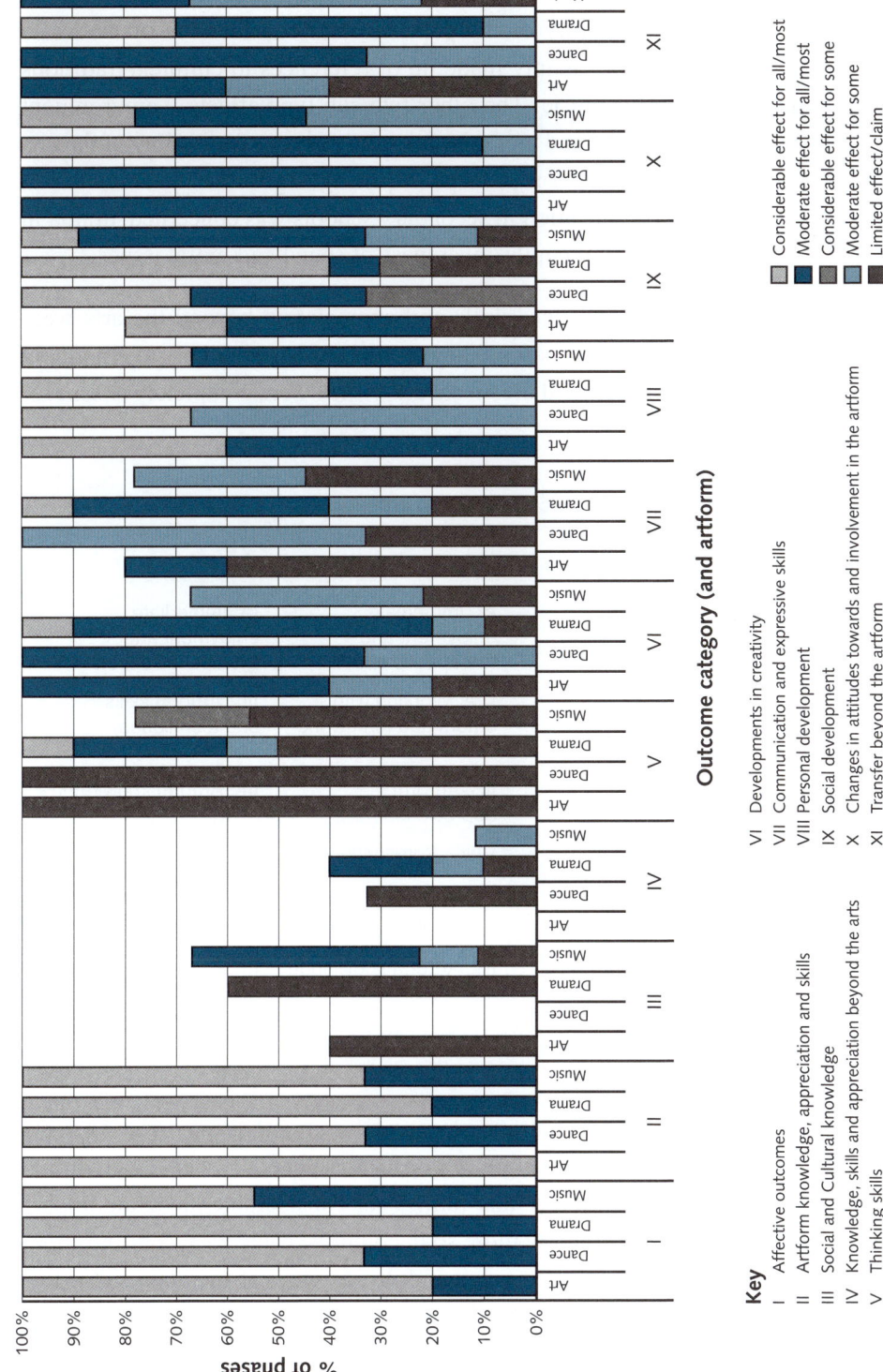

Outcome category (and artform)

Key

I   Affective outcomes
II Artform knowledge, appreciation and skills
III Social and Cultural knowledge
IV Knowledge, skills and appreciation beyond the arts
V   Thinking skills

VI   Developments in creativity
VII Communication and expressive skills
VIII Personal development
IX   Social development
X   Changes in attitudes towards and involvement in the artform
XI   Transfer beyond the artform

Key:
Considerable effect for all/most
Moderate effect for all/most
Considerable effect for some
Moderate effect for some
Limited effect/claim

Note: proportions are shown as a percentage of phases of each artform, to enable comparisons to be made, although caution must be employed because the numbers in each category are small.

For social and cultural knowledge music was the only artform where impacts were recorded for the majority of the pupils (either considerable or moderate effects for most). This was mainly made up of references to cultures, traditions and cultural diversity for music. The other two sub-type effects – environment and surroundings and social and moral issues were not prevalent in any of the artforms. The absence of the latter is perhaps surprising, since Harland *et al*. (2000) found that, as far as arts education in secondary schools was concerned, drama in particular seemed to develop pupils' awareness of social and moral issues.

Outcomes relating to knowledge, skills and appreciation beyond the arts were only evident in a minority of phases. They tended to be more likely to emerge in drama and dance than music and the visual arts – they were completely absent for the latter.

Table 2.5   The 'top five' sub-types of outcome in each artform

Visual arts	Dance	Drama	Music
IIC. Artform skills and techniques	IA. Immediate enjoyment and therapeutic effects	IA. Immediate enjoyment and therapeutic effects	IA. Immediate enjoyment and therapeutic effects
IA. Immediate enjoyment and therapeutic effects	IIB. Artform appreciation	IXA. Working with others and teamwork	IIC. Artform skills and techniques
IIA. Artform knowledge	IIC. Artform skills and techniques	IIB. Artform appreciation	IIA. Artform knowledge
IB. Sense of achievement, satisfaction and happiness	IXA. Working with others and teamwork	VIIIC. Self-confidence	IIB. Artform appreciation
IIB. Artform appreciation	IC. Sense of physical wellbeing	IIA. Artform knowledge	IB. Sense of achievement, satisfaction and happiness

Although all phases in the visual arts, dance and drama registered some effects relating to thinking skills, the strength of impact was generally weak, with drama being the only artform to achieve any ratings for considerable/moderate impact for most in some phases – slightly more so in cognitive capacities, concentration, focus and clarity than in problem-solving skills. In view of the claims that followed the debate on the so-called 'Mozart effect', the comparative paucity of outcomes in this broad category for music is worthy of note.

Similarly, all phases in the visual arts, dance and drama demonstrated some effects relating to developments in creativity, though the degree of impact was often not strong. Music was the only artform for which not a single phase posted considerable/moderate impacts on creativity for the majority of the pupils.

Within the broad category communication and expressive skills, outcomes relating to artistic communication and expressive skills were fairly low and ranked below those of generic communication skills. Indeed, outcomes for visual arts or music as tools for communication and expression were weak or unsubstantiated – for the visual arts this was at odds with the findings reported in Harland *et al*. (2000, p.266).

All phases in all artforms achieved personal development effects, though the strength of the impacts was less marked in the visual arts than in the other three artforms. Self-confidence featured more highly in drama than other sub-type effects in this broad category – it amounted to the fourth highest sub-type effect for drama. In other artforms different sub-types of personal development (particularly artform confidence) were ranked more highly than in drama.

In all phases of dance, drama and music there were impacts associated with social development and all the artforms posted appreciable proportions of phases where these effects were considerable/moderate for most pupils or young people. Reflecting the importance of group work in these artforms, working with others and teamwork appeared in the top five sub-type effects for drama and dance.

All phases in all artforms achieved effects relating to changes in attitudes towards and involvement in the artform and transfer beyond the artform – again with good levels of at least moderate impact for most pupils in all the artforms.

Artform variations

The distinctive characteristics of each artform's effect patterns are summarised below.

Visual arts

- This was the only artform for which artform skills and techniques surpassed immediate enjoyment and therapeutic effects as the main effect.

- Its top five sub-type effects were all located in artform knowledge, appreciation and skills and affective outcomes.

- It registered no effects under knowledge, skills and appreciation beyond the arts.

- Developments in creativity was ranked in the top ten effects for the visual arts (but was not present in this regard for drama or music). Pupils' accounts revealed that creativity in the visual arts was related mainly to feeling able to 'try out' or 'practise' given ideas or to explore ideas. In the visual arts, pupils' creative development also highlighted a realisation of the opportunity that the arts afford for creativity, some pupils having never thought about 'creating their own ideas' in art before.

- Additionally, ability to make aesthetic judgements had a higher ranking than in any of the other artforms. Furthermore, pupils' interpretative skills in the artform, whilst not ranked particularly highly, featured more so in the visual arts than the other artforms.

- The visual arts contained examples of negative impacts on pupils' attitudes towards the artform; as well as on pupils' self-esteem.

Dance

- The absence of artform knowledge from the top five sub-type effects in dance is conspicuous.

- The presence of working with others and teamwork and sense of physical wellbeing in the top five represents a distinctive feature of dance outcomes.

- Dance evidenced the least number of sub-type effects in the personal and social domains.

- Developments in creativity was ranked in the top ten effects for dance, but was not present in this regard for drama or music.

- Pupils' testimonies suggested that in dance (as with the visual arts), pupils' creativity was related mainly to feeling able to 'try out' or 'practise' given ideas or to explore ideas.

- Dance in particular had some 'negative' impact on pupils' sense of wellbeing – becoming tired or achy. While some pupils saw this as ultimately leading to better health and fitness, other pupils only articulated the immediate 'negative' impact.

- On the other hand, dance (along with music) had the greatest potential for transfer to current life.

Drama

Drama covered the fullest range of sub-type effects in terms of where there was felt to be an outcome for most or all the pupils – 29 of the possible 33 sub-types featured in this way. This was followed by visual arts (20), dance (17) and music (16). Drama also had the largest proportion overall of impacts that were felt to be considerable for all/most pupils – suggesting that drama has the potential for not only engendering a broad range of effects but also for 'strong' impact.

- The absence of artform skills and techniques from the top five in drama is striking.

- The presence of working with others and teamwork and self-confidence in the top five was a distinctive feature of drama outcomes. In other artforms different types of personal outcome ranked more highly, particularly artform confidence.

- For personal development and social development, drama had the highest proportion of phases where impacts were felt to be considerable for the majority of pupils.

- Drama had the greatest potential for transfer beyond the artform to life in school and to future life and work.

- Relatively speaking, drama was not strong in developments in creativity. In fact, an interesting distinction was made by pupils' ability in drama: weaker ability pupils were deemed to get no further than exploring and imitating others' ideas, whilst the higher ability pupils were seen to experiment with and adapt ideas given to them.

- Drama contained examples of negative impacts on pupils' attitudes towards the artform.

Music

- Whilst drama enveloped the fullest range of effects, music covered the least. It also included the highest number of phases with no effect in certain categories.

- Its top five sub-type effects were all located in artform knowledge, appreciation and skills and affective outcomes, echoing the top rankings for the visual arts.

- For social and cultural knowledge music was the only artform where it was felt that impacts were for the majority of the pupils (either considerable or moderate effects for most). One of the most notable differences was the high ranking of pupils' knowledge of cultures, traditions and cultural diversity – ranked 11th in music, but last, almost last (or absent) of the 33 sub-types of outcomes in all the other artforms.

- Music evidenced more sub-type effects in the personal and social domains (including artform confidence, self-esteem, self-confidence and working with others) in its 'top ten' than any other artform. In addition, outcomes related to social awareness of others (e.g. empathy) also ranked highly in music.

- Along with dance, music had the greatest potential for transfer to current life and for music this was also evident in terms of artform participation beyond school.

- For developments in creativity, music was the only artform where impacts were not referred to as being for the majority of the pupils; creative outcomes in music were ranked lower than in any other form.

- Music contained examples of negative impacts on pupils' attitudes towards the artform; as well as on pupils' self-esteem.

2.4.2 Do effects vary by type of educational setting?

Having considered the extent to which different types of effect resulting from the AEI initiative may have varied according to artform, this sub-section explores the extent to which variations were apparent according to the type of education setting involved, including:

- primary schools – five sites (incorporating a nursery and a special school) which hosted 13 phases

- secondary schools – five sites hosting 16 phases

- 'out of school' – two sites hosting three phases (mainly young people of secondary age).

The number of phases within 'out-of-school' settings was low, so results must be approached with considerable caution. As with the previous sub-section, we know of no similar analysis in the research literature.

Overall outcomes in different types of education setting

Figure 2.5 shows the effects reported within each of the different types of education setting, in terms of the proportions of phases where each outcome was cited and the strength attributed to it.

Figure 2.5   Proportions of phases where each broad type of effect was evident and their strength, by type of educational setting

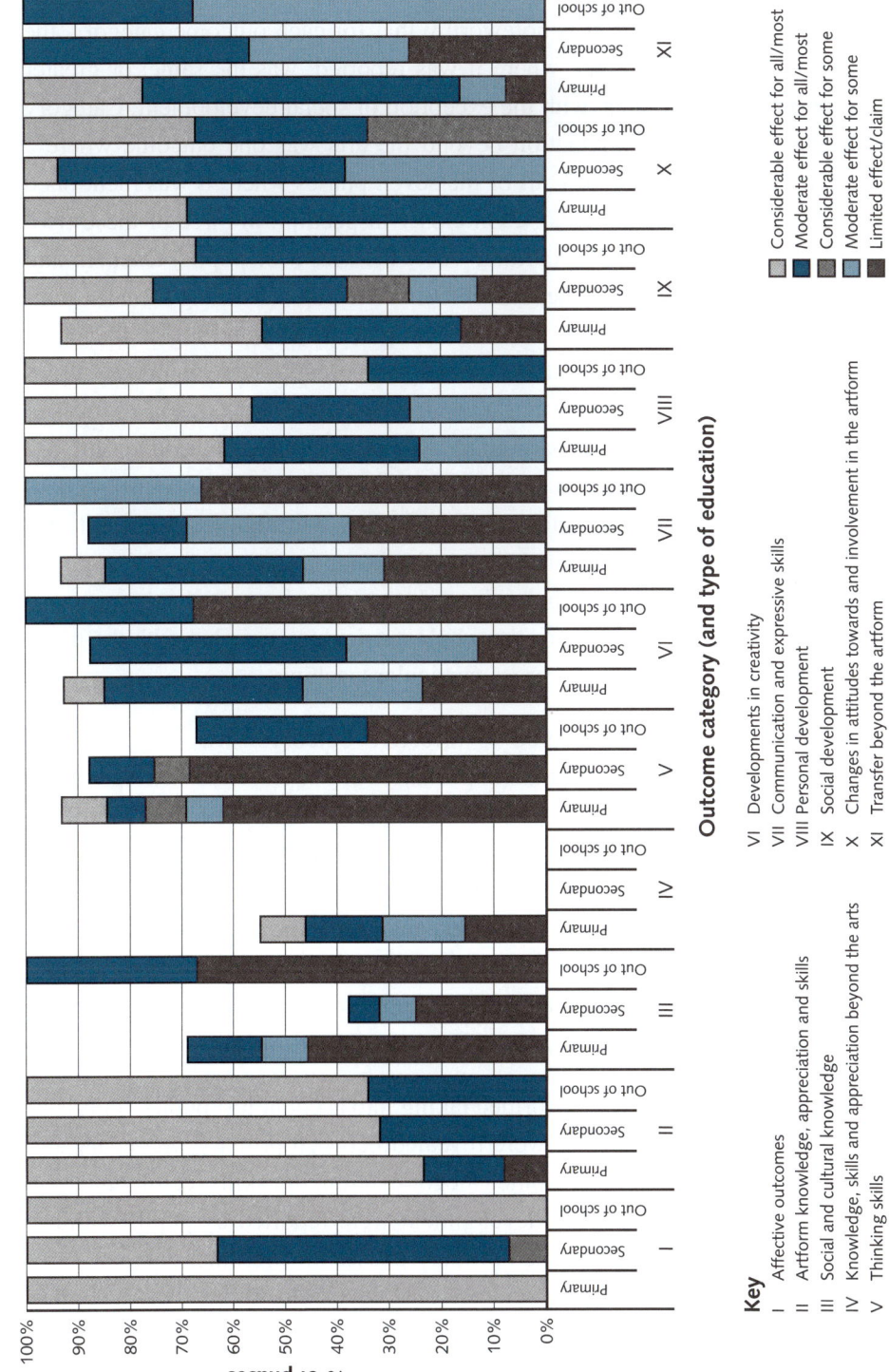

Outcome category (and type of education)

Key

I   Affective outcomes

II   Artform knowledge, appreciation and skills

III   Social and cultural knowledge

IV   Knowledge, skills and appreciation beyond the arts

V   Thinking skills

VI   Developments in creativity

VII   Communication and expressive skills

VIII   Personal development

IX   Social development

X   Changes in attitudes towards and involvement in the artform

XI   Transfer beyond the artform

Considerable effect for all/most

Moderate effect for all/most

Considerable effect for some

Moderate effect for some

Limited effect/claim

Note: proportions are shown as a percentage of phases of each artform, to enable comparisons to be made, although caution must be employed because the numbers in each category are small.

On balance, the differences between primary, secondary and out-of-school phases were limited. However, it is noteworthy that for each outcome category, the proportion of primary phases, where it was reported, was the same, or greater than that in secondary sites, with the exception of social development. Category knowledge, skills and appreciation beyond the arts was one outcome where a clear difference was apparent – all of the seven phases where it was mentioned took place within primary schools. On closer inspection, in three of these (two theatrical performances and a cultural visit) the views of pupils, teachers and artists were in agreement. References were made to pupils learning from the non-artform content of the phases – for example, from watching a theatrical performance pupils learnt about books and the colours of the rainbow (topics within the story). It seems likely that secondary and out-of-school phases focused more intently on the artform (particularly where they were embedded within a secondary school curriculum subject). None of the secondary or out-of-school phases involved participants watching performances with significant non-artform content – where artists did perform, the emphasis appeared more firmly on pupils observing and learning about the artform. It may also be a product of primary school teachers' responsibility for the whole curriculum, coupled with the traditional approach of 'topic'-based cross-curricular teaching.

The strength of impact attributed to affective outcomes was slightly more restrained in secondary schools than in primaries or out-of-school settings. Similarly, transfer beyond the artform was credited as being a considerable or moderate impact on the majority of participants within more primary than secondary or out-of-school settings. Social and cultural knowledge was cited as an outcome of a greater proportion of primary than secondary phases, although the difference was accounted for mainly by a larger number of phases resulting in a 'limited effect/claim' in this category. It was reported as an outcome from all three of the out-of-school phases, though at a similarly low level of impact.

When a similar analysis was performed taking into account just pupils' reports of effects, some clearer disparities were revealed between primary, secondary and out-of-school phases. Three outcome categories: thinking skills; communication and expressive skills and social development were reported by pupils within a higher proportion of secondary than primary phases. In two other outcome categories developments in creativity and personal development there was a similar, though less marked distinction. Since this pattern was not apparent amongst the views of teachers and artists, it is possible that the finding stems from primary pupils' limited articulacy in relaying these outcomes, rather than an actual absence of impact.

Sub-type effects within different education settings

Looking in more detail at the different sub-types of outcome reveals some subtle distinctions between those recorded as resulting from primary, secondary and out-of-school interventions. Initially, ranking the sub-type effects according to the number of phases where a considerable impact on the majority of participants was cited, followed by the number resulting in a more moderate impact on the majority, gives the top five sub-type effects for each type of education setting (see Table 2.6).

Table 2.6   The top five sub-types of outcome in each type of educational setting

Primary	Secondary	Out-of-school
IA. Immediate enjoyment and therapeutic effects	IIB. Artform appreciation	IA. Immediate enjoyment and therapeutic effects
IIA. Artform knowledge	IA. Immediate enjoyment and therapeutic effects	IIC. Artform skills and techniques
IIC. Artform skills and techniques	VIIID. Artform confidence	VIIID. Artform confidence
IXA. Working with others and teamwork	IIC. Artform skills and techniques	IB. Sense of achievement, satisfaction and happiness
IB. Sense of achievement, satisfaction and happiness	IIA. Artform knowledge	IIA. Artform knowledge IXA. Working with others and teamwork

Some variations in sub-type effects for the different settings are apparent.

* The top ranked outcome within secondary schools, artform appreciation was only sixth and tenth for primary and out-of-school interventions respectively. However, analysis solely on pupils' views brings this into the top five within all types of setting – pupils reporting it more often than teachers or artists in all types of education setting.

* Artform knowledge was ranked more highly within primary than secondary and out-of-school settings. Harland *et al.* (2000), however, suggested that artform knowledge was an important outcome of the in-school secondary arts curriculum. The implication may be that older pupils tend to have a higher 'baseline' in terms of artform knowledge than their younger counter-

parts, thus more limited scope for gaining new knowledge as a result of an intervention.

- Pupils' confidence in their own artform ability was placed third in the rankings for both secondary and out-of-school interventions. It was ranked 12th in primaries, characterising it as an outcome mostly associated with older pupils.

Further down the rankings, other differences were evident.

Overall attitudes to learning the artform were reported by some interviewees from all of the 32 phases. However, pupils' views indicated that 69 per cent of primary phases had affected the majority of pupils, compared with only 31 per cent of those in secondary schools. Having said this, secondary phases resulted in more reports of changes in participation in the artform beyond the normal school day and changed attitudes towards careers in the artform. This probably reflects older pupils' greater concerns with their future and ability to determine their own leisure activities. Although younger pupils appeared to have gained improved attitudes towards the artform generally, this did not appear to have transferred to out-of-school activities or thoughts about future careers.

Self-confidence was reported as resulting from 92 per cent of phases in primary schools compared with 69 per cent in secondary schools, though the rankings were broadly the same. However, this mainly represented the views of artists. Pupils' views showed the reverse, with secondary phases leading to the most reports of increased self-confidence for the majority of participants.

Transfers to current school life were reported by interviewees within all of the 32 phases and overall, interviewees within 85 per cent of primary phases referred to an impact for the majority of pupils (compared with only 44 per cent within secondary schools). This was particularly evidenced by teachers – perhaps the best placed to identify such an effect, with more limited corroboration from artists, or pupils themselves.

In addition to the numerical variation in terms of the numbers of phases where each type of effect was reported, there were also variations in the actual contents of each sub-type when examined in terms of primary, secondary and out-of-school educational settings. For the most part it appears this was related to the ages of the pupils involved and the sophistication of their prior learning and experience. Two typical examples may be cited.

Artform skills and techniques

The differences here were about the level of sophistication of the skills and techniques developed.

Primary pupils referred to:

- learning to play drama games
- starting to use and care for musical instruments and equipment
- 'cutting and sticking'
- using clay.

Secondary pupils' skill development was more specific, including:

- reading music
- rhythm
- ensemble playing
- making felt and batik
- writing and performing poems
- controlling facial expressions and non-verbal communication
- stage awareness, dance moves and choreography.

Working with others and teamwork

Different discourses to describe working with others and teamwork were employed by primary and secondary pupils. Primary pupils described being more able to get themselves into groups or find a partner, knowing how to help others and learning how to work with other people. Those in secondary schools talked in more depth about listening to each other, cooperation, negotiation, managing group situations and being better at working with people than they would normally.

Comparing the outcomes of AEI with those from in-school arts teaching

Looking solely at pupils' views, a broad comparison can be made between the rankings of effects resulting from regular in-school arts teaching, as reported in Harland *et al.* (2000) and those from AEI interventions in secondary schools. This is limited to a broad comparison, because the typology of effects presented here and the method of assessing the breadth and strength of each has been developed somewhat from the original. However, ranking the effects according to the number of phases where the majority of pupils cited a major impact, then by the number of phases where the majority cited a more modest impact and comparing this ranking with that presented in Harland *et al*. (2000) highlights some important issues.

Artform appreciation was the top-ranked effect from AEI interventions – much higher than the 14th it was ranked as a result of the arts curriculum in secondary schools. Pupils identified that working with an artist had increased their appreci- ation of the artform – particularly in terms of their extended awareness of the potential repertoire or scope of the artform. This could be due to the fact that interventions often introduced a new genre or style in an artform, or a new range of skills, rather than supporting something that the teaching staff in school already did. The teachers often chose to focus interventions on giving the pupils a different experience within the artform that the school could not easily provide, for example new instruments in music, felt and batik in art, etc. Using artist- based partnerships to explore a dimension to the artform not covered in the normal in-school curriculum could be seen as the curriculum 'enrichment' or 'compensatory-deficit' approach.

Outcomes related to technical skills and capabilities within the artform were ranked by far the highest as a result of the secondary arts curriculum (Harland *et al*., 2000), considerably above the next-ranked item, enjoyment, in terms of the number of citations it received. In the AEI interventions, these two effects were reversed – with immediate enjoyment and therapeutic outcomes increasing dra- matically and being ranked second, pushing artform skills and techniques into third. The emphasis that pupils placed on their enjoyment of the experience of interventions might be expected as they were often viewed as being different, new and exciting – outside the realms of the regular arts curriculum. The slight shift away from learning new skills and techniques is a little more difficult to explain. It may be that each phase of an intervention involving a relatively short- term artist input may have limited the amount of time pupils were actually able to spend developing their skills in the artform, thus hampering perceptions of their improvement in this area.

One effect where AEI interventions seemed to result in lower levels of impact was developments in expressive skills (ranked fifth as a result of regular teaching compared with 25th for artistic expression as a result of AEI interventions). This may, again, be related to the short-term nature of the individual phases – it may be that for self expression to develop, a longer-term and more regular relationship needs to be established between the pupils and the individual from whom they are learning.

The results of the above comparison may signal some important policy implications – they suggest that, at secondary level at least, the distinctive 'added value' of arts interventions (as practised within the AEI) centre on their capacity to offer heightened degrees of enjoyment and fulfilment, along with their scope to raise and broaden appreciation of the artform.

2.4.3 Do outcomes vary by cost, location or type of intervention?

Variation by cost

In order to broadly examine the relationship between the cost of providing each phase within the AEI interventions and the reported outcomes, each phase was classified into one of three broad cost bands:

- Low: under £500 (10 phases)

- Medium: £500–£1500 (10 phases)

- High: over £1500 (12 phases).

The proportion of phases within each of these bands reported as leading to each type of effect and their strength, were then compared. There were few clear distinctions by level of investment, particularly within pupils' reports of outcomes – with only artform skills and techniques and self-esteem resulting from a higher proportion of phases and at a higher level of impact within high cost phases. Teachers supported the views of pupils – demonstrating cost-associated increases in strength and/or breadth of these outcome sub-types, as well as working with others and teamwork, immediate enjoyment and therapeutic outcomes and sense of achievement, satisfaction and happiness. However, there was an apparent cost-associated decrease in both breadth and strength of the outcome artform appreciation, suggesting that this effect – and strong forms of it – were less likely in higher cost phases. This may indicate that in higher cost phases artform learning substitutes skill acquisition for artform appreciation. Accounts from artists endorsed pupils' and teachers' views which pointed to higher cost projects resulting in more reports of effects within artform skills and techniques. Apart from this, the absence of major variations in the outcomes of arts interventions according to costs suggests that, in general, factors other than the total level of investment (such as the way in which funds were deployed) may be more influential in determining pupil outcomes. These other factors are discussed in Chapter 4.

Variation by location

A similar analysis was performed in order to determine the extent to which outcomes from interventions located within the two different EAZs differed.

In terms of communication and expressive skills, the views of pupils, artists and to a lesser extent, teachers coalesced in such a way that these effects, particularly generic communication skills, were more often developed in Bristol interventions. Similarly, within personal development, self-confidence, artform confidence and sense of maturity were more often evident in Bristol, although self-esteem was an outcome from more phases with a stronger level of impact in Corby. Teachers' and artists' views broadly supported this pattern, except in the case of artform confidence which was identified more often by artists in Corby than Bristol.

Participation in the artform beyond school was a more common outcome in Bristol, with the views of teachers and artists corroborating those of pupils – perhaps an indication of the greater opportunities for arts participation in Bristol compared with Corby.

Variation by type of intervention

Initially, the 12 interventions in which artists worked directly with pupils (excluding the 'teacher development' interventions) were conceived as comprising four of each of three broad types:

- one-off, short term
- series – where the same group of pupils experienced a series of short-term inputs in different artforms over a period of time
- sustained developmental – where the same group of pupils experienced inputs in a single artform, to support incremental learning.

In reality, some of these types proved less appealing to the schools involved, or more difficult to organise, such that what actually happened in practice did not always reflect what was planned. For example, because of problems in one school the planned developmental series in art eventually comprised only one phase from which sufficient data could be collected – thus it was re-classified as a one-off. The interventions which actually occurred were:

- one-off (five interventions)

- series – multiple artform (four interventions, between two to six phases each)

- developmental – single artform (three interventions, two in drama with three phases each and one in music with five phases).

It seemed that not all developmental series interventions, based on a single artform, were viewed by teachers and artists as a cohesive series where each phase built on the last with the intention of 'incremental learning'. In practice, the intervention planned as developmental in music actually involved five distinct music experiences with five different musicians, the order of which was not deemed to be important by the music teacher – they were not planned in order to advance outcomes in a developmental way. It is worth noting that the length of individual phases also varied considerably – from a one-hour long performance to a full term of one-hour lessons or a week long residency.

Outcomes from individual phases within different types of intervention

An examination of the proportion of phases within each type of intervention which resulted in reports of each outcome type revealed no major differences. There were, however, some interesting minor distinctions in that knowledge and appreciation beyond the arts was most often apparent within one-off phases, whereas social development and thinking skills both gave stronger results in the individual phases of series and developmental interventions.

Pupils' views exposed the greatest difference in terms of the two sub-types of thinking skills (cognitive capacities, concentration, focus and clarity and problem-solving skills), which received the most frequent and strongest nominations in the individual phases of developmental interventions. Teachers' and pupils' views revealed similar increases in working with others and teamwork within series and developmental interventions. Artists described this outcome more strongly from developmental interventions, compared with both one-offs and series. Teachers and artists both reported stronger effects in terms of social awareness of others from developmental interventions. However, all of these differences were felt to be more associated with the predominance of drama phases (particularly those involving pupils' active participation rather than passive watching) within series and developmental interventions, which resulted in strong outcomes in these areas. On closer examination, knowledge and appreciation beyond the artform was probably more strongly associated with interventions in primary schools than with the type of intervention.

The sequential nature of phases within interventions was considered. Were some outcome types developed in later phases of series or developmental interventions but not during earlier phases or one-off interventions?

The only difference amongst pupils' reports of effects was within changes in attitudes towards and involvement in the artform. Accounts of improvements in attendance and behaviour during artform activities and, to a lesser degree, participation in the artform beyond school were more frequent during the later phases of series and developmental interventions. This might suggest that, over the course of series and developmental interventions, pupils were becoming more aware of, or keener about, meeting the expectations of them in terms of behaviour and attendance during sessions and more inclined towards participation in the artform outside school.

Teachers' views often revealed outcome peaks (particularly in terms of effects on the majority of participants) within second and third phases and a tailing off in those occurring fourth or later. For example, in terms of artform knowledge, six out of 11 first or one-off phases resulted in a reported impact on the majority of pupils. In phases occurring second (in series or developmental interventions) the figure was six out of seven phases, but for those occurring fourth or later it had dropped to only two out of seven. Developments in creativity and communication and expressive skills (both sub-types) saw similar reductions during later phases.

Again, artists' nominations of effects were most frequent and often strongest during phases occurring second or third within series or developmental interventions. Tentatively, this might suggest that there is an optimum number of two or three phases within a series or developmental intervention, or that additional strategies are required to maintain momentum over the later stages of interventions involving more than three phases.

The accumulation of outcomes from different types of intervention

Having considered the outcomes of individual phases occurring within different types and at different points within interventions, here we explore the accumulation of effects from the 12 pupil-related interventions overall. The effects were ranked (on the basis of the number of phases resulting in considerable and then moderate effects for the majority of pupils where multiple phases were involved).

Once the interventions are viewed as a whole programme rather than as discrete individual phases, it is acknowledged that there were major distinctions between the range and strength of the effects which each type of intervention generated. In general terms, the one-off interventions where pupils had only one opportunity to experience an effect resulted in a narrower range of effects reported overall than those where pupils experienced multiple phases and therefore had more than one chance to make gains in each category. For example, according to teachers, primary pupils experiencing a one-off intervention where they watched a theatre performance did not experience social development. The series in the primary special school included an analogous phase involving a performance and the effect was similarly absent. However, three other phases in the series, involving different activities, resulted in reports of this outcome, to some degree, for the majority of pupils. It would seem, therefore, that including a range of different types of phase within series or developmental interventions may result in a broader possible range of effects overall.

It was difficult to identify distinct differences between the effects most highly or least highly ranked within different types of interventions. Outcome categories thinking skills and communication and expressive skills were the only broad outcome types which were absent from the majority of one-off interventions, but present in most series and developmental interventions, though they were both generally weak.

In addition to the increased overall range of effects from series and developmental interventions, some effects were reported as a result of more than one phase, but generally it was difficult to find evidence of cumulative learning or incremental development (e.g. pupils' enjoyment of phases within series or developmental interventions did not appear to be deeper than within a one-off phase, although they experienced that same level of enjoyment more times). We could only locate two main exceptions to this general absence of cumulative learning that could be connected with different types of intervention: one related to artform skills and techniques; another to working with others and teamwork.

Artform skills and techniques was one of those effect types which was closely linked with the artform involved. In series interventions involving different artforms in each phase, a range of different skills and techniques were developed, but to a relatively limited extent. For example, in the primary special school, pupils learnt how to do dance exercises, take photographs and use cameras, play rhythms on African drums and skills in working with clay. In a secondary series, pupils learnt how to do drama 'scenes', make felt and batik, compose songs with music and words and play musical instruments, perform dance moves and steps, write and perform poems and techniques with sound and images involved in live art. In these cases, pupils' skill range was broadened, but each skill was not necessarily developed incrementally over multiple phases.

The focus within developmental interventions was on the same artform in each phase. Within the primary developmental drama intervention pupils learnt drama games and basic theatrical skills of taking on a character and understanding scripts during the first phase. The second phase consolidated their skills in drama games and developed into acting out situations and role playing. The third phase continued to develop pupils' theatrical skills, with one teacher commenting 'they are like little actors now' – demonstrated through a play that they helped to devise and perform. This example suggests a developmental progression in skills – starting with knowing drama games, through being able to act a small scene or role play, to being able to perform a play that they were involved in devising. One of the actors leading the sessions said 'to be successful in learning you have to keep coming back to it … as your understanding changes you will reuse a skill in a different way and that is a major benefit of having worked over a long term with these children'. There was also a sense that the pupils would not have made the same gain in terms of skills and techniques from the third phase if they had not previously experienced the first two.

Working with others and teamwork was identified particularly in connection with drama and dance phases and as such was a repeated outcome from phases within developmental drama interventions. It is acknowledged that drama relies heavily on pupils working together, whilst other artforms are often viewed as more individualised pursuits. However, this outcome was also frequently cited in connection with phases in series interventions involving other artforms where working together and teamwork were supported or required. Looking in more detail revealed that pupils who were given multiple opportunities to work together in groups during arts interventions experienced a greater sense of 'camaraderie' and 'shared experience' than those involved in very short one-off phases. This affected pupils' working relationships with each other and also with their teachers and the artists involved. Pupils' skills in working with others and teamwork appeared to deepen (rather than new or different skills being developed) with each phase during an intervention. There may be important implications here for the social inclusion agenda – in this context, arts interventions with multiple phases appear to have brought pupils closer together and improved their working relationships both with each other and with their teachers. There is some evidence that the enhanced sense of community and belonging engendered, coupled with increased peer pressure, may reduce pupils' disaffection and improve behaviour.

It appears, on balance, that series and developmental interventions result in a wider range of effects for pupils overall than one-off phases. In addition, the same types and sub-types of effects were often reported as resulting from series and developmental interventions on a repeat basis. Some of these repeats represented reinforcement of the effect during each phase, whilst others involved a subtle shift of emphasis within the category or development of the effect in slightly different ways. Some interviewees were also clear that later phases of series or developmental interventions would not have been possible or successful without pupils having experienced earlier ones. To a limited extent, this would suggest that the effects from these longer interventions, involving multiple phases, did, in certain respects, amount to more than simply the sum of their individual parts, often despite limited linkage between phases or deliberate planning to this end. Perhaps, because of this, the overall evidence for significant degrees of incremental development was not compelling.

2.5 Outcome routes and developmental learning

By way of advancing the discussion of cumulative learning, this section reports on the possible routes within and between types and sub-types of outcomes. Previous research has documented current and retrospective views on the outcomes of arts participation (Harland *et al.*, 2000), but from a mainly static viewpoint. This research explores the scope for moving towards a more organic and developmental perspective, taking forward previous research in two ways. First, by analysing pupils' responses to questionnaires prior to and after the phase (pre- and post-), the 'distance travelled' by pupils is considered. Second, by following a sample of pupils through the multi-phase interventions (both in a single artform and in different artforms) a more developmental perspective of the learners' progress may be constructed. Developmental or hierarchical routes 'through' the outcomes are tentatively suggested and illustrated with examples experienced by some of the pupils and young people.

2.5.1 Exploring the 'distance travelled'

Changes in attitudes towards the artform and personal characteristics

Pupils and young people in the secondary and out-of-school interventions completed questionnaires, pre- and post-phase. Questionnaires were administered in 16 phases, in seven of the 12 pupil-targeted interventions (see Appendix 2 for an example of a questionnaire).

Changes in pupils' attitudes were tracked through pre-and post-items in two fields: their attitudes towards the artform and towards themselves and their personal characteristics. This pre- and post-analysis was possible in nine of these phases, where ten or more same respondents filled in questionnaires at both pre- and post-stages. The key findings, which are summarised below, contain some unexpected results.

On the whole, pupils had slightly less favourable attitudes towards the arts and about themselves after the phase (or intervention, if single artform) compared to before, although it should be noted that their attitudes generally remained on the positive side of the scale. Except for the item 'I'm quite a confident person', shifts from pre- to post- scores more often moved in a negative rather than a positive direction. Interestingly, every single shift in the secondary-developmental drama intervention moved in a negative direction and yet this achieved good effects overall. The sizes of the shifts were different in the various interventions, but on the whole, these were negative (e.g. 'I look forward to coming to school' showed a negative shift in more phases than a positive shift).

In terms of attitudes towards the arts, the most notable change in this regard occurred for the item, 'I really enjoy … I really dislike [the artform] at school' (and in one case, post-intervention ratings were tipped towards the 'dislike' end of the scale). This apparent downturn in pupils' attitudes towards the arts is somewhat intriguing. Paradoxically, enhanced enjoyment of the artform in the context of the interventions (according to interview data) may have resulted in less favourable attitudes towards the artform in school lessons. Pupils apparently form the opinion that the artform as they experience it within the in-school curriculum is not as stimulating or captivating as that experienced in the arts interventions – or is simply not available within the normal school curriculum. These results elevate the significance of the findings reported earlier (see 2.2.2) from the interview data regarding negative effects, specifically in connection with changed attitudes to the school version of the artform. The evidence suggests that schools, artists and brokers of arts-education partnerships need to pay much greater attention to the issue of how highly engaging and enjoyable interventions will impact upon pupils' attitudes to the artform in the school, once the intervention is over.

The risk that such interventions could lead to pupils feeling less positive towards, more critical about, or more frustrated by the school's offering in the artform needs to be carefully assessed and managed. In particular, if negative attitudinal effects on pupils are to be averted, crucial questions concerning the means by which pupils' heightened awareness and raised expectations of new approaches to artistic creation can be satisfied beyond the life of the intervention need to be addressed in the earliest stages of project conception and planning. For teachers, the results send the message that arts interventions are likely to affect the way that pupils see and feel about their exposure to that teacher's normal practice and curriculum provision. If they are to avoid the intervention stimulating more negative and critical constructions of the normal school diet, it would seem unwise for teachers not to get fully involved in designing, planning, helping execute, sustaining and learning from the intervention and the artist's input.

The downward trend in perceptions of 'self' was evident in many of the items. Pupils in one particular phase (occurring at the start of their secondary school careers) became less favourable in their attitudes on all 16 items about self (e.g. self-esteem, understanding themselves, self-image at school, ability and in relations with others).

The chief positive change in self-perception was for the item: 'I'm quite a confident person ... I'm not very confident'. However, looking at certain individual phases (rather than the whole sample of pupils), there was a cluster of positive change around personal and social developments (impacts mapping and to some extent communication and expressive skills in the model of effects).

It should be stressed that these items explored general perceptions of self and were not explicitly linked to the arts or AEI. Clearly, there are likely to be several factors other than the experience of the AEI intervention at play in these patterns of responses pre- and post- intervention. In between times, pupils have got older, progressed through their schooling – by half a term or so and sometimes up to an academic year – and assumed other activities and life-experiences. Indeed, other research indicates that there is a general downward trend in secondary school pupils' enjoyment of the curriculum, across all subjects, starting at the time between year 7 and year 8 and continuing, in some instances, through to year 11 (see Harland *et al.*, 2002 and Lord, 2003). Other indicators of pupils' attitudes towards school also suggest this trend (for example, perceptions of progress, enjoyment of school, see Harland *et al.*, 2002).

It is perhaps tantalising that these arts interventions appear not to have affected pupils' perceptions of themselves more positively (although it should be noted that their perceptions about themselves were also on the whole slightly more positive than negative). It raises the question, have these projects succeeded in ameliorating any gradual decline in self-esteem and self-image at school as pupils get older? In terms of attitudes towards their 'selves' and school (such as self-image at school, looking forward to school and finding lessons interesting) results would suggest not, though a control group would be needed to assess whether the decline may have been steeper without any arts interventions. However, against this sobering backcloth of generally declining levels of positive self-esteem, the high impact of the arts interventions (according to the interviewees' testimony) on exactly these qualities of personal development takes on new significance and meaning. Whilst these results testify to the improbability of arts interventions alone arresting any longer term downward trend in attitudes towards self-esteem and self-image at school for many children in these EAZ areas, they also highlight two other points: firstly, the critical need for educational experiences that address the problems of low self-esteem and poor self-image and secondly, the manifest power of arts interventions to make substantial contributions to countering these downward trajectories, if only temporarily. Clearly, they also underline the case for devising longer-term strategies that could ensure that developments in self-esteem and self-image were sustained over time.

Perceptions of outcomes – questionnaire data

The questionnaires also sought the pupils' and young people's perceptions on 22 different statements describing outcomes from the interventions (these statements were designed to exemplify the main effect types outlined in the model at the start of this chapter). They were rated as either 'no', 'a little', 'a lot' or 'not sure'.

In general, the questionnaire results reflected the interview data for outcomes on pupils, with one exception: the item … 'helped me to be more creative and imaginative'. According to the questionnaire data, this ranked within the top five of 22 categories as having impacted on pupils 'a lot', but in interviews, developments in creativity were nominated with less fervour. In part, this discrepancy between the interview and questionnaire data may reflect the fact that questionnaires were only completed in half the number of phases in which interviews were conducted and the particular type of phases in which it was possible to administer questionnaires. Nevertheless, this finding does need to be borne in mind as a qualification to the earlier evidence presented on the frequency and strength with which developments in creativity were registered.

Accumulation of outcomes

Another gauge of the distance pupils travelled was suggested by the interview data. A number of respondents (mainly teachers and pupils and some artists) in the series and developmental interventions were interviewed as a final follow-up to their whole experience of AEI. Their perceptions indicated that overall, pupils had accumulated artform skills, self-confidence and the skills for working with others and teamwork. In some cases these appeared to have had knock-on effects, such as the 'gelling together' of a class of primary school pupils, or pupils with the confidence and willingness to have a go at new things – not just in the artform experienced, but generally in their wider experiences. Such outcomes were not apparent, or at least, not fully recognised until the latter phases of multi-phase interventions – suggestive of both developmental outcome and certain outcome routes to achieve these effects. It is to both these areas – development within and between outcomes that we now turn.

2.5.2 Routes within outcome categories: a developmental perspective

Which effects are developmental?

Earlier we considered the possibilities for reinforcement of outcomes or incremental learning from interventions mounted in different ways (for example, whether one-off, series or developmental, see section 2.4.3). We now turn to interviewees' own perceptions of development in the outcomes achieved. In our interviews, the concepts of 'continuity and progression' were explored with pupils through the use of such terms as a sense of build up of learning, of skills, of follow-on, or of one thing leading to another.

Over all types of phases and interventions, it proved difficult to identify an appreciable number of examples of developmental or cumulative learning. In particular, pupils or young people seldom described continuity or progression in their learning. In the context of AEI, this is probably a very significant finding, since from the outset, attempts were made to foster interventions that would facilitate sustained or developmental learning.

Despite the general absence of cumulative reported outcomes, a number of interviewees (mainly artists and teachers, but also some specific pupils) did recognise developmental progress. Representing exceptions that underscored the general trend, accounts of cumulative outcomes were recorded in the following key areas (the most frequently nominated in this regard are listed first):

• working with others and teamwork

• artform confidence

• artform skills and techniques

• artform knowledge

• artform appreciation

• self-confidence.

Working with others and teamwork was the most frequently referred to in terms of developmental or incremental outcome and almost exclusively within drama, although also noted by some interviewees as developing throughout a multi-artform series.

In addition to examples of positive development, there were several instances where interviewees felt that not only had they not gained incrementally from a previous phase, but that they had actually gained less than in the previous phase. Examples were to be found in:

• immediate enjoyment and therapeutic outcomes (examples in multi-artform series and same artform developmental interventions)

- working with others and teamwork (pupils were felt not to build on the relationship they had developed with the artists in the previous phases and indeed to regress in some way)

- artform skills – pupils' 'baseline' had regressed since the previous phase of a developmental intervention.

How are the effects developmental? Are there hierarchies in the subtypes?

It was very difficult to establish from the interviews any precise developmental routes or hierarchies within outcome types. However, we have already seen in Section 2.4 how each phase of a developmental drama intervention focused on different aspects of artform skills and techniques, such that by the final phase skills could be drawn together to devise and perform a piece. There was a strong indication in this intervention that artform knowledge and artform appreciation were developed alongside artform skills and techniques.

Developments in artform knowledge and skills – interconnections

Whilst gaining basic skills employed in drama games, pupils also visited the theatre enhancing their appreciation of the stage and understanding of 'characters' (IIA and IIB). In the second phase of the intervention, alongside developing skills for role play, pupils advanced their ability to interpret plays (IID Interpretative skills). Finally, whilst gaining theatrical skills, pupils recognised how a play 'all fits together' – with the scenery, costumes, stage directions and so on (IIA and some IIE).

This example seemed to encompass all the type II effects as interconnected and developmental, each one building on and feeding into another.

However, such interconnections by no means exemplified any generalisable outcome routes within this category of effects (i.e. artform knowledge, appreciation and skills). Other interventions saw impacts on pupils' artform skills but with little effect in the realms of artform knowledge (for example, pupils gained the skills and techniques to play the steel pans but gave no indication of having learnt about the cultural, historical or contemporary context of West Indian or street carnival music). In contrast, other interventions enhanced pupils' artform knowledge and appreciation, but with little or no skill development (this occurred particularly in those projects where pupils were responsive participators – watching a performance, or discussing the artform, as opposed to active participation).

Perhaps the most coherent depiction of developmental routes within outcome types occurred for developments in creativity, although hardly any pupils seemed to have experienced the full range of possible effects suggested by the model, or as portrayed by their teachers and the artists. A suggested hierarchy is illustrated below from the two developmental drama interventions.

Developments in creativity – a possible hierarchy

- Capacity to be imaginative or inventive (e.g. invent your own ideas).
- Ability to explore (e.g. explore and use given ideas).
- Capacity to expand and experiment (e.g. adapt own and others' ideas).
- Developments in risk-taking.

Pupils' confidence levels in one type of outcome appeared to be a precursor to moving to the next level of creative development. For example, the first phase of the primary drama developmental intervention was deemed to spark pupils' imagination and provide excitement in using their own ideas (apparently something they had rarely had the opportunity to do before); by the second phase pupils were using their own ideas freely, even outside of the artform in their story-writing and by the third phase they were more willing and confident to try new ideas in drama (almost risk-taking). An interesting distinction in the secondary drama developmental intervention was made by the teacher with regard to pupils' ability: weaker ability pupils were deemed to get no further than exploring and imitating others' ideas, whilst the higher ability pupils were seen to experiment with and adapt ideas given to them (in later phases, using ideas gained from earlier phases).

It is worth noting that not once was there exemplification of enhanced risk-taking by pupils (the 'deepest' level of effect here) as a result of the AEI interventions, although it was alluded to in terms of pupils being more willing to have a go. This is in contrast to the findings in Harland *et al*. (2000:107) where pupils gained the confidence to experiment, take risks and be 'outrageous' in the arts.

Developments in creative capacities appeared to be aided by interventions that were extended beyond the one-off model. However, the sustainability or longevity of the effects after the intervention was less certain and it may well be that the incremental development of creative skills was dependent upon the specific context of the artistic medium. Certainly, there was little testimony to transferability outside of the artform (although some primary school children did feel that drama had helped them become more imaginative when playing games or 'pretending' at home).

Other suggestions of hierarchies, pre-cursors or outcome routes were across outcome categories and it is to this area that we now turn.

2.5.3 Routes between outcome categories: a developmental perspective

Clusters of outcomes

On analysing the interview data, some clustering of outcomes was apparent. These were not necessarily examples of routes between outcomes, but illustrate the kinds of outcomes that occurred together in the same phase or the same intervention.

Self-esteem, enjoyment and sense of satisfaction and fulfilment seemed to occur together and where enjoyment was high 'in the moment', there was also improved attitudes towards learning the artform.

In many cases, increases in self-esteem were closely aligned with gains in confidence and with a sense of satisfaction and fulfilment ensuing from pupils' perceptions of the quality or success of products they had made, or performances they had taken part in.

More often than not, where there was testimony to high levels of social development there was also evidence of skill development in the artform. On the other hand, there were instances of enhancements in artform skills and techniques with little social development.

Impacts in the realms of empathy and social awareness of others occurred together with enhancements to working with others and teamwork. However, several interventions led to gains in terms of working with others with little impact upon pupils' social awareness of others (empathy, tolerance etc). This particularly begs the question, is social awareness of others a higher order outcome than working together and teamwork?

Generally, impacts on pupils' artistic communication and expressive skills occurred with developments in creativity. These areas also occurred with artistic skills and techniques and there was some suggestion from a few interviewees that creativity in particular could not be enhanced without developments in artistic skills first. What is certainly the case is that it was extremely rare for developments in creativity to be referenced more forcefully than impacts on pupils' artistic skills and techniques by any interviewees in any of the phases. Interestingly though, in no cases did developments in creativity occur more 'strongly' in later phases of multiple phases interventions than earlier phases (although as we have seen above, there were subtleties in the type of creativity being espoused as the developmental interventions progressed).

Cumulative learning?

Whilst offering fuel for speculation, the above clusters only point to co-occurrence in outcomes. In themselves, they provide no evidence of cumulative or developmental learning. In fact, in spite of meticulous searches through the data, examples of learning being progressed from one outcome to another were extremely rare, whether subjectively perceived by the participants or identified by researcher analysis. Only a handful of examples, be they for whole classes or individuals, could be elicited from the data and these are outlined below.

> ### Sense of achievement and confidence leading to 'more willing to have a go'
>
> In some multiple phase interventions teachers believed that pupils' gains in confidence to participate during early phases had enabled them to more fully engage in those which followed. Pupils' sense of achievement and confidence, gave rise to them being more willing to have a go; not only in the same artform, but in other artforms and for some, more generally in terms of 'trying new things'. For some pupils, this manifested 'far' from the site of application, for example, in other lessons ('speaking up in class', 'having a go'), or being keen to find a new club to join out of school, even if one's friends would not be there.

done before. By the final phases, Jack's confidence and sense of achievement had received a real boost, so much so that he was upset at missing a performance as part of the project due to illness. Being able to express his thoughts and feelings about the projects and to recognise his own achievements were deemed important outcomes by his teachers, who felt it was rare for him to admit anything going his way, or to express his enthusiasms and disappointments.

Jack was felt to have made demonstrable progress personally and without the initial springboard of therapeutic effects and the seeds of self-esteem, it is possible that he would not have gained in as developmental a way from the subsequent phases.

Longevity and sustainability in learning outcomes

If, apart from such rare examples, the evidence suggested that the interventions rarely generated cumulative or developmental learning from one outcome to another, was there evidence of broadly the same type of learning outcome being sustained or developed over time? By examining interviewees' views at different points in time – during and some time after the event – the sustainable nature of the outcomes can be considered. This represents a development to the analysis used in Harland *et al*. (2000), which focused on pupils' views of current impact and not necessarily of the impacts resulting from a previous point in time. Most interviewees recalled the same types of outcomes when interviewed some time after the projects as they had done during or immediately after the experience. However, when asked whether those impacts had been experienced since the project, the extent to which impacts continued varied. Table 2.7 shows examples of the variation in longitudinal nature of some the outcomes.

There was some sense that outcomes in the realms of artform knowledge and skills were for the long-term in terms of building blocks for future work – for example, should pupils take GCSE music.

In the first two phases of the primary drama intervention there was a limited sense of the effect on self-expression being developmental – becoming more sophisticated in the second of the phases. This intervention was the only example where teachers reported a noticeable change in pupils' artistic expression in lessons afterwards.

An indicator of whether the effects were likely to be sustained was perhaps a sense of how 'far' from the site of application (or extent of transfer) that the effects were felt.

Table 2.7   Variation in the longevity of affective outcomes

Immediate/short-term	
Enjoyment/therapeutic	Affective outcomes 'in the moment' – 'buzz', 'enthralled', 'feeling calmer'

Intermediate	
Enjoyment/therapeutic	Some pupils continued to 'feel calm' into lessons immediately following the arts experience.
Achievement, satisfaction and happiness	There was some sustained 'happiness' or 'excitement' in multi-phase projects, in terms of pupils looking forward to the next project.

Long-term	
Achievement, satisfaction and happiness	In a couple of isolated phases, pupils described being 'happier' in the long-run for the arts experience they had had. In one instance a teacher recognised a 'happier child'.

Illustrations of two ways in which effects were sustained in this regard were evident: (i) initial wide range of outcomes ('near' and 'far' from the site of application) leading to sustainable effects 'far' from the site of application and (ii) initial wide range of outcomes ('near' and 'far') leading to 'near' effects being sustained.

> ### Initial wide range of outcomes ('near' and 'far') leading to sustainable effects 'far' from the site of application
>
> During the first few phases of this multi-phase intervention, Graham gained a wide range of outcomes. These included outcomes that were 'near' to the site of application, for example artform knowledge and skills and the impact on his ability to focus and concentrate on the task and those that were a little further from the site of application such as personal development (e.g. sense of maturity and willingness to apply himself to the task). Impacts were also evident 'far' from the site of application, with increased concentration and motivation to work harder in other lessons.
>
> By the final phase of this intervention, Graham was keen to express his pleasure at having been involved throughout and felt that he had finally made particular improvements in his artform skills and techniques (an area he found difficult). However, the intervention had not affected his overall attitude towards involvement in the artform – he remained clear that it was an area not for him. Instead, Graham realised that he had gained skills for working with others and for applying himself to a task even if it was difficult and he seemed optimistic that these would stand him in good stead for the next part of his school career.

Initial wide range of outcomes ('near' and 'far') leading to more focused individual (i.e. 'near' outcomes are the ones which remain)

In the first phase of this developmental drama intervention, Mark seemed to make gains across the widest range of effects depicted by any of the pupils. He felt he had gained artform knowledge and skills, better concentration and thinking skills, the ability to incorporate other people's ideas with his own, self-confidence and teamwork skills. His comments showed great sensitivities to others, as well as to development in his own work and habits. He felt these skills and attitudes would transfer to other areas of learning and was prepared to put more effort in to his schooling as he had realised that could lead to getting more out. Initially, Mark experienced these impacts 'everywhere', not just in drama.

It was somewhat surprising then, that by the final phase of the intervention, the impacts on Mark were in the field of drama only – he experienced enhancements to his personal and social skills in drama lessons but not elsewhere. Mark was more discriminating in where he wanted to focus his energies, having led drama workshops for younger pupils and hoping for a career in drama. It is possible that the initial broad range of effects led directly to this focus and enhanced positive attitudes towards the artform – having tasted what he might be capable of and now having a goal within the arena of the artform itself.

It is clear from the above examples, that sustainability of effects depends on individual pupils' and perhaps to some extent their attitudes and predispositions to the artform and to learning. However, longevity and sustainability of learning are also dependent upon the extent and nature of arts education provided by the school or host institution and in that respect any legacy left by the artists for teachers and their organisations is a crucial consideration. It is to that area we turn in the next chapter.

2.6 Summary

The chapter began by offering a framework of 11 broad categories for discussing the effects and outcomes for pupils and young people achieved (or not achieved) by arts interventions.

The most frequently and strongly reported effects in the interventions were:

- affective outcomes, especially enjoyment, pride and a sense of achievement

- artform knowledge, appreciation, skills and techniques

- personal development, especially self-esteem and self-confidence

- social development, particularly teamwork and awareness of others.

Although enhanced self-esteem was often cited as an outcome, the questionnaire results showed that secondary pupils had slightly less favourable perceptions about themselves and about their attitudes to school and learning after the phase compared to before. The powerful impact of arts interventions on pupils' personal development has to be seen against a backcloth of generally declining levels of self-esteem and self-image at school for many pupils, especially in areas of social and economic deprivation. Taken together, the findings highlight the need for longer-term strategies that sustain developments in such qualities as self-esteem, as well as the capacity of arts interventions to make a substantial contribution to this objective.

Other outcomes that were identified in some interventions with some regularity and with moderate levels of impact included:

- developments in creativity (the only broad outcome to be bolstered by the questionnaire results)

- changes in attitudes towards and involvement in the artform

- transfer effects beyond the artform (e.g. impacts on general performance and attitudes to schools; effects on current leisure and extra-curricular activities; or projected changes for future adult life and careers).

The effects that were nominated least frequently and with limited intensity were:

- knowledge, skills and appreciation beyond the arts – of particular note was the absence of this outcome in secondary schools

- social and cultural knowledge

- thinking skills

- communication and expressive skills.

Although comparatively rare, negative effects were also evident. The most notable of these centred on shifts towards less positive attitudes towards the artform in general or, more specifically, as it was taught within the school curriculum.

In general, there was a fairly high degree of correspondence between aims and outcomes. Where aimed for, outcomes were more strongly achieved than where they were not aimed for and some of the least commonly cited aims reflected the lowest profile pupil outcomes: social and cultural knowledge, thinking skills and general communication and expressive skills. However, there were perhaps higher profile outcomes in the broad category 'personal development' than had been aimed for (particularly for self-confidence and self-esteem), whereas there was a lower profile for creativity compared with other types of outcome than had been aimed for. Outcomes such as improvements in attitudes towards and behaviour in the artform, transfers to life in school and to self-esteem were the most likely types of outcome to be achieved even where they were not aimed for. On the other hand, knowledge and skills beyond the artform and outcomes related to social and cultural knowledge were unlikely to be achieved unless they were a specific aim.

Each of the artforms displayed distinctive configurations of outcomes. From a comparative perspective, the visual arts were particularly strong on outcomes associated with artform skills and techniques, but weak on knowledge, skills and appreciation beyond the arts. Developments in creativity, aesthetic judgement making and interpretative skills featured more highly in the visual arts than any other artform.

Dance was relatively strong on teamwork, physical wellbeing and creativity effects, but weak on artform knowledge and overall personal and social development. Dance (along with music) had the greatest potential for transfer to current life.

Drama displayed the greatest potential for generating a wide array of effects, as well as for 'strong' impacts. Drama was comparatively strong on teamwork, self-confidence, overall personal and social development and transfer effects to life in school, future life and work, but weak on artform skills and techniques, as well as creativity development.

Music produced the narrowest range of effects. Music was comparatively strong in artform knowledge, appreciation and skills, social and cultural knowledge, personal and social development. It was especially weak in creativity development.

Turning to differences between phase of schooling, while artform appreciation and increased confidence in their own artform ability was more prevalent among pupils in secondary schools, primary schools were stronger in enhanced artform knowledge and monopolised knowledge, skills and appreciation beyond the arts as an outcome.

Focusing only on secondary schools, comparisons were drawn between the effects of the AEI interventions and those of the normal in-school arts curriculum (Harland *et al.*, 2000). Compared with the latter, arts interventions were more likely to deliver artform appreciation and high levels of enjoyment, but less likely to achieve expressive skills.

The outcome of knowledge, skills and appreciation beyond the arts was most often apparent within one-off phases, especially those in primary schools, whereas social development and thinking skills were more evident in the individual phases of series and developmental interventions, the latter of which were biased towards drama. Accounts of improvements in attendance and behaviour during artform activities and, to a lesser degree, participation in the artform beyond school were more numerous during the later phases of series and developmental interventions. Teachers' and artists' views often revealed outcome peaks within second and third phases and a tailing off in those occurring fourth or later.

Unsurprisingly perhaps, one-off interventions resulted in a narrower range of effects reported overall than those where pupils experienced multiple phases, including developmental formats. However, thinking skills and communication and expressive skills were the only broad outcome types that were absent from the majority of one-off interventions, but present in most series and developmental interventions, though they were both generally weak.

Overall, it was difficult to find evidence of cumulative learning and incremental development. Even examples of sustained learning of the same outcome were not in plentiful supply. In particular, pupils seldom described continuity or progression in their learning and only a limited number of 'outcome routes' and other exceptions to this trend could be identified. In the context of AEI, this is significant, since interventions that would facilitate sustained or developmental learning were deliberately encouraged. However, as a pointer to future practice and policy, the few examples of cumulative learning that were evidenced were more likely to be found in developmental interventions or multi-phase ones that were, to some extent, conceived as sequential.

Notes

i   It should be stressed that any increases in motivation were not classified here. The types of outcomes categorised as 'affective' were the internal feelings and emotions characterised by enjoyment and therapeutic outcomes. Motivational outcomes were typified by intent to change or act on something and were categorised within the realms to which they related, for example, personal maturity, motivations towards the artform and motivations towards school more generally. However, later in the report (e.g. see 2.5.3) we explore the possibility of 'outcome routes' like the affective ones leading to others such as increased motivations. As we shall see, whilst generally it was difficult to find many examples of such progression in learning, there were cases where initially high affective outcomes were followed by enhanced motivations to learning in the artform concerned, as well as other artforms.

ii These were perceptions offered by teachers and pupils – no conclusive objective evidence (e.g. test results) to substantiate these opinions was provided.

3 Outcomes for teachers and artists

3.1 About this chapter

While the previous chapter set out the evidence on the outcomes for pupils and young people, this chapter considers the outcomes for teachers, schools and other host institutions (3.2), as well as those for artists and arts organisations (3.3). An overview of this chapter's structure is set out below.

3.1.1 Overview

Outcomes for teachers, schools and host institutions (3.2)

A typology of outcomes developed from an established model of continuing professional development (CPD) effects is presented, with descriptions of how these were exemplified in the AEI interventions. An overview of which outcomes were most evident in the interventions follows. Finally, this section compares effects accruing from those interventions that were targeted mainly on pupils and those which primarily had a teacher development focus.

Outcomes for artists and arts organisations (3.3)

Using the same typology of outcomes as for teachers, this section describes and analyses how the interventions impacted on the artists involved (and, where relevant, their organisation). An overview of the least and most prevalent artist outcomes occurring in the interventions concludes this section.

The chapter concludes with a summary of the main findings (3.4).

3.2 Outcomes for teachers, schools and host institutions

The previous chapter considered the effects on pupils of having participated in arts interventions either in schools or in out-of-school settings. The first part of this chapter (3.2.1) moves one stage further to explore what effect, if any, these interventions had within two key spheres of influence – on the school or host organisation as a whole and on the teachers and youth workers directly involved. It draws on evidence from interviews with participating teachers and youth workers, coupled with the views of artists providing the inputs and other key members of schools and host organisations. Eleven interventions, comprising 32 individual phases (excluding one of the out-of-school interventions where there was little involvement of a host organisation) are considered. In addition, the second part (3.2.2) of this section explores the effects of interventions classified as being primarily for the purpose of providing teachers with CPD.

3.2.1 Effects on teachers and host institutions in the interventions mainly for pupils

Teachers made many references to the ways in which AEI interventions had affected them, with only one instance of a teacher suggesting that he had gained little specifically from it (though later made references where impacts were clearly implicit). Artists made far fewer references to effects on teachers, as might be expected given that few had maintained their relationship with the teachers following the intervention. Moreover, many of the remarks made by artists appeared to be essentially aspirational – based more on what they hoped teachers to have gained, rather than on evidence of their actual gains.

Initially, effects on teachers and youth workers were examined according to a typology of CPD outcomes devised by Kinder and Harland (1991). Although it is acknowledged that teachers' development was generally not the main objective of most AEI interventions, it was found that this typology required only minimal adjustment in order to effectively capture the full range of outcomes from these interventions. The remainder of this section considers nine main types of effect:

- career development
- material and provisionary outcomes
- informational outcomes
- affective outcomes
- motivational and attitudinal outcomes
- new awareness and value shifts

- knowledge and skills

- impact on practice

- institutional and strategic outcomes.

The original model acknowledged the closely interrelated nature of these impacts and that developments in one area often facilitated those in another. This was particularly apparent in terms of outcomes acting as a catalyst for actual changes in teachers' classroom practice. The implications of the extent and types of impacts both identified and not identified within each overarching category are considered.

Career development

This category was added to the original typology in order to encompass the small numbers of teachers' and youth workers' references to interventions impacting on their career development. It was the least commonly cited type of outcome (in eight phases), though particularly influential for some individuals. The main type of impact within this category comprised increased status or professional recognition for the interviewee within their school or organisation. For some, the recognition implicit in being selected to manage the intervention was the key. Two teachers felt that managing interventions had given them 'another string to my bow' and enhanced their curriculum vitae – one of whom had actually gained a new post. Others had taken on new responsibilities or broadened their role within their current organisation.

Interventions had spurred several teachers and youth workers to reflect on their own careers and professional development. A youth worker who had not experienced such a project before said 'if this is something that young Corby people need, then I would like to go and do the training to make sure that I am doing it properly for them'. For an experienced art teacher, taking part in a textiles workshop had reaffirmed her career choice, though the converse was true for a primary school teacher trained as a dancer who questioned 'why aren't I doing a job like that?' after watching a theatre performance. However, this teacher had been inspired to try to incorporate more dance and drama into her classroom practice.

Material and provisionary outcomes

Material and provisionary outcomes – relating primarily to teachers' acquisition of different types of resources, was a relatively infrequently reported outcome from AEI interventions. Furthermore, the acquisition of such resources was sometimes merely an intention expressed on the part of a teacher, which in some cases did not appear to have been pursued even some time after the intervention.

The resources that teachers had acquired took a number of different formats. Three phases had resulted in teachers possessing written information – assembled from notes they had written during interventions and a 'resource pack' containing lesson plans provided by the artists. Musicians visiting the primary special school left a CD of their own music and donated a balaphon (a type of African xylophone) they had been given on their last trip to Africa, whilst the school had sought additional funding and purchased djembe drums for general use. Two teachers alluded to their plans to use products of interventions (textile banners and a published book of pupils' poems) as resources providing illustrative examples when teaching similar topics to other groups. Their emphasis was on demonstrating what pupils had been able to achieve, thus raising pupils' aspirations.

Finally, there were two instances where teachers explained that working with artists had enabled them to make greater use of equipment already available in the school. One had become the only member of the school staff who knew how to use the ceramic kiln and art teachers in another school had learnt how to use a printing press they had mistakenly deemed to be broken. The teachers' increased knowledge had enabled them to feel confident utilising this specialist and previously under-exploited equipment within their own classroom teaching and also support others in its use.

Informational outcomes

This type of outcome was among those least commonly cited. The main type of information that teachers gained related primarily to the artists or arts organisation with whom they had worked and future opportunities to work with them that might exist. One teacher described the artist as an 'outside expert' on whose expertise the school would be able to draw should the need or opportunity arise. These new relationships had also provided teachers with details of other networks of artists or arts organisations and sources of information they could access.

Affective outcomes

This category acknowledges teachers' emotional response to the AEI interventions – a reported outcome in around four-fifths of phases. Artists made few such references, though some negatively. For example, a drama workshop leader recognised a teacher's disappointment at pupils' poor behaviour during an intervention. In another case, a dancer described how a session provided for teachers had been 'personally challenging individuals to go places that they didn't really want to go'.

Teachers themselves also made a small number of negative remarks, mostly conveying some degree of envy – either of artists' artistic abilities – 'I wish that I was skilled enough in guitar to do what [the artist] did' – or the positive response and 'instant respect' they had evoked in pupils. One teacher described feeling 'rattled' – experiencing self-doubt based on the immediate success of the artist–pupil relationship. Another, impressed by the outcomes of a project involving professional dancers, felt unable to try working in a similar way for fear it would 'go to pot', without professional input. It seems there are two possible repercussions of these negative responses – teachers may either be spurred into action to change their own practice, or with their professional confidence having been undermined, be less willing to acknowledge the potential for change.

Despite this, teachers' affective responses to AEI interventions were positive, with most describing interventions as an enjoyable experience. For some, the sense of achievement gained from successful experiences and outcomes of interventions resulted in increased motivation to undertake similar projects in the future, coupled with confidence in their ability to manage them effectively should the opportunity occur. For others, increased confidence was actually manifest within their own practice. Some teachers who were not artform specialists had gained confidence and an impetus to introduce the artform into their lessons, one saying, 'I feel it is do-able', having stated before the intervention that 'I would rather run a mile than teach drama'. A small number of more experienced artform teachers referred to increased confidence to incorporate different methods or activities into their practice, having observed the artist using them successfully. There were other examples where teachers perceived artists' approaches as having been less successful, declaring 'I wouldn't do it like that' providing them with reassurance which 'confirmed the good things about my practice already'.

Motivational and attitudinal outcomes

For many teachers, changes in motivation and attitudes towards the arts were an obvious consequence of their positive affective responses described previously. In some cases, particularly in secondary schools, teachers described being 'inspired' by artists delivering interventions, depicting them as 'a breath of fresh air' and bringing 'completely new fresh ideas into school'. Some specialist and highly experienced artform teachers appreciated the opportunity to work alongside artists as professional equals, one saying that 'they keep me above the school water, so that I don't drown in GCSE and the national curriculum'. Others in a similar position described interventions as providing 'rejuvenation' and 'the injection that I need'. Teachers who were less experienced in the artform were more general about their respect for artists' skills and their enjoyment of observing professional artists working with their pupils.

The main ramification of this category was an increase in teachers' desire or enthusiasm to recreate or build on the experience of interventions. Two described this exclusively in terms of wanting to do similar projects, establishing a longer-term relationship or working with other professional artists and in one case this had already occurred. However, encouraging over-reliance on curriculum enhancement entirely through external input (highly dependent on funding), rather than changes to everyday classroom practice, might prompt concern about long-term sustainability. Other teachers had applied their new-found enthusiasm for the subject in lessons following the intervention, particularly in terms of planning related lessons for pupils directly involved. Whether this enthusiasm would be sustainable or result in long-term changes to the teachers' practice remained to be seen. There were also suggestions that teachers expected their improved attitudes and motivation to influence the way they approached the artform or topic, or teaching generally, in the future.

One distinct negative impact on motivation and enthusiasm was raised by two secondary school teachers (one art, one drama) who experienced frustration at not being able to replicate the interventions within the constraints of the school curriculum. An intervention where pupils were taken off-timetable to undertake a one day textiles workshop had reinforced a teacher's belief that

> *the way we teach in secondary school is stupid really. There should be more days where you do one thing all day and there are connections between other subjects ... ultimately they* [pupils] *would get more from it.*

New awareness and value shifts

Gains in new awareness, sometimes leading to actual shifts in teachers' beliefs or value systems, were identified in over three-quarters of all AEI phases and this placed it fifth in teachers' rankings of the different types of effects. There were two main sub-types of new awareness: their new sensitivity towards pupils as a result of observing them during interventions or sharing the experience and new awareness related specifically to the artform involved. Perhaps surprisingly, teachers focused more on the former. Artists also alluded to both sub-types of outcome.

Common responses conveyed teachers' 'seeing pupils in a different light' and being surprised or 'amazed' at what they had achieved – particularly as a consequence of involvement in performances during dance and drama interventions. The opportunity for teachers to observe pupils and their responses to interventions – particularly the chance to witness individuals working in different contexts – seemed acutely influential. 'Sometimes you are so close that you don't see things' and 'you see potential in children that you haven't seen before' were two notable examples, which may then have had a bearing on how teachers approached their classes in the future. Others illustrated the benefits of teachers and pupils sharing a learning experience, resulting in a deeper relationship and empathy between them and in teachers becoming more aware of pupils' perspectives and attitudes towards learning. The headteacher at the primary special school acknowledged that 'a lot of the time we do ask children to do things that perhaps we as adults would feel quite nervous about'.

In some ways, teachers' new awareness of pupils was closely linked to increased recognition of the educational potential of the arts, both in terms of active participation and also artistic consumption. Two primary teachers, as a result of pupils watching theatrical performances and a nursery teacher in reference to a museum visit, recognised that such opportunities 'ought to be part of the learning experience' which supported pupils' cultural development.

New awareness directly relating to the artform included examples such as changed perceptions of turntablism as an artform, viewing dance as 'not just ballet and country dancing', art as 'not just about being able to draw' and 'what drama can be' and how it could enhance the curriculum. A deputy head said 'it put dance back on the map for me as a manager'. It was difficult to determine the extent to which teachers' new awareness and changes in beliefs had actually been translated into changes in their practice in the classroom. This type of outcome was particularly evident amongst teachers with more limited experience or artform specialisation and also those who might have found it most difficult to translate gains into practice. It was noticeably absent or limited as a result of secondary school interventions, where the advanced baseline level of teachers' artform awareness may have restricted their scope for improvement.

Knowledge and skills

Another reason for the slightly lesser attention focused on teachers' gains in new awareness may be its close and progressive relationship with knowledge and skills. New knowledge and skills was the most commonly reported outcome of AEI interventions for teachers, asserted both by artists and teachers themselves and it may be that the true extent of gains in new awareness is concealed within teachers' references focusing on this more concrete manifestation.

Teachers reported increases in knowledge and skills linked directly to the artform as a result of 25 individual phases of interventions, with gains in knowledge about an artform and its practice being slightly more evident than practical skills. Teachers described having learnt about the techniques and processes involved in practising the artform, such as the creative process of writing a poem or selecting photographs for display in an exhibition, how to use particular equipment including digital cameras, kilns, or printing presses and knowledge about the historical, contemporary or cultural context of the artform. Where they had actively participated, teachers also had new skills in doing drama, dancing, making textiles and using specialist equipment, as well as interpreting and evaluating artistic performances or products.

As in the case of new awareness, new knowledge and skills were particularly evident amongst teachers and youth workers who had little or no previous experience of the artform, though those with such experience had broadened their knowledge and skills in some cases. For example, an art teacher who specialised in painting had expanded her repertoire to include new skills and knowledge relating to textiles, including felt making and batik.

In addition to their knowledge and skills about an artform, teachers also described knowledge and skills pertaining to artform pedagogy. As demonstrated later (see Chapter 5), observing and taking part in interventions had provided them with the opportunity to observe the ways in which artists worked with pupils, how learning was facilitated and how pupils responded to different activities. As a result, teachers described knowing more about different or novel ways of approaching teaching the artform, new activities that they could incorporate and which types of activities had worked particularly well with their pupils, as well as how to encourage pupils to engage with arts activities. Many also referred to gaining new ideas or 'picking up tips' from the artists that they could use in their own practice. One described learning an important lesson about the benefits of pupils learning about poetry through engaging with the creative process and writing their own poems, rather than the more traditional method focused on reading poems written by others.

However, the development of actual skills in teaching the artform was less immediately apparent than increases in knowledge. Whilst incorporating a supportive or participant role for teachers, the design of many interventions where artists took the lead clearly limited the opportunities for teachers to develop or practice teaching skills. It seems likely that this would have serious implications for teachers being able to implement changes in their own practice as a result of gains in awareness, values, motivation, enthusiasm and knowledge, particularly given that the relationship with the artist generally came to an end at precisely the point where teachers may have benefited most from the artist's support to implement such changes. The outcomes of an alternative model, where teachers and artists worked closely in partnership to 'team teach' pupils are considered in 3.2.2 below and in Chapter 5.

One specific type of new knowledge and skills that teachers had developed as a result of AEI interventions related to their abilities in managing projects of this type. This was clearly in evidence in some series and developmental interventions where changes were made to the ways in which later phases were designed, planned and managed as a result of earlier experiences, such as incorporating regular feedback sessions between artists and teachers and opportunities for artists to visit schools before projects commenced. By the end of one series intervention the deputy head responsible for its management acknowledged that the school now had a good planning model for projects involving professional artists. All types of phases resulted in teachers and artists suggesting improvements that could have been made to their organisation and management, which may have enabled them to successfully host or participate in similar projects in the future.

Impact on practice

Impacts on teachers' own practice in the classroom were the second most commonly reported type of outcome as a result of AEI interventions, mentioned in connection with 28 out of 32 phases. However, in contrast to the Kinder and Harland (1991) model, which ultimately identified long-term changes in teachers' practice, often the changes that were observed resulting from AEI were more immediate, where teachers had built directly on interventions or their content, which, in reality, may not have signalled actual changes in their practice for the long term. In addition, other references to change were expressed in the form of intentions to make changes, or the recognition that changes were possible, which had not yet resulted in concrete changes having been made. This ranking as the second most frequent outcome might considerably over-emphasise the true extent to which AEI interventions were able to make significant, long-term and sustainable changes to teachers' own classroom practice.

Twelve interventions appeared to have resulted in teachers' making actual changes to lessons, particularly in terms of the way they taught or the activities included. Some now focused on modelling their pedagogy on that of the artists they had worked with, examples including: being more direct with pupils; demonstrating and showing them what they were expected to do and new methods of providing encouragement, with one teacher saying 'you mimic it, take it in, assimilate it and take it further'. Others had replicated whole projects, or 'nicked' individual activities and exercises that artists had introduced such as 'hot-seating' in drama, vocal warm-ups in music and 'mirroring' in dance. In secondary schools it was sometimes apparent that these were being incorporated into the teacher's general repertoire, with groups of pupils other than those directly involved in the intervention. For teachers in primary schools, the impetus was often simply to make more opportunities for the arts within the curriculum – sometimes introducing it as a learning vehicle in other curriculum areas or school assemblies. It is possible that these changes, if teachers found them to be beneficial within their own lessons, may constitute the more long-term developments.

One specific way in which teachers had changed, or intended to change their practice related directly to their new awareness of pupils and what they were able to achieve. Several teachers described how this new awareness had made them question the level of challenge provided by their own classroom practice and make additional demands on pupils. In addition to one teacher who said 'knowing that they [year 7 pupils] can work with text and character means that I'm going to be more willing to do that in the future', others simply used the experience of the intervention itself as a point of reference to remind pupils what they were capable of, thus inspiring them to work harder in lessons generally – 'I know you can do this, I've seen you do it, now do it now'. Several also described how the 'shared experience' of the intervention had improved their relationship with and understanding of the pupils who were involved – particularly apparent in the case of a youth worker who now had more credibility with young people attending the youth club which hosted an out-of-school intervention.

However, for some teachers it was clear that, although their intent was to change their practice, in reality, this might take some time to achieve. In secondary schools this was often related to the necessity of having department-wide schemes of work that could not be overhauled on an ad hoc basis, requiring dissemination and discussion coupled with broad departmental support. Another teacher also suggested that despite the will to change, some teachers – particularly those who were more cautious or anxious about the arts – might require a succession of professional inputs before being able to implement change, saying 'each time someone comes in it gives you that little push'.

Institutional and strategic outcomes

This final section explores the impacts that were more widely experienced by the schools or organisations where they were hosted. It is acknowledged that many of the effects described up to this point may be experienced collectively, or cascaded to other staff within schools or host organisations. For example, there were several examples of teachers' sharing new resources that they had acquired or developed as a result of interventions, or 'reporting back' to other staff.

However, there were some outcomes of a more strategic nature, which acted directly on the organisation as a whole. This broad type of outcome was ranked third in terms of the number of phases where it was recognised by teachers, with some types of outcome in this category reported as resulting from 27 out of the 32 phases, though actual descriptions varied considerably and, as with impacts on practice, some seemed tenuous.

The most common type of outcome in this category, though impacting in numerous different ways, comprised the interventions' contribution to developing the culture of the school or host organisation. One developmental intervention in primary drama, for instance, appeared to have had a particular influence in terms of artists working within the school becoming 'more the norm' and acting as 'a catalyst to do other things'. This was similarly experienced in series interventions in primary schools and the out-of-school setting – where the multiplicity of activities had raised awareness about the benefits of undertaking a range of different projects and young people having 'an array of different experiences'. The desire to maintain such experiences in the future and extend them to other young people was plain. However, this type of belief, at an organisational or strategic level, was considerably less apparent as a result of the secondary series intervention, where there was little obvious linkage between the phases. Each phase was hosted within a different curriculum area, as a result being viewed as separate projects, with the consequence that impacts on the wider culture of the school as a whole were not clearly defined.

The way in which the arts were provided for within host organisations was the other major area of impact in this category. There were two specific references to teachers exploring opportunities to expand extra-curricular activities in the arts, based on interventions. These were outnumbered by teachers expressing more general intentions to write new schemes of work, new policies, or address the planning of the arts curriculum for the future. It is acknowledged that in order to be effective many of these activities required a considerable investment of both staff and time at school level and widespread support across the organisation, possibly accounting for the limited evidence of such changes already having taken place.

There were a small number of comments about how such projects had, or could, enhance the general reputation of the school. Several interventions had been publicised in school newsletters and others had involved performances open to parents and the wider community, or visible products such as textile banners and a published book of pupils' poems. A youth worker involved in an out-of-school intervention exemplified it as being 'another gold star for the youth service in terms of the things we provide'.

Overview

Although teachers described a wide range of different effects of AEI interventions on themselves, it is clear that most regarded effects on pupils to be their main focus. Very few teachers explicitly acknowledged interventions as providing them with a professional development opportunity, in the same way that they would regard attendance at a training course or in service training (INSET) session. Nevertheless, a wide range of effects on teachers and their schools were reported. The range of different outcomes experienced by teachers and the number of phases leading to teachers' reports of each are shown in Figure 3.1.

Figure 3.1 The number of phases resulting in each type of outcome for teachers

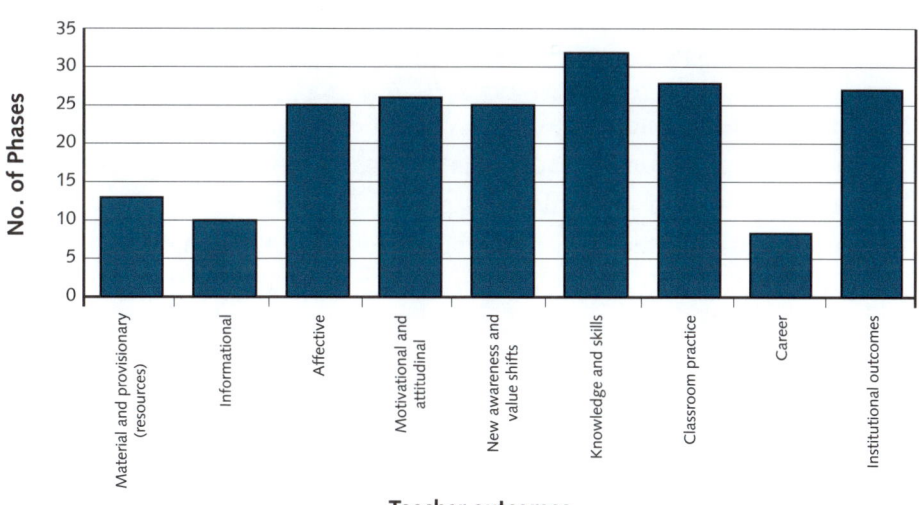

Corresponding closely with the effects experienced by pupils, most teachers regarded AEI interventions as having been a positive and enjoyable experience, which had improved their attitudes, confidence and enthusiasm towards the arts – either generally, or within an educational context. Interventions had also provided teachers with knowledge and skills and an impetus to make changes within the classroom. However, there was little evidence on which to determine whether many of these changes were deeply embedded, long term and ultimately sustainable. More than one teacher referred to having an increased desire to incorporate the arts into regular classroom practice following an intervention, but experiencing barriers to making changes in reality. The low incidence of teachers describing new resources and information from interventions, on which they could draw afterwards, may also have exacerbated this situation.

To what extent might other types of intervention involving professional artists be a more appropriate means of providing support for change in the host institutions? It is to these questions that we now turn, when examining the effects of interventions established with CPD as the central aim.

3.2.2 Outcomes of teacher development interventions

This section considers the outcomes of the three interventions (nine phases) focused primarily on providing CPD for teachers. All of these interventions took place in primary schools, two centred on dance and the other on visual art. The outcomes for teachers themselves and any consequent effects on their pupils are considered. Because of their age and often limited practical involvement in the interventions, pupils were not interviewed.

On balance, the overall categories of teacher effects reported as resulting from these interventions were broadly similar to those resulting from interventions where artists worked primarily with pupils. Teachers gaining knowledge and skills and changing their teaching practices were still the most common outcomes. Critically, teachers involved in these interventions mentioned impacts on their career or professional development no more often than their counterparts where projects relied on artists working with pupils. The main difference was the increased frequency with which teachers reported gaining material and provisionary outcomes on which they could draw following the interventions – perhaps one way in which artist and teacher acknowledged the professional development aspect. One of the interventions also resulted in informational outcomes relating to the dance curriculum and its teaching provided by a dance educator who mediated the relationship between teachers and professional dancers involved in each phase.

In practice, the actual delivery of the nine phases varied considerably – four involved work solely between teachers and artists, the remaining five involving artists and teachers working together with pupils in different ways.

Phases exclusively involving artists and teachers

Two of the interventions began with phases solely involving teachers and artists, though the experience and resulting outcomes varied. In one school a teacher and a learning support assistant took part in sessions with a dancer over two terms (classified as two phases, but considered together). Following the general trend, the main outcome they experienced was an increase in knowledge and skills relating to the artform and its teaching. This was well supported with resources on which they could draw afterwards. Both members of staff had enjoyed the sessions, gaining in confidence and both were enthusiastic about continuing to pursue the artform (both in school and beyond). Their initial trepidation had also provided an insight and new sensitivity towards pupils' learning experiences, which one felt had influenced her classroom practice across the curriculum. However, the focus on the 'salsa' style of dance posed particular challenges in terms of its level of technical difficulty and although the members of staff were serious in their intent to incorporate dance more within the curriculum and had basic plans for how this might be achieved, these developments had not yet come to fruition. The teacher said 'we haven't got anywhere near enough skills yet to come into school now and start teaching it … I'm not prepared to do it unless I'm doing it well and I'm not doing it well at the moment'. In addition, there was no clear evidence of dissemination within the school. For both of these reasons, effects on pupils were noticeably absent.

In the other example, all of the school staff took part in sessions provided by two different dancers, coordinated and supported by a dance educator. The first, where the dancer focused on imparting the possibilities and methods for teaching dance within the primary curriculum, was generally felt by teachers to have been more successful than the second, where the dancer delivered a session much as she might to pupils with the teachers somewhat unwillingly taking on the pupil role. The teachers experienced similar outcomes to those in the previous example – increased knowledge and skills in dance, but more especially in teaching dance and to some degree increased motivation and enthusiasm. The intention to incorporate more dance within the curriculum was already part of the school development plan and there was evidence that some of the teachers who were more experienced or open to dance had been 'trying things out' in the classroom following the sessions. This may have been facilitated by the accessibility of the basic style of dance involved (in contrast to the 'salsa' style attempted in the previous case) and the explicit links that were made with the national curriculum. One teacher explained that 'I just found myself remembering things that [the dancers] had done and using them … these things were springing into my mind as I was teaching'. Where this had occurred, pupils were reported as gaining a wide range of outcomes from participation in dance lessons, one of the teachers also saying, 'I enjoy it more because I am getting more out of it'. The dancer delivering the first session recognised that some of the teachers were more inhibited and found dancing in front of their colleagues uncomfortable, saying that, rather than heavily curriculum-based teaching, 'possibly what the teachers need a bit more of, at this stage, is just to enjoy dance themselves', recognising their more limited gains in enthusiasm and motivation.

Phases involving artists, teachers and pupils

Following on from the phases where teachers and artists worked together outside the classroom, both interventions concluded with a phase where teachers and artists worked together to 'team teach' a group of pupils. In the intervention where a teacher and support assistant had focused on salsa, the final phase comprised teachers and artist working together with a small group of gifted and talented pupils to produce a dance performed in a school assembly. The teachers took an increasing role in leading the group as they prepared the dance for the performance, whilst direct input from the dancer decreased. The main outcomes represented a consolidation of the teachers' previous learning alongside considerable increases in their confidence to teach dance in practice. The dancer also acknowledged that the teachers had experienced a sense of ownership of the final performance – 'it was their piece that they had been trained to lead and create … they were therefore stepping into that role as artists themselves'. However, although the project had impacted on the pupils involved and other pupils and parents who had seen the performance expressed an interest in taking part in salsa activities, longer term impacts on the teachers and the school as a whole were difficult to determine. At the end of the project the teachers' intentions regarding the delivery of dance within the curriculum and provision of an extra-curricular salsa club were still at an early embryonic stage.

It must also be noted that a basic variation of this model was apparent during the primary special school series intervention – where one of the school's main aims was raising the profile of the arts across the curriculum. During two phases artists provided a separate INSET session for teachers, prior to their working with the pupils, based on some of the activities that they would be using. Though the later sessions with pupils did not involve 'team teaching', the teachers had the opportunity to observe the artists working with the pupils in a classroom situation, at the same time feeling more confident about what was going to happen and more able to support pupils appropriately as a result. This was particularly important within the special school setting, where pupils often required more individual attention during sessions than could be provided exclusively by the artists. The teachers felt that incorporating CPD had enhanced outcomes for both themselves and the pupils.

The remaining teacher development intervention exemplified a slightly different model, though still involving teacher and artist working together with pupils. On first inspection, the phases of the intervention resembled very closely the usual format of AEI interventions that were not specifically addressing teacher development – where the artist worked primarily with pupils. The outcomes reported were also similar, to some extent. However, it was clear that this intervention represented a very close collaboration between teacher and the three different artists involved – particularly in the planning stages. Furthermore, although the artists generally took the lead role during the delivery of the sessions with pupils, opportunities for the teacher and artist to reflect and evaluate each session shortly afterwards and plan together for the next formed a vital element of the programme.

The teacher, already a practising artist, and the arts coordinator in the school had chosen deliberately to work with artists working in aspects of the visual arts with which she was less familiar, including digital imagery, ceramics and textiles. The new skills and knowledge of these media and their application in the classroom and the reaffirmation of her enthusiasm and motivation for the arts resulted in the teacher expressing her firm intentions to incorporate what she had learnt into her own practice – both as an artist and as a teacher – thus extending her repertoire. Whether the intervention could be justified solely on this basis, given the teacher's already considerable experience and enthusiasm for the arts, remains to be seen. However, it had also influenced the purchase of a new digital camera and ceramic kiln, as well as providing the teacher with a 'soapbox' from which she promoted the arts with renewed vigour, thus raising awareness and influencing the attitudes of other staff within the school as a whole. Wherever possible the teacher had disseminated what she had learnt to other staff, who gained new knowledge and skills as a result and were 'enthused' about incorporating elements of the projects into their own work. It may be, then, that where an experienced member of staff worked with an artist and cascaded learning to other members of staff might be a model by which wider impacts on the school could be attained. The arts coordinators' continued presence in the school after the intervention might also contribute to the long-term sustainability of the outcomes achieved.

Overview

Looking at the different models of teacher development interventions and the outcomes that resulted from them revealed some clear differences which, as might be expected, seemed closely related to the backgrounds of those taking part and the activities incorporated into the sessions. These models incorporate different elements of successful teacher development as described by Joyce and Showers (1982):

- study of the theoretical basis or rationale of new teaching methods

- observation of demonstrations of the methods by 'experts'

- practice and feedback in protected conditions

- coaching one another (i.e. learning through on-the-job support) within the school as new methods are introduced.

The evidence suggests that phases based solely on activities involving teachers and artists (excluding pupils), resulted in teachers' gaining considerable knowledge and skills and having enhanced enthusiasm and motivation for the artform. However, only the more experienced teachers, or those particularly enthusiastic about the artform prior to the intervention, seemed able to translate these outcomes into practice in the classroom, with very limited immediate impacts for pupils as a consequence.

This is not to decry the importance of the outcomes teachers did experience and these phases clearly provided a useful starting point for interventions also progressing to include pupils. Phases also involving pupils provided an ideal opportunity for teachers to observe artists teaching (in the primary special school series intervention) and for some the chance to experiment with new found skills and knowledge in a classroom environment with the support of the artist.

The final model, where an artist worked with the school arts coordinator, already an experienced artist, demonstrated how development could be cascaded as a result of successful collaboration between teacher and artist which was observed by colleagues within the school. The sustained presence of the arts coordinator after the intervention, able to act as a 'peer coach' for other staff and offer on-the-job support, coupled with the intervention having reaffirmed her belief in the arts as an educational tool, may also contribute to the long-term sustainability of these outcomes.

3.3 Outcomes for artists and arts organisations

Similar to the effects on teachers, schools and host organisations presented above, this section addresses what artists and, where appropriate, the arts organisations of which they were a part, gained from their participation in AEI interventions. The analysis is based on interviews with teachers and artists in connection with all 15 interventions (including the three focused on teacher development) comprising 42 individual phases in total. To what extent did AEI interventions provide artists with an opportunity for their own professional development?

Corresponding with the pattern of reports of effects on participating teachers, artists themselves were the most forthcoming about the outcomes they had experienced. Teachers made very few references and, similar to artists' views of the effects on teachers, where such remarks were made they often appeared to represent what teachers expected or presumed artists to have gained from their involvement, rather than any objective, evidence-based reality.

There were only two instances where artists explicitly stated they had gained nothing from their participation in the interventions. In one of these cases gains had been made at an organisational level. In the other, a freelance musician involved in the secondary developmental music intervention accounted for the lack of impact by acknowledging that the class teacher had taken the leading role, to the extent that 'essentially it wasn't my project, I just came in and did what was necessary ... it wasn't a significant piece of work for me'. All other phases resulted in artists describing at least a small number of effects that they had experienced, though in general terms effects on artists were less frequent and appeared less substantial than those on pupils and teachers. Some artists who viewed arts education work as their fundamental raison d'être, professional arts educators in essence, identified few notable impacts of AEI interventions on themselves, suggesting that there was limited scope for gaining outcomes which were distinctive from those already gained from their previous work.

Effects on artists and arts organisations were classified according to the same range of headings as those on teachers, schools and host organisations. However, it was recognised that though comparable in part, effects on artists within the nine broad categories were often quite different from those experienced by teachers. The remainder of this section addresses each of these broad categories of outcome in turn.

Career development

Impacts on their own career development were more often recognised by artists than they had been by teachers – perhaps reflecting the greater extent to which artists viewed AEI interventions and similar arts education projects as an important or substantial element of their career. However, only two artists felt that the interventions had influenced their own professional practice as an artist. A factor possibly accounting for this lack of impact was the number of artists who were either heavily involved in arts education work with limited focus on solely artistic practice, or already highly experienced and successful artists who regarded education work as a distinct and separate element of their work.

More often, artists described how AEI interventions – and their own affective response to them – had caused them to reassess or reflect on their careers, in some cases bringing about or planning changes as a result. Several who had particularly enjoyed interventions felt more certain of their current position, or had an increased desire to take on further work of a similar nature. Conversely, for one artist, a less positive experience had validated his decision not to become a secondary school teacher, despite having completed an initial teacher training course.

Artists also described impacts on their reputation or status – both individually as educators and at an organisational level, a few identifying the specific benefits from being involved in a large research project in connection with the Arts Council, the EAZ and NFER.

Material and provisionary outcomes

This was the least frequently mentioned outcome of AEI interventions for artists – cited in only three cases. One had acquired a new computer software package for digital image manipulation on which the intervention was based, whilst another had purchased clay for personal experimentation prior to a ceramics project. In the final example, an artist considered the file of notes and planning produced during a radio project to be a valuable resource to develop in connection with similar future projects.

The limited extent to which artists reported material and provisionary outcomes may not pose a major cause for concern. Many of the artists were highly experienced – as either professional artists or arts educators – and may have had little scope, or indeed cause, to make additional gains in this area. The attitude of some school staff towards the artists as 'provider' of interventions, rather than a collaborative partner, may further have inhibited the sharing of material and provisionary resources in this way.

Informational outcomes

Artists' gains in terms of new information were similarly limited, raised in only five cases. Four artists delivering interventions in Bristol reported having more information about arts activities and opportunities in the area, one of whom put this down to the relationship established with the Arts Council and EAZ with the prospect of increased networking and an accessible source of information. This was particularly important for the three living locally. As reported earlier, a small number of teachers from both areas reported that they had gained similar information about local opportunities. None of the artists who delivered interventions within the Corby EAZ reported such gains, which may perhaps be related to the more limited opportunities and networks available. In Corby, artists were drawn from a far wider area, few living locally, such that they may not have sought, or seen the benefit of links to a region some distance from their own location.

The final example of information that an artist had gained resulted from the close association and dialogue between artist and teacher during an intervention focused specifically on the teacher's development. The teacher had shared information with the artist relating to the school's arts policies and the 'artsmark' award. It is perhaps surprising that artists with limited experience of delivering arts education projects, or for whom interventions extended their experience into new areas, did not report further gains in terms of new information – particularly information about the arts curriculum or its practice in schools. As with material and provisionary outcomes, a common attitude of teachers and schools equating artists with 'experts' responsible for delivering interventions, rather than collaborative partners who could also benefit from their involvement, may have been an inhibiting factor. Alternatively, it may be that artists working in schools on a regular basis had little scope for such outcomes.

Affective outcomes

Artists' emotional or 'affective' response to interventions was their second most frequently reported outcome from AEI interventions – being mentioned in connection with 31 individual phases. That said, although 26 phases resulted in some form of positive emotional response being described by artists, the outcome of 13 was negative in some way.

The most common positive affective outcome described by artists was an increase in their levels of confidence to deliver arts interventions. This was particularly apparent amongst artists who were less experienced at delivering arts education, or who had broadened their repertoire in some way. Ways in which this broadening was manifest included working with different ages or abilities of pupils, mediating new material or projects with an alternative structure or duration and in some cases providing training for teachers rather than work with pupils. Working with pupils with severe emotional and behavioural difficulties in the primary special school had been a new experience for the majority of artists involved and though at times described as 'difficult' emotionally, several had also been 'inspired' and reported a considerable sense of achievement which gave them increased confidence and an enhanced desire to take on similar work in the future.

A sense of achievement or satisfaction and enjoyment of interventions were the other main types of positive emotional response to interventions described by artists. Both were often based on the enthusiasm or enjoyment of interventions openly exhibited by pupils or the quality of artistic products or performances that had resulted. Artists also reported effects in this area as a result of being able to pass on their knowledge and passion for their artform. Actors involved in the primary developmental drama intervention had experienced a distinctive sense of satisfaction and enjoyment from getting to know teachers and pupils well, having worked with them for a longer period of time than was usually possible. The class teacher also acknowledged that the actors appeared more relaxed with the pupils during the second phase of the project than during the first.

Artists' negative responses generally relayed their frustration or disappointment relating to particular projects and often provided an impetus for future improvement. A small number of difficulties were relayed in terms of planning and arranging interventions, though for others frustration resulted from the challenge of pupils' discipline and lack of focus during sessions. Examples included an artist who was frustrated at not being more involved in the actual delivery of the intervention (the lead role being assumed by the class teacher) and one who would have appreciated more opportunity for communication and reflection with the teacher. These difficulties often had a knock-on-effect for the products or outcomes of interventions, the limits of which sometimes resulted in artists' disappointment. For example, the final phase of the secondary developmental drama intervention was described as something of an 'anticlimax'[i], whilst a musician delivering a phase within a series acknowledged, with hindsight, that his initial expectations of what pupils could achieve may have been unrealistic. A small number of artists completed interventions with their confidence as arts educators, or faith in schools as educational establishments, slightly undermined.

Motivational and attitudinal

It is clear that for some artists their affective response to AEI interventions had important ramifications for their future motivation and attitudes. In general terms, the majority of changes to artists' motivation and attitudes were positive, linked with a positive report of their experience and affective response to the intervention. One noted that working with children 'always affects my enthusiasm'. However, not all of the phases where artists recorded an affective response produced a corresponding change in attitudes or motivation. The numbers of artists who were already highly motivated towards providing arts education work, some of whom experienced an affective response which merely reinforced their attitudinal perspective rather than bringing about an actual change may be a contributory factor.

Nineteen phases resulted in artists reporting a positive impact on their motivation and attitudes – the majority of comments relating specifically to arts education work. Some, for whom interventions represented a deviation from their usual work, were encouraged to increase their involvement, wanting to 'continue inspiring pupils'. One said, 'I am actually increasingly fascinated by education … I have just made a choice to take on more teaching work rather than artistic work' and another, 'I want to be able to introduce this activity into more schools'. Despite this, as with career development, only a small number of artists intimated that interventions had given them renewed impetus or ideas for their own artistic work.

New awareness and value shifts

This was the most frequently reported outcome of AEI interventions for artists, relayed in connection with 34 of the 42 phases. It comprised a wide variety of different sub-types, though most were at the more basic end of the spectrum representing new awareness, rather than more profound effects shifting artists' deep-seated beliefs and values, albeit that the distinction was somewhat blurred on occasion. It is notable that this top-ranked outcome for artists was not experienced universally, in contrast with the top-ranked outcome for teachers (new knowledge and skills) which resulted from all AEI phases. This reflects the general pattern of AEI interventions having a more limited effect on artists than on teachers and pupils, but might also be an indication that there was less uniformity in the outcomes artists experienced, perhaps related to the diversity of their backgrounds and current practice in both the arts and arts education.

Most of artists' references in this category relayed new awareness of alternative teaching styles and methods, or of specific factors that had been either beneficial or detrimental to the perceived success of the intervention. These outcomes were mentioned most often by artists for whom interventions were extending their practice in some way – working in ways which were new to them, with different groups of pupils, or in different settings. One artist, reflecting on a project in the primary special school, highlighted the importance of 'responding to what you are seeing', but also learning that pupils with severe emotional and behavioural difficulties often behaved unpredictably and this was not necessarily an indication of their real attitude towards activities or what they gained from them. As a result of their new awareness, some artists had modified their practice over the course of interventions, though one noted that 'you can have all sorts of rules about good practice, but actually putting them into effect in certain situations is jolly hard work'. Some artists modified their practice during sessions and their flexibility and creativity may have facilitated their responsiveness. It was also noticeable that where interventions involved multiple sessions, artists had sometimes made major alterations to plans for later sessions based on their new awareness of what had, or had not worked during those occurring previously.

Several artists had become more aware of their own learning needs and expressed a desire to undertake training in education work, classroom and behaviour management being a common focus. Some artists had clearly found managing pupils' behaviour during interventions more challenging than expected, with one saying 'it's made me realise that I need to get some sort of proper group motivation training' and another 'perhaps if I find a suitable course for artists – how would you go into a classroom … I might go on something like that'. This raises an immediate question about artists' backgrounds and the availability of suitable arts education training for those who wished to develop in this way. Artists' recognition of the value of training was tangible and one described the realisation that 'I am not just an artist when I go into school, I am also a teacher'.

It is perhaps surprising that whilst AEI interventions had prompted some artists to consider additional training, very few considered the intervention itself as an opportunity for professional development. Again, this may be related to the depiction of artists as delivering interventions, rather than collaborative partners working alongside teachers and host organisations. References to new awareness of the arts curriculum in schools were notably absent, whilst only a small minority mentioned seeing schools or teachers in a new light or with increased

the arts–education interface: a mutual learning triangle?

awareness of the difficulties they faced. It is possible that artists were already very aware of these issues, although an alternative picture is that artists assuming the role of intervention provider, with aims focusing heavily on outcomes for pupils and teachers, limited the extent to which they sought, or recognised having gained such new awareness as a result. A similarly small number of remarks were made which related to artists' own artistic practice (as distinct from education work). One suggested 'it might give me a shove into stopping fiddling and being bold' with her own art work, whilst a theatre company acknowledged drama workshops as enabling them to 'flex ourselves a little bit and take risks'. Another had been awakened to 'the possibilities with my work'.

Knowledge and skills

Very closely related to new awareness and value shifts, gaining new knowledge and skills was another very commonly cited outcome for artists, resulting from 29 individual phases, (albeit quite minor gains at times). As might be expected, given the educational remit of the interventions, the vast majority of artists' references were to impacts on their knowledge and skills in providing arts interventions, rather than related to their own artistic practice. Several merely identified improvements in their 'teaching skills' generally, giving no further explanation, with a small number of teachers also intimating that 'the more [education work artists] do, the better they get'. However, it was often very difficult to distinguish where the effect was exclusively the acquisition of knowledge and where the new knowledge had actually been translated into new skills in practice and for this reason they are addressed together.

One of the main emphases of artists' remarks was to their increased knowledge and skills relating to different types of pupils. New knowledge included understanding different pupils' capabilities and how they might be expected to respond to different activities. This was comparable to the new awareness and sensitivity towards pupils experienced by teachers, though for artists (who generally did not have a long-term and continuing relationship with the pupils) it was manifest as knowledge of pupils at different ages generally, rather than awareness of particular groups of pupils or individuals. Closely linked were increased skills in working with different types of pupils – knowing how to engage with them and tailor activities to suit. This sometimes involved changing the timescales of sessions, breaking tasks down into smaller sections and setting specific tasks that were not 'woolly' in their interpretation. Other knowledge and skills related to teaching cited by artists included: knowledge about the pace of sessions and what activities worked in a short space of time; how to motivate and communicate with pupils; classroom and behaviour management; how to improvise and be flexible and having patience.

It is clear that some of the longer interventions had given artists the opportunity to experiment with different strategies of working with pupils in the classroom and reflect on which had proven the most successful. During this process artists refined their skills and gleaned new knowledge of strategies they could draw on in similar situations in the future. Such refinement was not immediately apparent as a result of many shorter interventions, though some artists' prior experience included the delivery of a range of short projects from which they had gained similar (and in some cases broader) knowledge and skills, over time. Another factor which appeared to facilitate some artists' development in this area was the active involvement of the regular class teacher, or other members of school staff. One artist said of a teacher 'she is fantastic at getting them to listen, creating appropriate boundaries, giving them a structure to work in … which I learnt a lot from'.

A small number of references were made to artists gaining new ideas for delivering the artform, with one teacher suggesting that artists might gain ideas from 'just watching the things that they [the pupils] can do'. Two artists described this type of learning. However, the majority of artists' references to new ideas related to phases which involved several different artists simultaneously, where those involved had learnt and gained ideas from observing each others' practice.

Artists within ten phases referred to gaining new knowledge, skills or ideas contributing to their artistic development. For several this had involved gaining new skills and knowledge about using different media (digital imaging, ceramics, acapella singing) or different equipment. Two (one in music and one in drama) also referred to enhancing their artform skills through practice during the sessions. Three reported gaining new ideas for their own practice, one specifically from observing a pupil's response to an activity. As with career development, the limited effects reported here may be linked to the high levels of skills already possessed by many artists (such that there was little potential for development) and the numbers who focused mainly on providing arts education, placing less emphasis on their own artistic development.

Impacts on practice

This category encompasses impacts on artists' practice following interventions and also the intentions to adapt their practice that artists expressed. These outcomes were often linked to those of new awareness and new knowledge and skills and were cited by artists themselves in connection with 26 out of the 42 individual phases.

The majority of artists' responses were based heavily on the opportunity that interventions (and in some cases the associated research interviews) had provided for them to reflect on their arts education practice. One said 'it made me think about how I am as a teacher', with several others in accord about the benefit of continually questioning their work or what they hoped to achieve in the future. In one case, an artist recognised that the intervention had 'allowed me to look at my work and see where I ought to go with it in terms of education'. Another, involved in delivering a teacher development intervention, said 'teaching things to someone else who is going to be teaching does make you look at what you are doing more closely'. Such reflection prompted some artists to express intentions to change their arts education practice – suggesting how interventions they were involved in could have been improved, or how they might best plan and deliver similar projects in the future. This was particularly prevalent where interventions represented a chance for artists to extend their education practice.

However, it was often exceptionally hard to determine whether artists' intentions regarding change had been translated into reality and which aspects of their practice had been affected. One artist said: 'I have completely changed my practice … that is going to make a difference for every project that I will do in the future' and another: 'I think it has fed into the work I have done since', with neither expanding on the actual changes made. More obvious developments included: dancers who had chosen to undertake work which allowed them to develop activities from the intervention one stage further; an actor using an intervention as an example during teacher INSET sessions and a visual artist who said: 'I'm more keen to ensure that I have the opportunity to meet up with the teachers at least for a couple of sessions, before I get involved with the children'. For a small minority, the change in practice consisted of maintaining an active relationship with the school or host organisation.

It seems likely that this outcome was not more prevalent because some artists had little scope for such development – particularly those for whom AEI interventions typified the education work in which they were routinely engaged and already highly experienced. Others implied that their practice was naturally based on the sum of all their past experiences, but could not identify specific changes as a result of the AEI intervention. However, there were also indications that changes in artists' practice might develop over a longer period of time than that allowed by the research. Some artists working on a freelance basis and balancing arts education work with their own artistic practice, further constrained by the need to make a living, had not yet been able to take on projects allowing them to implement changes they had identified as beneficial.

Organisational and strategic outcomes

When the outcomes of AEI interventions for teachers were described, this category encompassed those effects which were experienced at the level of the school, or for teachers as a whole – over and above those directly involved in the intervention. However, many of the artists delivering AEI interventions worked primarily as individuals on a freelance basis (or as members of small groups of similar artists). In these cases, the outcomes they experienced were centred mainly on themselves as individuals, thus appearing within the previous eight categories. The categories of career development and organisational and strategic outcomes were often particularly blurred. Artists associated with larger arts organisations (analogous to the relationship between teachers and schools) were in the minority. Opportunities for AEI interventions to impact on arts organisations were limited compared with opportunities to impact on schools, though some organisational or strategic impact was cited by artists as a result of 19 out of the 42 individual phases.

The majority of artists' references related to the implications of AEI interventions for arts education work. Several referred to their desire to maintain links with the schools they had worked with, particularly where the interventions had occurred over a longer period of time than was usually possible, or to establish similar long-term projects with other schools. The possibility of arts organisations providing training for those involved in delivering arts education work was also suggested in a few isolated instances. As described in the section relating to career development above, several artists felt that AEI interventions had raised the status of the organisation as a whole. For two theatre companies producing shows directed at young people, this focused on ensuring future bookings – either in the intervention school, or in others via 'word of mouth'. A similar per-

Figure 3.2   The number of phases resulting in each type of outcome for artists

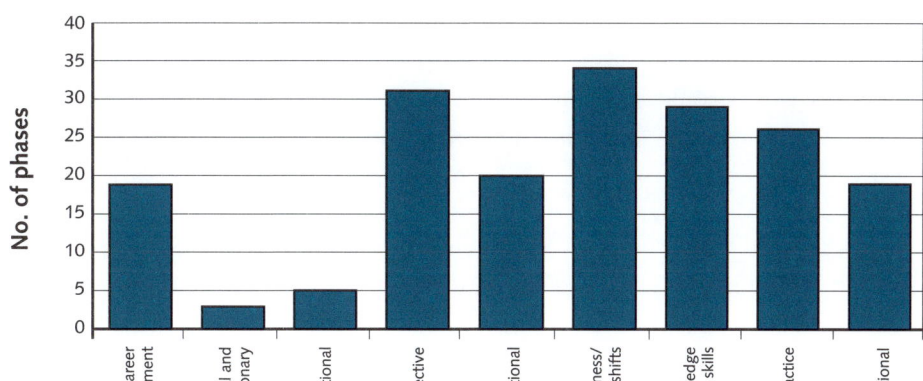

spective was endorsed by a youth worker involved in a different intervention who said 'I was so impressed by the work that [the artists] did, I recommended them to another organisation … to do some work with their young people'. Another example of a change in status was mentioned by an actor and a dancer who both described how the interventions they took part in had raised the profile, within their respective companies, of arts education work undertaken in parallel with their main artistic output.

It appeared that AEI interventions made a very limited contribution to the development of arts organisations' own artistic output. For a small number of artists interventions had provided new ideas for future performances and in one case an artistic director described how each performance of a show gave the company an opportunity to refine it in the light of the audience's response. In another case, one of the two dancers who delivered a project in the primary special school described how their shared experience had 'made us stick together as a team' which had contributed to deepening their relationship during their own dance performance. In general terms, though, the prior expertise of arts organisations in terms of their own artistic output might suggest it would be unrealistic to expect such an outcome to occur.

Overview

Artists described a very wide range of outcomes that they themselves had experienced as a result of participation in AEI interventions, though in general terms these effects appeared less frequent and substantial than those on pupils and teachers. On closer examination many appeared to be of an immediate or short-term nature, with only a small minority of artists reporting more significant changes which could be deemed to be of a deep-seated or longer-term nature. Figure 3.2 shows the distribution of different types of outcomes nominated by artists.

It is clear that new awareness and value shifts (particularly awareness of factors which had influenced the success of interventions or their own training needs) and immediate affective outcomes (including enjoyment and satisfaction and increased confidence in delivering arts education) were those most frequently cited outcomes for artists. Given this high incidence of affective outcomes, the more limited reports of increased motivation and enthusiasm may seem surprising, but for the fact that many of the artists were already highly motivated and enthusiastic prior to the interventions. This suggests that for some artists AEI interventions might merely reinforce levels of motivation and enthusiasm which were already high.

New knowledge and skills and changes in their own practice relating to the provision of arts education were also common, whilst a small minority of artists relayed developments linked to their own artistic practice. However, many of these effects were relatively minor and it was often difficult to discern the extent to which real changes had been implemented in artists' practice following the interventions. Perhaps in spite of this, almost half of the 42 individual AEI phases resulted in artists describing some form of career development and a wider impact for the organisation of which they were a part.

Several factors may be responsible for limiting the effects that artists experienced as a result of their participation in AEI interventions. The first is their general levels of experience – both as artists and often also as arts educators. This may have limited the scope that these artists had for gaining new outcomes as a result of the intervention. In turn, this may have influenced the way in which artists were viewed within the schools or host organisations where interventions were mounted. Artists often seemed to be depicted as the 'experts' who delivered interventions, whilst teachers and schools were the more passive 'recipients' of their work. Some artists also subscribed to this viewpoint and the resulting lack of active collaboration may have restricted what artists were able to learn themselves from their involvement in the interventions.

3.4 Summary

3.4.1 Outcomes for teachers, schools and host institutions

In the pupil-focused interventions

Teachers widely considered effects on pupils to be the main focus of the interventions and very few explicitly acknowledged interventions as providing them with a CPD opportunity, in the same way that they would regard a training course. Most described a wide range of different effects on themselves.

The most frequently nominated outcomes were:

- enhanced knowledge and skills, with gains in knowledge about an artform and its practice being slightly more evident than improved practical skills; these effects were particularly prolific amongst teachers and youth workers who had little or no previous experience of the artform, – artform pedagogic techniques and skills in managing arts interventions were also developed

- impacts on classroom practices, with several teachers describing how they had modelled their own teaching on the artists, though the extent to which teachers were able to make significant, long-term and sustainable changes remains an open question, as several references here appeared more like 'promises' to change in the future

- institutional and strategic outcomes, though often quite tenuous, which impacted directly on the organisation as a whole, especially evident in multiphase interventions where sequential links were planned for.

Other outcomes (not far behind in frequency terms) comprised:

- motivational and attitudinal outcomes, with many testimonies to teachers' desire or enthusiasm to recreate or build on the experience of interventions

- affective outcomes, including some negative emotional responses (e.g. envy, or their confidence undermined), as well as the more prevalent positive reactions

- new awareness and value shifts, often seeing the pupils or the artform in a new light and more likely to be evident among primary and less specialist teachers than secondary and more specialist colleagues.

In the teacher-focused interventions

The overall categories of teacher effects associated with these interventions were broadly similar to those resulting from interventions where artists worked primarily with pupils. Teachers gaining knowledge and skills and changing their teaching practices were still the most common outcomes, though the same doubts about the degree and sustainability of the changes also surfaced here, as did the encountering of obstacles to implementing changes in practice. Interestingly, teachers involved in these interventions mentioned impacts on their career or professional development no more often than their counterparts where projects focused on pupils. The main difference was the increased frequency with which teachers reported acquiring material and provisionary outcomes on which they could draw following the interventions – perhaps one way in which artist and teacher acknowledged the CPD aspect.

The evidence suggests that phases based solely on activities involving teachers and artists (excluding pupils) resulted in teachers gaining considerable knowledge and skills and having enhanced enthusiasm and motivation for the artform. However, only the more experienced teachers, or those particularly enthusiastic about the artform prior to the intervention, seemed able to translate these outcomes into practice in the classroom, with very limited immediate impacts for pupils as a consequence.

In contrast, phases that also involved the artist working with pupils provided an ideal opportunity for teachers to observe artists teaching and for some the chance to experiment with new found skills and knowledge in a classroom environment with the support of the artist.

The final model, where an artist worked with the school arts coordinator, already an experienced artist, demonstrated how development could be cascaded as a result of successful collaboration between teacher and artist which was observed by colleagues within the school. The sustained presence of the arts coordinator after the intervention, able to act as a 'peer coach' for other staff and offer on-the-job support, may also contribute to the long-term sustainability of these outcomes.

3.4.2 Outcomes for artists and arts organisations

There were only two instances where artists stated they had gained nothing from their participation in the interventions. All other phases resulted in artists describing at least a small number of effects that they had experienced, though generally effects on artists were less frequent and appeared less substantial than those on pupils and teachers. Many of the effects cited by artists appeared to be of an immediate or short-term nature, with only a small minority reporting more significant changes which could be deemed to be of a deep-seated or longer-term nature. In particular, experienced arts educators identified few notable impacts of AEI interventions on themselves, suggesting that there was limited scope for gaining outcomes which were distinctive from those already gained from their previous work.

The outcome most frequently mentioned by artists centred on new awareness and value shifts. Most references in this category relayed new awareness of alternative teaching styles and methods, or of specific factors that had been either beneficial or detrimental. Several artists had become more aware of their own learning needs and expressed a desire to undertake training in education work, classroom and behaviour management being a common focus. However, it was noted that whilst AEI interventions had prompted some artists to consider additional training, very few considered the intervention itself as an opportunity for professional development. Again, this may be related to the depiction of artists as delivering interventions, rather than collaborative partners working alongside teachers and host organisations.

Artists' affective response to interventions was the second most frequently reported effect, most with some form of positive emotional response being described by artists, but about half had outcomes which were negative in some way. The most common positive affective outcome described by artists was an increase in their levels of confidence to provide arts interventions. A sense of achievement, satisfaction and enjoyment were the other main types of positive emotional response mentioned by artists. Artists' negative responses generally relayed their disappointment relating to particular projects. A small number of difficulties were relayed in terms of planning interventions, though for others frustration resulted from pupils' indiscipline and lack of focus. For some artists their affective response had important ramifications for their future motivation and attitudes. In general terms, the majority of changes to artists' motivation and attitudes were positive.

Gaining new knowledge and skills was another very commonly cited outcome for artists, albeit quite minor in scope for many. The vast majority of artists' references here were to impacts on their knowledge and skills in providing arts interventions (e.g. understanding different pupils' capabilities), rather than related to their own artistic practice. There was evidence that longer interventions had allowed artists to reflect on their practices and refine them in a sustained and incremental manner. Testimonies to this type of effect made up many of the comments categorised under impacts on practice.

Notes

i As we describe later (see 4.2.3, continuity and progression), this seems to be caused, in part at least, by holding a performance of the pupils' work part way through the intervention.

4 Factors that affect the outcomes for pupils and young people

4.1 About this chapter

This chapter and Chapter 5 focus on the second aim of the study, examining what components of AEI interventions were said to bring about and underpin those outcomes outlined in Chapters 2 and 3. Factors associated with pupil outcomes are examined in this chapter, while those relating to teacher and artist outcomes are covered in Chapter 5.

4.1.1 Overview

What affects pupil outcomes? (4.2)

A typology of some 20 factors relating to pupil effects is first presented. As in Chapter 2, the variation with which the 20 factors were actually nominated by our samples of teachers, artists and young people is next outlined. The focus is on how often [frequency] and with what degree of emphasis [strength] these factors were mentioned. Illustrations and first-hand accounts of high- and low-ranking factors are relayed, as well as discussion of any differences in emphasis between the three sub-samples. How these different viewpoints may have implications for future interventions is also raised.

This is followed by a delineation of how nominated factors varied by artform, type of setting, location and type of intervention.

The section concludes with a discussion of how interviewees explicitly associated certain factors with particular pupil outcomes and explores the implications of any notable differences between the perspectives of the three sub-samples.

The chapter concludes with a summary of the main findings (4.3).

4.2 What affects pupil outcomes?

4.2.1 Investigating factors of effectiveness

A wide range of factors were cited as being associated with outcomes of arts interventions for young people. We begin by presenting a typology comprising some 20 different perceived factors and then describe the frequency and strength with which these were reported. The relative importance of individual factors is then examined by artform, by phase of schooling, by intervention type and by EAZ.

A typology of factors of effectiveness for pupils

What did interviewees see as making a difference to pupil outcomes? Unlike the model of effects on pupils presented in Chapter 2, the order in which the following effectiveness factors are set out is not deliberate and does not denote a conscious attempt to signal any developmental sequence.

1 Individual pupil factors

Individual pupil factors include the young people's familiarity with the artform and/or familiarity with the artist's teaching approach, in or out of school. It also covers SEN, gender, ethnicity and aptitude for the artform.

2 Behaviour

This category refers specifically to pupils' behaviour and their response to the artist, as a group or as individuals, during intervention activities.

3 Whole-school factors

Salient whole-school factors include the extent of senior management support and the status of the artform in the school.

4 Artist factors

Factors relating to the artist cover personal characteristics such as cultural background, or whether the artist was seen to belong to the same generation as the participants. This category also covers the artist's professional background and experience of education work with particular age groups. The significance of the artist's 'authenticity', as a professional earning a living by practising the artform, also features here.

5   Pupils' sense of privilege

The sense of privilege refers to the opportunity to work alongside a professional artist and the pupils' awareness that they had been chosen or singled out for inclusion in the intervention.

6   Enjoyability

This category embraces all the references made to 'fun'. It distinguishes between intervention features that were referenced as 'comic', i.e. made people laugh and those that made the experience enjoyable more generally, in terms of its appeal for the group of participants involved.

7   Venue

The venue (either in or out of school) could be a significant factor. In some cases, privacy from other peers or staff in school could be important. In others, novelty could be the salient feature: many pupils had little experience of cultural venues outside school.

8   Time

This category refers to the timing of the intervention, in relation to the school day, term or academic year and the amount of time devoted to the intervention as a whole.

9   Relevance to pupils

The relevance factor comprises the appeal of something new or exciting, as well as the extent to which features of the intervention coincided with pupils' current interests or hopes for the future.

10 Manageability for pupils

This factor refers to conceptual or physical difficulty and emotional vulnerability, all of which were frequently, though not invariably, associated with pace. The value of a challenge also belongs to this category.

11 Content

This factor covers the experience of learning about different artform elements (such as colour and rhythm), as well as associated terminology and artform processes. In addition, it covers the experience of encountering a broader repertoire of styles within the artform and the professional arts world and insight into what it means to be an artist, including what the role entails. It also embraces enhanced appreciation of products and performances.

The opportunities to develop technical skills, have hands-on experience and practice also feature in this category, together with the cultural and historical context of the artform. Knowledge and skills relating to other areas of the curriculum are also included.

12 Artists' pedagogy

This category embraces a number of different elements. The quality of explanation and the nature of feedback; the use of resources; the provision of opportunities for creativity; the extent to which pupils were allowed ownership of activities and the artist's flexibility to pupil needs were all seen as important aspects of the individual artist's approach to teaching.

13 Continuity and progression

Continuity and progression are considered as factors, both within the intervention itself and also in terms of links perceived between features of the intervention and the school curriculum (either within the same artform or with other curriculum areas).

14 The role of the final product

The final product is characterised as a performance or a display of some kind, in which degrees of formality may vary. As a factor, there was variation in the degree of emphasis intended and the way in which it was perceived by participants.

15 Group size

This factor refers to working group size overall and also for specific activities: whole class, small groups or pairs.

16 Group composition

Working groups for specific activities could be selected either by the artist and or the teacher, or by the pupils themselves. Thus, pupils might be working with friends, or with people who were unfamiliar to them. The degree of trust and mutual respect between pupils also appears in this category.

17 Pupil–teacher relationship

The pupil–teacher relationship factor covers the level of trust between teacher (or youth worker) and pupils in the phase or intervention, in relation to the teacher's role as participant, facilitator, or observer, or provider of reassurance or control.

18 Artist–pupil relationship

This category refers to aspects such as the artist's charisma and any distinctive features that set the artist apart from the pupils' normal teacher, (including differences in pedagogy). It also covers the development of mutual trust and respect between artist and pupils.

19 Artist–teacher relationship

This refers to the quality of systems of communication, the extent to which professional values were explicitly shared and accommodated and the extent of any ongoing discussion once interventions were in progress.

20 The role of planning

Planning referred to preparation for the intervention by artists and teachers, including consideration of their respective roles for its duration and any provision for follow-up.

4.2.2 Frequency and importance of factors perceived to be causing pupil effects in the AEI

Equipped with this typology, we can now examine which factors were perceived to be more or less important across the AEI interventions. Which factors did the pupils most frequently identify? Were these factors also identified by teachers and artists? How strongly were these factors perceived to be causing an effect?

This section addresses these questions through analysis of pupil, teacher and artist responses across 33 phases of the AEI interventions. Two kinds of factor ratings are identified and discussed – those mentioned most frequently by interviewees and those given particular emphasis.

As Figure 4.1 and Table 4.1 show, it is artists' pedagogy that emerges as the most frequently mentioned factor by all types of interviewee. Manageability, type of content, relevance, artist–pupil relationship and pupil factors were also mentioned in a high number of phases.

Overall, whole-school factors, artist–teacher relationship, the role of planning and artist factors were the least frequently referenced factors in relation to pupil outcomes.

Figure 4.1 and Table 4.1 also highlight that there are notable differences between the three sub-sample's perspectives. Enjoyability and group size were frequently perceived by pupils to be contributing to effects. In contrast, it was time and group composition that were most frequently referenced by artists, while teachers gave a higher ranking to continuity and progression and role of the end product.

Figure 4.1   In how many phases did pupils, teachers and artists mention each of the broad categories?

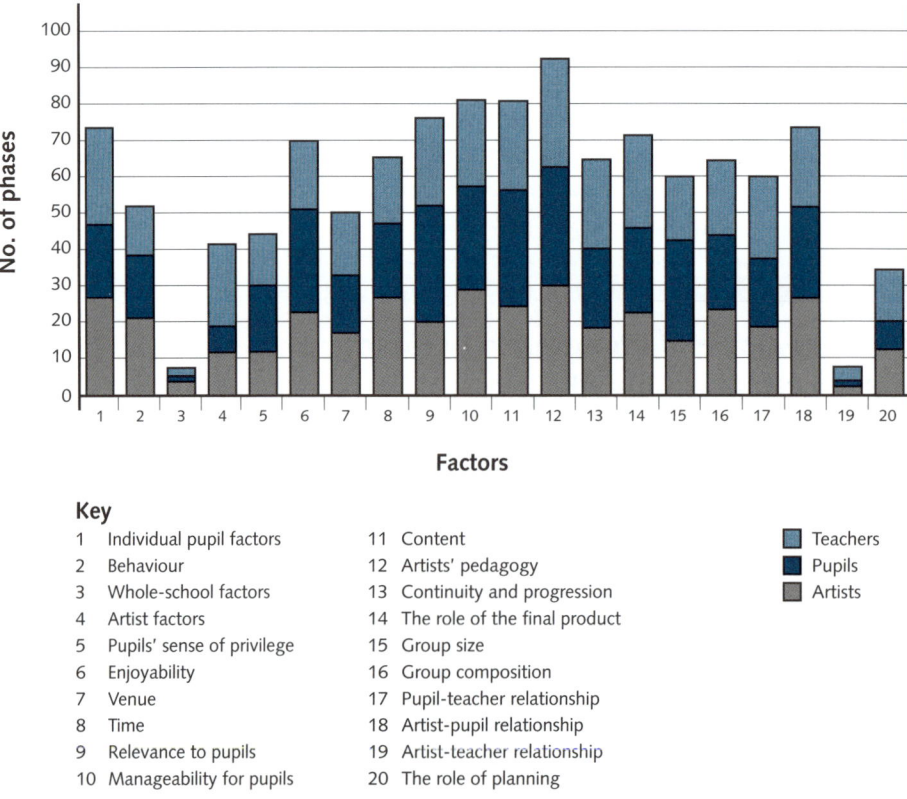

Key

1	Individual pupil factors	11	Content
2	Behaviour	12	Artists' pedagogy
3	Whole-school factors	13	Continuity and progression
4	Artist factors	14	The role of the final product
5	Pupils' sense of privilege	15	Group size
6	Enjoyability	16	Group composition
7	Venue	17	Pupil-teacher relationship
8	Time	18	Artist-pupil relationship
9	Relevance to pupils	19	Artist-teacher relationship
10	Manageability for pupils	20	The role of planning

Teachers
Pupils
Artists

Table 4.1   Did the pupils, teachers and artists mention the same factors with similar frequency?

Factors identified by pupils	Number of phases	Factors identified by teachers	Number of phases	Factors identified by artists	Number of phases
Artists' pedagogy	33	Artists' pedagogy	29	Artists' pedagogy	30
Type of content	32	Pupil factors	26	Manageability	29
Relevance	32	Continuity and progression	25	Pupil factors	27
Enjoyability	28	Role of end product	24	Artist–pupil relationship	27
Manageability	28	Relevance	24	Time	27
Group size	28	Manageability	24	Type of content	25
Artist–pupil relationship	25	Type of content	24	Group composition	24

But how important or influential was each factor felt to be in causing or contributing to pupil effects? As with pupil effects in Chapter 2, frequency of reference should not be the only rating method. The intensity or strength of response also had to be considered and this shows a somewhat different picture. Indeed, some of the factors mentioned less frequently overall were seen as particularly influential in the phases where they were operating: respondents spoke of them with particular emphasis and as generating an array of effects. As Table 4.2 and Figure 4.2 show, the factors perceived as most strongly influencing pupil effects again varied according to pupils, teachers and artists.

Table 4.2   The strongest perceived (more important) factors according to pupils, teachers and artists

Factors identified by pupils	Number of phases	Factors identified by teachers	Number of phases	Factors identified by artists	Number of phases
Artists' pedagogy	33	Artists' pedagogy	24	Artists' pedagogy	28
Type of content	23	Type of content	11	Pupil factors	14
Relevance	12	Manageability	11	Type of content	13
Group size	11	Role of end product	10	Role of end product	9
Artist–pupil relationship	10	Pupil factors	10	Continuity and progression	7
Manageability	10	Continuity and progression	9	Time/enjoyability (jointly)	6

Note: This table shows the number of phases in which sub-samples perceived each factor as 'being very important' or 'being important' (see legend in Figure 4.2)

Figure 4.2   Strength of perceived factors, by number of phases

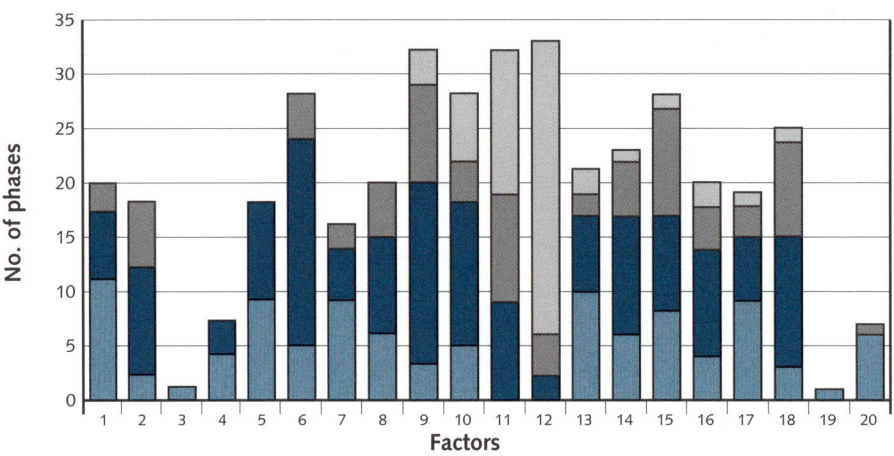

Strength of perceived factors for pupils

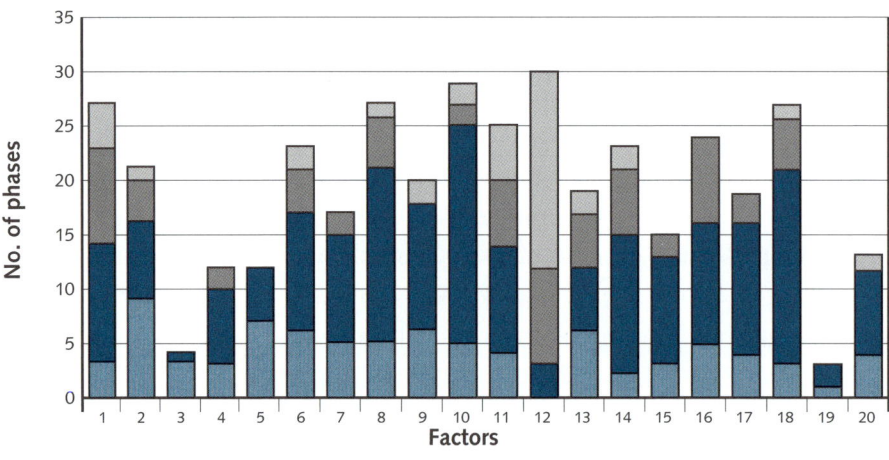

Strength of perceived factors for artists

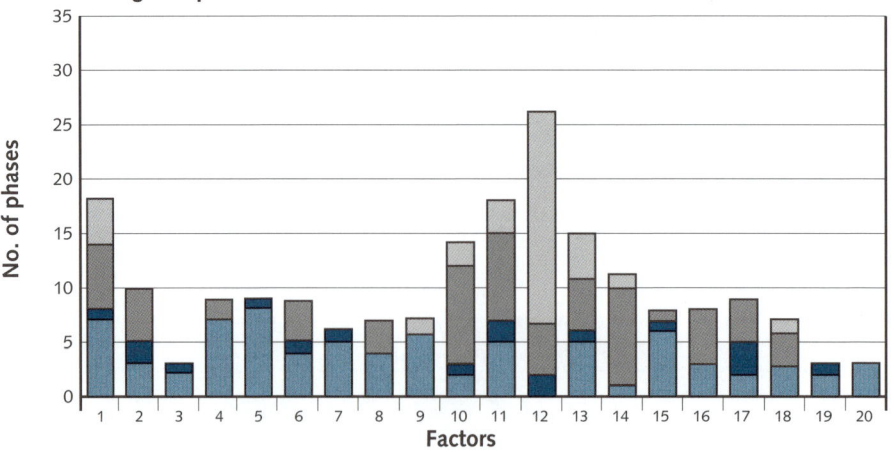

Strength of perceived factors for teachers

Key

1	Individual pupil factors	11	Content
2	Behaviour	12	Artists' pedagogy
3	Whole-school factors	13	Continuity and progression
4	Artist factors	14	The role of the final product
5	Pupils' sense of privilege	15	Group size
6	Enjoyability	16	Group composition
7	Venue	17	Pupil-teacher relationship
8	Time	18	Artist-pupil relationship
9	Relevance to pupils	19	Artist-teacher relationship
10	Manageability for pupils	20	The role of planning

■ Perceived as being very important

■ Perceived as being important

■ Perceived as being less important

■ Perceived, but importance not acknowledged

This 'intensity' rating method reveals that artists' pedagogy was once again the most referenced factor by all types of interviewee. Type of content is also universally perceived as having a particularly strong influence. Interestingly, where teachers and artists noted content, it was felt to be of particularly high importance for producing pupil effects.

Within the top six rankings, no other factors emerged commonly from all three groups. However, the role of the end product, continuity and progression and pupil factors, are seen as particularly influential by the teachers and artists. Manageability was perceived as important by the teachers and pupils.

To summarise, by combining analysis of frequency of references with strength of response, the factors with the overall highest profile emerge as:

- artists' pedagogy (factor 12)
- type of content (factor 11)
- manageability (factor 10)
- emphasis on the end product (factor 14)
- pupil factors (factor 1)
- relevance (factor 9)
- artist–pupil relationship (factor 18)
- continuity and progression (factor 13).

The factors with the lowest profile overall:

- artist–teacher relationship (factor 19)
- school factors (factor 3)
- role of planning (factor 20)

- artist factors (factor 4)

- pupils' sense of privilege (factor 5).

We now turn to the key features of these high and low profile factors.

4.2.3 Factors affecting pupil outcomes: what did they comprise?

This section now offers an illustrative discussion of the factors highlighted as having a particularly high or low profile in the previous section. It unpacks what were the distinctive features within each factor and examines any variation in pupils', artists' and teachers' references to these features.

Factors with a high profile

Artists' Pedagogy

Overall, as the previous section revealed, it was artists' pedagogy that emerged as the most influential factor across all the interventions and from the accounts of pupils, artists and teachers. However, the three sub-samples did highlight different features within this factor.

Pupils identified quality of explanation from the artist most frequently and most intensely and then nature of feedback. The quality of explanation was often a reference to an artist's willingness to repeat or offer alternative explanations and also the ability to relate to the pupils' everyday lives. For instance, a dancer had used everyday analogies to explain ways of moving, 'as if your feet were stuck in superglue and you had to get them out'. Perhaps such comments could be seen as reflections of the artist's flexibility to pupils' needs, which, as shown below, was more explicitly articulated by teachers and by the artists themselves. The nature of feedback was often a conspicuous feature of performing arts interventions, where pupils may have felt particularly exposed and in need of encouragement. Demonstration, as a way of explanation, was also frequently, if less intensely, cited; as, too, was the experience of artform-specific resources provided by the artist, such as microphones and mixing desks, or the 'rainbow-coloured' pages of the 'giant book' used in a theatre production.

Flexibility to pupils' needs and responses was the aspect of pedagogy rated most highly by artists. For instance, a musician who had realised that a song was too difficult for a group of primary pupils said he 'had to keep taking out words in the script'. Another artist explained his open-ended approach to some pupils with SEN involved 'trying it again and again whilst looking out for signs of boredom or thinking "well, this isn't going to work today" and moving on to something else'. Provision of opportunities for creativity was the feature of their pedagogy rated second with artists. To one theatre worker, inviting pupils to use their creativity meant eliciting concepts and ideas from the children in order to write a play. A ceramics specialist introduced pupils to working with clay in order for them 'just to find out what you can do and let their own creativity sort of go wild'. Allowing pupils ownership of the activity was also cited frequently by artists. For some, it was a priority 'to make (pupils) aware that they are making the choices and that is what makes it their piece of artwork'. Where this was absent, negative outcomes might accrue. In one case, for example, some pupils expressed disappointment that although they had contributed initial ideas to a piece of work for performance, the artist had 'changed' them in accordance with his/her own pre-conceived ideas.

Overall, for teachers, opportunities for creativity was the feature of artists' pedagogy that attracted the most references, followed closely by quality of explanation and its closely associated flexibility to pupils' needs. With reference to creativity, some teachers of dance and drama openly acknowledged their sense of inadequacy in relation to improvisation and personal interpretation of experience through the artform. One teacher had particularly appreciated how, under an artist's guidance, pupils were 'given a general theme and encouraged to develop it in their own way'. Degrees of formality or ethos were also noted by teachers particularly in certain instances: for example, an informal approach had been seen as 'the best way to capture the young people's attention' in one out-of-school intervention.

Content

Content emerged as the second most important factor overall, with some variation in emphasis also apparent. For pupils, hands-on experience was the most strongly and frequently perceived aspect. For many pupils, the 'best bit' was undoubtedly 'doing it': 'playing the drums' or handling the clay, 'because it's all squidgy and soft'. Accordingly, 'the worst bit' was the sense of frustration when the artist 'just carried on speaking, instead of doing it'. While hands-on experience evidently impressed pupils most, two other aspects of content, the development of technical skills and the historical/cultural context of the artform, (e.g. 'learning songs from different countries') were consistently, if less emphatically referenced. There were also several instances where the content of a particular phase of the intervention emerged as very strongly referenced. For instance, first-hand experience of the natural world had caught the imagination of a group of pupils during a photography expedition, for example, while participants in another intervention recalled the significance of health and safety precautions, 'not to do it like that … you will hurt yourself bad.'

Artists particularly stressed substantive (or overall) content as a key feature influencing outcomes. For instance, a theatre education worker explained that a group of primary pupils had experienced 'different ways of working, exercises, routines and vocabulary specific to drama' and the pupils' unsolicited references to 'acting' and 'actors' in their interviews perhaps corroborated this assertion. Substantive content was also nominated most important by teachers; although they did not mention it as frequently as artists, when they did they were more emphatic. One teacher, for example, was very enthusiastic about a visual art phase and praised the way pupils had been shown how to look at sculpture as a piece of art and how to consider 'shape, texture and colour'.

The difference between pupils' perceptions here and those of artists and teachers, suggests that if substantive (artform or non-artform) content is their priority, practitioners could make it more palatable to pupils through closer and more consistent attention to other type of content, offering them hands-on experience for example and making a connection with real life through appropriately pitched references to historical and cultural context.

Manageability

The term 'manageability' here refers to conceptual and physical difficulty and also to emotional vulnerability. Pupils of all ages were sensitive to manageability if it became a personal issue. For instance, a participant in an out-of-school intervention observed that activities had been conceptually 'pitched too young' for him because they had 'made it very simple for everybody to learn'. Physical difficulty confronted a number of younger primary pupils involved in elaborate cutting and modelling activities and was of acute concern to very young children, for whom the mastery of physical coordination, 'each little movement' as a nursery teacher explained, was a very new and precarious accomplishment. It was individual pupils rather than artists or teachers who articulated the emotional vulnerability of different individuals in different situations. For example, less physically skilful pupils had felt uncomfortably exposed in situations demanding energetic display or physical agility. In other interventions, some children had not enjoyed the more boisterous group participation activities, 'all of the children push in together and I get pushed over'.

Pupils often associated manageability with pace. For instance, the relentless speed of an animated dialogue with the audience in a theatre performance, punctuated by frequent appeals for help and commentaries on rapidly executed changes of costume, seemed to have struck one child as a verbal onslaught and impeded his ability to understand its significance. He said 'the man talked too much' and he would have preferred him to 'be quiet for a bit'.

Pupils in two secondary interventions, one in drama and one in dance offered an interesting contrast in their response to the rapid pace of learning intrinsic to the artist's demands for them to develop their own interpretations of particular themes through physical expression. One group who were already 'quite confident' according to their teacher and accustomed to such an approach in school artform lessons, had relished the level of concentration the artist expected, 'like an exam, but it was good'. In the second case, the extent to which an artist had really had to 'push' the pupils, resulted in their disappointment that there was 'not enough time to learn or practice' in order to overcome their inhibitions and 'develop our own ideas'.

In spite of voicing their anxieties over aspects of activities that had particularly taxed them, many pupils volunteered their appreciation of a challenge; although they had felt 'very nervous' or that they 'couldn't do it' at first, they had persevered. 'We pushed ourselves' because it was required and were 'proud' of what, in spite of the difficulties, they had been able to achieve. They evidently responded positively to high expectations.

Sometimes, artists highlighted the value of challenge, whilst recognising the need for success: 'I don't think there's anything wrong with it being difficult as long as it's not a goal that they can't reach'. The need to 'pitch' work appropriately, be 'responsive to' and 'develop from (pupils') level' was also noted in some instances.

The role of the end product

Teachers and artists were unanimous in assigning considerable importance to the final product, be it a performance in dance or music intervention, or a work of art completed during a visual arts intervention.

It was noteworthy that artists and teachers referred more frequently and more emphatically to the final product than pupils, with teachers actually giving this factor a higher rating overall than artists. There were references to the benefits of a public performance being valuable as 'something to work towards' or 'focusing minds wonderfully'. The higher rating by teachers and artists of this factor may have been because they were able to see the final product as a component of the intervention in advance of the actual event itself to a greater extent than pupils: the ability of young people to think ahead and to anticipate the future, is perhaps not as well-developed as that of adults. This view gains credence from the fact that the strongest expressions of this factor's importance came from pupils who were responding when the end product was imminent (and often emerged in short-term interventions or within single phases of multi-artform interventions). Pupils then agreed it was 'good' to have a 'proper performance' to work towards. It was seen as helpful to learning, to have a sense of progressing towards a final goal. One girl struggled to articulate her sense of crescendo in this type of incremental structure, stating 'I achieved putting it all together, it's something I can't really explain'. Thus, perceptions of the final product as a final destination or conclusion to a narrative also recurred persistently throughout the pupil data, but not with any special emphasis.

Individual pupil factors

Within this factor, pupil's familiarity with the artform was nominated by pupils most forcefully. A boy in an out-of-school intervention attributed the fact that he had found the 'theoretical' side of the artform more appealing than his peers to a well-established personal interest. Participants in a dance intervention thought they had been less daunted than those new to dance by the 'moves' the artist had asked them to learn because they already attended dance classes.

While artists referred to this familiarity factor as affecting outcomes slightly less frequently than teachers, they did mention other pupil factors, such as pupil's familiarity with the teaching approach, and SEN more frequently than pupils or teachers. The teacher interviews corroborated the impression drawn from pupils that specific individual factors, such as gender, could be influential when linked to certain learning tasks. For example, a music teacher in a series intervention reported that the boys had found playing instruments in front of the girls 'intimidating'; they were reluctant to 'take risks', or work in mixed groups and 'stuck together'.

Relevance

Within the category of relevance, the notion of 'new' was repeatedly referred to across all interventions: pupils nominated the stimulating effect of sheer novelty by contrasting it with the accustomed timetable, divided into lessons following a predictable pattern for weeks or months at a time. 'Getting to know all the new things about art' working with cloth, clay, willow and bamboo, had been a memorable experience for one boy with SEN, while primary pupils elsewhere had delighted in drama sessions spent learning 'new games'. Older pupils highlighted relevance to current interests, which was closely associated with the crucial perceived need to conform to their peers; opportunities to be radio presenters had really appealed to one group because 'it gets everyone to, like, join in …'.

Artist–pupil relationship

Views on the artist–pupil relationship, though less pronounced in their expression than those on artists' pedagogy and intervention content, were frequent enough to rank it among the most important factors. However, compared with highly specific concepts such as nature of feedback and hands-on experience, younger pupils in particular may have had difficulty in both conceptually defining and orally articulating it. Across series and developmental interventions there were references to the sense of trust and mutual respect generated between artist and pupils, to the artist's attitude to the relationship and to the differences perceived between the artist and the pupils' normal teacher. The comments from three pupils in a secondary developmental intervention showed appreciation of the artists' ability to gain their trust while retaining an effective discipline: 'they were more like our mates', 'they listen to us ', 'they were nice, but strict – that was good', ' they treated us like people'.

Artists' references to this factor were slightly more emphatic than those of pupils. Like the pupils, several individuals drew attention to the importance of the delicate balance between building trust and retaining control. One artist noted the licence allowed by their 'novelty' and artistic identity to be more adventurous and 'innovative' than teachers 'under pressure' from the statutory curriculum.

Teachers' comments on this factor also recurred throughout the data, particularly in reference to series and developmental interventions. A teacher involved in a short-term intervention with very young children praised an education officer's (artist's) skill repeatedly for the 'natural way' he/she developed 'rapport' with a group to whom she was a total stranger.

Cumulatively, interviewees' perceptions seemed to confirm that the more that contact was sustained with the artist over a period of time (whether a sequence of sessions within a single phase or over a number of phases), the more the quality of the relationship is highlighted. In addition, for younger children and those in special education, accustomed to the security of the closer adult-child relationship which develops through spending the entire school day with a single teacher, the artist–pupil relationship may be especially critical.

Continuity and progression

A perceived factor emphasised by some teachers was continuity and progression, perhaps unsurprising in view of the overriding demands of curriculum 'outcomes' on teaching time. They considered continuity and progression within the intervention itself; for example, teachers in two separate developmental interventions expressed dissatisfaction with the order of the phases. In one case, where the pupils' public performance had taken place in the second phase, the teacher concerned believed this had inevitably caused the activities of the third and final phase to be experienced as something of an 'anti-climax'. Pupils' own comments corroborated this view. Continuity and progression were also seen in terms of the links the intervention made with the rest of the curriculum, either with the same artform or with other curriculum areas. A primary teacher remarked that the content of a drama intervention was 'relevant to their SATs story-writing', that the pupils did 'lots of art work' based on the intervention and that they used 'history and geography skills' when researching themes for the story.

What other factors were important?

Other factors were deemed to be important, though they tended to be accentuated to varying degrees by each of the sub-sample of interviewees. Pupils, for example, regarded enjoyability, group size and group composition as important, whereas artists felt that time issues and also group composition were particularly influential.

Enjoyability was cited by pupils across most phases, with accounts of the experience being literally 'funny', or comic, as in a drama performance for primary pupils, or with references to the pleasure of working in a new way because it involved an exciting venue or a sympathetic rapport between artist and pupils.

Group size had been a very strong factor in one primary intervention. This was a very unsettled group of children; their comments on the first two phases, which were very positively rated for trust between artist and pupils, suggested they derived a much needed sense of security from activities where the class had worked harmoniously together 'like a family group' towards a common goal. In marked contrast, many of them had been distressed during the third phase by the fact that the artist had had considerable difficulty (which he/she had acknowledged in interview) in controlling 'the naughty ones'. The adult-pupil ratio was particularly important within some interventions, contributing to a number of negative experiences for pupils. For example, within one secondary dance phase pupils were frustrated and annoyed with the lack of attention they received from the artist 'she kept saying "I will be over in a minute" and it was like 10 minutes later and she said it again. So we didn't really get much'. Within another intervention the teacher would have liked a smaller adult-pupil ratio in order to help every child pursue 'a train of thought'. Adult-pupil ratio was rarely cited by teachers as being influential, possibly as they were generally less involved than the artists or pupils and therefore less likely to experience this factor first hand.

Group composition as a factor included such aspects as choice of working groups, unfamiliarity with the group and trust or respect between pupils who would not necessarily be used to working together. Pupils and artists perceived this factor more strongly than teachers. Although not strongly perceived, working with new people over a period of time, within or between phases, seemed to have made an impression on pupils whenever it occurred and on some secondary pupils in particular. While some pupils valued 'getting dead close' through working with friends, others noted how working with strangers required a continuous process of conceptual adaptation and adjustment in order to accommodate 'how different people are ... and just to get on well with people and what to do and what not to do, what to say and what not to say'. A number of artists emphasised the importance of generating trust and respect between pupils. In dance and drama interventions, this could mean trusting a partner to give physical support in a sequence of 'moves'. In other interventions it involved 'making decisions with peers, listening to one another'. A teacher present as an observer during sessions of a secondary intervention noted how pupils from different year groups had gradually gained confidence in working together and had 'built up relationships'.

The factor conspicuously noted by artists was time. This could relate to the length of individual sessions within a particular phase: for example, one musician felt that 'an hour is too short' as there was not enough time for the pupils 'to be creative … they want to carry on'. Nor was there enough time to fully establish an artist–pupil relationship. The significance of time for artists also related to the overall length of an intervention. Another artist had felt under pressure from the expectation to produce a performance within three weeks and present it to the rest of the school. This was seen to have seriously compromised the artist's original aim which was to give the pupils enough time to familiarise themselves with a new style of the artform in order to be sufficiently confident to improvise their own ideas on a particular theme.

What factors received least nominations in relation to pupil effects?

Five of the twenty from the factor typology particularly stand out and are now discussed.

Artist–teacher relationship

When pupil outcomes were under discussion (and notably in interventions where teacher development was not the main focus), this category emerged with very few references. It is not surprising that pupils rarely mentioned something of which they would not have been directly aware. However, notably, a single young person in one phase of an out-of-school intervention, did draw attention to the 'disconcerting' effect, 'you don't know where you are', of conflicting instructions caused by failures in artist-youth worker communication.

Very few artists and teachers specifically referred to their relationship as a factor that impinged on pupil outcomes; where evident, these were from series or developmental interventions. Most of the comments expressed an appreciation of trust and mutual respect. The only negative reference, from a teacher who felt that artists had 'ignored' his/her ideas and suggestions, indicated the potential for discord inherent in the process of planning interventions and accommodating one another's professional values. The rarity of perceptions of this factor may suggest that in pupil development interventions, teachers and artists attached little importance to it. As an essentially transient encounter, their relationship may only have registered when it yielded unanticipated benefits or adverse effects. In contrast, when the artist–teacher relationship was considered as a factor for effects on teachers and artists, it was given correspondingly more weight.

Whole-school factors

Nominations for this category were particularly sparse. However, in the few interventions where they were located, they suggested that factors such as the extent of senior management support and the status of the artform in the school could dilute or dissipate the quality of the experience for pupils. According to one artist, the low status of drama in one school had meant that individual pupils had been withdrawn from occasional sessions throughout a series of workshops in a drama phase in order to participate in other things in school. Elsewhere, the low profile of dance in the school appeared to have precluded the possibility of any structured follow-up work to channel pupils' burgeoning enthusiasm. Conversely, a sympathetic approach from senior management at another site had been valued as a direct support in releasing pupils from their normal timetable, an unpopular decision with some other teachers.

The role of planning

Planning emerged as a slightly stronger perceived factor than whole-school or artist–teacher relations. While very few references were made with any emphasis, several aspects of planning recurred in the responses of interviewees. Amongst teachers' nominations, preparation for the intervention and provision for follow-up attracted the highest number of references. Artists also mentioned preparation most frequently. The degree of understanding of one another's roles during the intervention was identified occasionally by both groups.

Pupils' views were restricted to comments on follow-up: these, though few in number, were telling. A number of pupils in one of the short-term interventions shared a feeling of frustration, 'I want to carry on with it but …. it finished'. Even where follow-up had been provided, it was sometimes experienced as antipathetic to pupils' needs. In one intervention, 'the worst thing' had been 'making hats' the same afternoon. Elsewhere, one boy, along with his peers, had followed a comic and visually colourful theatre performance with delight and riveted attention. He said he had 'hated (being) … asked to write something down' in the follow-up session immediately afterwards. For him, this dour expectation had summarily dispelled his exhilaration and jolted him too suddenly back into the real world.

From the pupil perspective, it seems that the appetite for follow-up may vary according to the nature of the intervention and that in any case, some kinds of follow-up may be less palatable than others. In endeavouring to ensure some kind of follow-up work to an intervention, findings here suggest teachers may need to respect participants' need for sympathetic activities which allow them to 'come down to earth' gradually after what may be an intense and unfamiliar experience. Conscientious attempts to produce specific outcomes too quickly could, for some pupils, prove counter-productive.

Artist factors

The nomination of this category was also much more in evidence among teachers and artists than among pupils. Some artists specifically intended to 'demystify' their artform, or erase prevailing 'stereotypes' relating either to the artform and/or to the artist's cultural background. Others were very conscious of an ambivalence in their role: they felt that the fact that they were artists, but were 'working in an educational setting' could be confusing for pupils, who sometimes expected them to behave like teachers. One artist reported that the children 'seemed to respect me as someone who knows what they are doing'. Interestingly, this was reflected in a pupil's appreciation of this artist who did 'better stuff' than their normal teacher because he/she 'knows how'.

Teachers made twice as many references to artist factors as did the artists themselves. This appears to underline the fact that for teachers, as well as for pupils, the intrinsic value of the intervention was associated with the professional identity of the artist as an artist. However, a closer look at the references here revealed how focused teachers were with the artist's skills and experience in classroom management and their ability to relate to a particular age group. An artist who had completed a postgraduate certificate in education had made a favourable impression in this respect, while elsewhere another's lack of understanding of pupils' needs was criticised.

While appreciating the special contribution of an artist's expertise, teachers' comments tended to emphasise the artist's proficiency or lack of it in areas of pedagogy. Although artists may earn respect from pupils, for superior levels of expertise in the artform, the teachers' professional perspective suggested this alone would not guarantee a positive experience of the artform. This is borne out by the fact that artists' pedagogy emerged as the single most important overall factor.

Pupils' sense of privilege

Although this factor was not forcefully or frequently expressed, it formed a discernible strand in the data. Very few references emerged from artists and there were not many more from the pupils themselves. However, pupils' comments suggested this could be an important factor for specific individuals.

A pupil's sense of privilege was sometimes akin to artist factors, such as the opportunity to work directly alongside a professional artist. One pupil was thrilled that he/she 'got an opportunity to work with (artists) which was almost famous and dead confident ...', another was 'shocked by their coming to work with us' and was 'very nervous as well as very excited ... feeling mixed.'

In other cases, the sense of privilege related to the fact that he/she, as an individual, had been selected to take part, which as a boost to their self-esteem, affected the way they approached the experience. In an intervention where pupils commented positively on the artists' high expectations of them, several thought the confidence and self-belief they had gained from being 'picked' had helped them rise to the occasion.

In some instances, the sense of privilege was closely aligned to an appreciation of being trusted with a special responsibility, or ownership. Pupils in one phase had been entrusted with cameras to take home and use to practise; many of them spontaneously confided that the artist 'let us take them home'. Both teacher and artist alluded to this temporary ownership as an integral feature of the experience.

In sum, consideration of the most and least important perceived factors reveals that pupils, teachers and artists frequently emphasised different aspects of the broad main overall categories. It emerged that the importance of certain factors could be related to specific phases of interventions, or to particular individuals. The inter-relationship of factors was also evident. This will be reconsidered in the section where factors are cross-referenced with effects (see 4.2.8).

4.2.4 Are factors artform-specific?

In this section we consider whether certain factors emerged as having particular significance for the different artforms. The four most common artforms in the AEI interventions were:

- visual arts (including photography)

- dance

- drama (including theatre)

- music.

Again it is worth noting that results for dance need treating with caution, as only three phases are included in that particular artform sub-sample.

Table 4.3 and Figure 4.3 show there is some similarity in the ranking of influential factors across the artforms and they reflect the ratings overall as described in 4.2.2. Factors such as artists' pedagogy and type of content rank highly across all the artforms, with factors such as role of the end product and pupil factors also surfacing.

Table 4.3   The five highest profile factors affecting pupil outcomes by artform

Visual arts	Dance	Drama	Music
Artists' pedagogy	Artists' pedagogy	Artists' pedagogy	Artists' pedagogy
Type of content	Manageability	Continuity and progression	Pupil factors
Pupil factors	Type of content	Manageability	Type of content
Role of the end product	Group composition	Type of content	Role of the end product
Relevance	Role of the end product	Artist–pupil relationship	Continuity and progression

As the results clearly show, the relative status of these factors did vary according to artform. For example, whereas end product, pupil factors and relevance were considered particularly influential in the visual arts, continuity and progression, artist–pupil relationship and manageability were rated highly in drama, where pupil factors were ranked lower. (Drama's high rating for continuity and progression may be related to the fact that six of the ten drama phases in the study were single artform series interventions where the degree of continuity between phases could be expected to be seen as particularly significant.) Music, where pupil factors were ranked comparatively high, shared several affinities with art, except continuity and progression were ranked higher. Dance was distinctive in that manageability and group composition were ranked higher than many other factors.

In addition, within the broad factor categories, it was notable that different aspects were emphasised by different artforms.

Figure 4.3 Average strength of each factor by artform

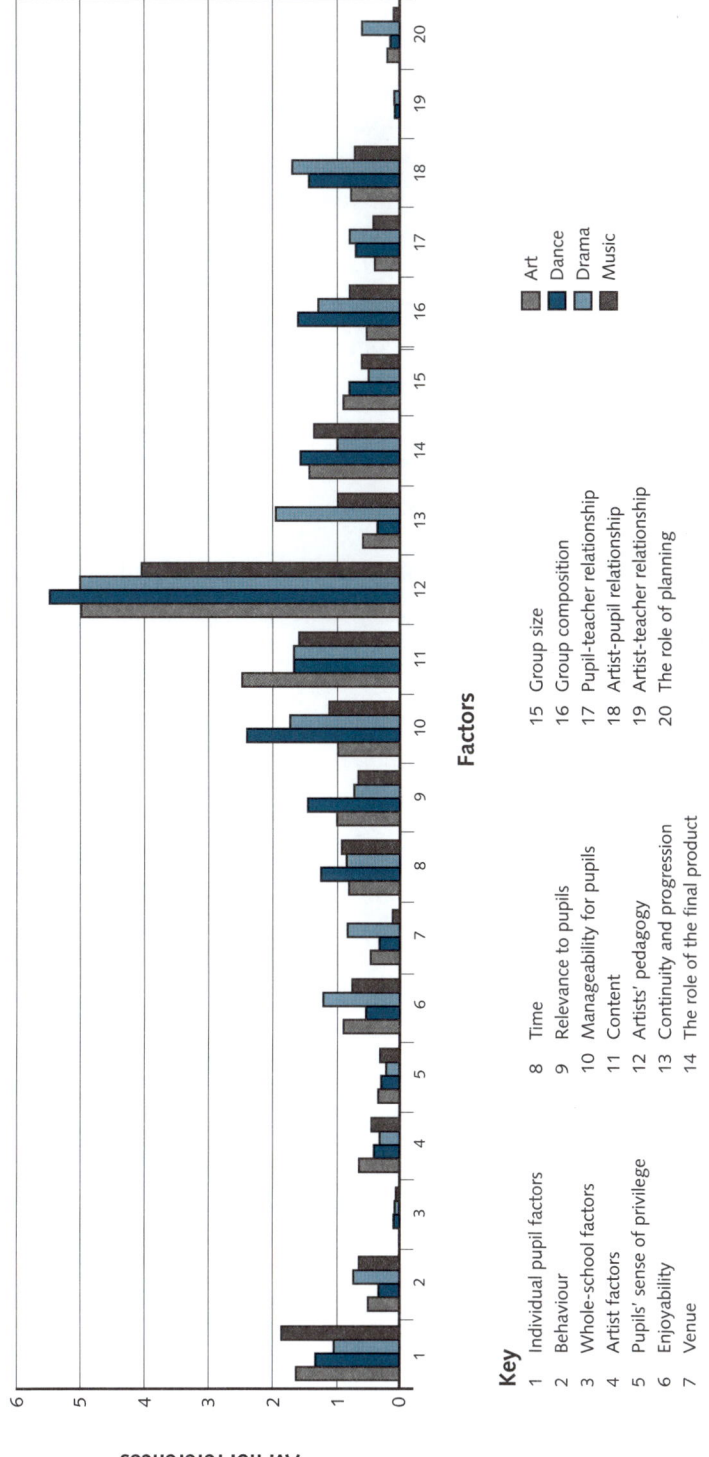

Factors

Key

1 Individual pupil factors
2 Behaviour
3 Whole-school factors
4 Artist factors
5 Pupils' sense of privilege
6 Enjoyability
7 Venue

8 Time
9 Relevance to pupils
10 Manageability for pupils
11 Content
12 Artists' pedagogy
13 Continuity and progression
14 The role of the final product

15 Group size
16 Group composition
17 Pupil-teacher relationship
18 Artist-pupil relationship
19 Artist-teacher relationship
20 The role of planning

Within the top ranking artists' pedagogy factor, it was noticeable that respondents from visual arts interventions particularly referenced allowing pupils ownership of the activity, the artist's flexibility to pupils' response and needs and the use of artform-specific resources as particularly important. In contrast, the provision of opportunity for creativity and self-expression was an aspect of pedagogy emphasised in dance interventions and also important in drama and music. Within drama, the atmosphere created and nature of feedback were cited as important.

Type of content was also strongly reported. Common to all artforms was the significance of the overall substantive content (themes and technical knowledge). Within visual art phases, the opportunity for hands-on experience and within music, the inclusion of historical and cultural contexts was mentioned frequently as contributing to effects. In drama, a combination of hands-on experience and practice emerged as being very important aspects of content.

Within the broad category of pupil factors, it was pupils' ability that was singled out in the visual arts, while for music, gender emerged as an aspect influencing pupil outcomes.

In dance and to a lesser extent in drama phases, group composition was perceived to be particularly influential, though this may reflect greater use of groups in these artforms. In dance, how familiar the group were with the other group members was highlighted and, in drama, it was the levels of trust or respect between pupils that offered the greatest contribution to the overall importance.

4.2.5 Are important factors specific to type of educational setting?

This section explores the extent to which variations in the saliency of factors occur according to the type of educational setting. The results for the out-of-school interventions should be treated with caution due to the low number of phases they hosted.

Figure 4.4 and Table 4.4 demonstrate influential factors by phase of schooling and by type of educational setting. All but five of the factors influencing pupil outcomes were referenced more intensely in primary settings than those located in secondary or out-of-school settings. This may be related to the more holistic, pastoral day-long contact between teachers and pupils at primary level compared to the more limited subject-based contact of secondary. Factors given equal or more emphasis in other settings were emphasis on the end product, group composition, pupils' sense of privilege, time and pupil–teacher relationship. In the latter case, it was the out-of-school phases that attributed the greatest importance to it. The role of the 'host adult' (teacher or youth worker) in controlling behaviour and the trust and respect between pupils and host adult were deemed particularly important aspects, suggesting where participation is mainly voluntary, this relationship between participants and the 'host adult' could be particularly significant. Emphasis on the end product and group composition may similarly need special attention in these non-statutory situations.

Figure 4.4   Average strength of each factor by phase of schooling

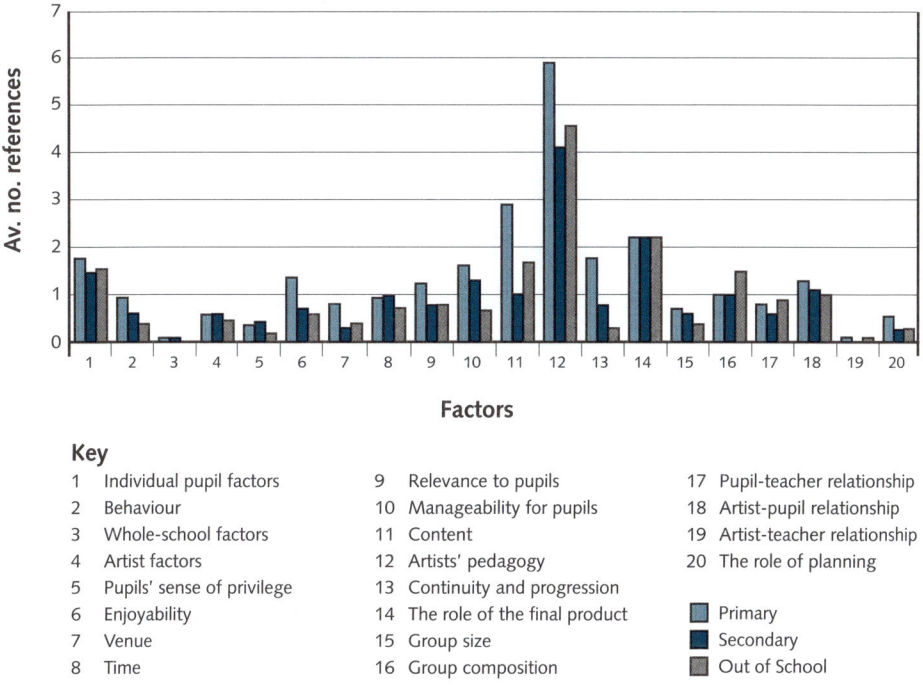

Key

1	Individual pupil factors	9	Relevance to pupils	17	Pupil-teacher relationship
2	Behaviour	10	Manageability for pupils	18	Artist-pupil relationship
3	Whole-school factors	11	Content	19	Artist-teacher relationship
4	Artist factors	12	Artists' pedagogy	20	The role of planning
5	Pupils' sense of privilege	13	Continuity and progression		
6	Enjoyability	14	The role of the final product		Primary
7	Venue	15	Group size		Secondary
8	Time	16	Group composition		Out of School

On balance, the differences between primary, secondary and out-of-school interventions are limited. Common factors prevail although their importance varies. For example, manageability and pupil factors were ranked higher at secondary level than at primary level or out-of-school settings, suggesting that individual pupil factors in secondary interventions are felt to influence the outcomes they achieve. Pupil's familiarity with the teaching style, their personality and their aptitude were highlighted as important features at secondary level. In out-of-school interventions, there was more focus on the personality and age of the participant, while within primary settings, it was the pupils' general ability and individual needs. Group composition emerged as a high profile factor in out-of-school interventions suggesting that the intricate dynamics of the peer group are particularly influential factors in settings other than at school.

Table 4.4   The five highest profile factors affecting pupil outcomes by educational setting

Primary	Secondary	Out of school
Artists' pedagogy	Artists' pedagogy	Artists' pedagogy
Type of content	Pupil factors	Role of the end product
Continuity and progression	Manageability	Type of content
Pupil factors	Artist–pupil relationship	Pupil factors
Manageability	Type of content	Group composition

Type of content and continuity and progression were given relatively high ratings for strength as factors in primary schools.

Artists' pedagogy remained the most important factor across all educational settings, with the provision of opportunities for creativity and self-expression being features particularly rated. Nevertheless, some variations did occur between settings. The artists' flexibility to pupil response and needs was deemed particularly important at primary level. At secondary level and in out-of-school settings, it was the nature of feedback that was rated important, (which may be related, as above, to the age of the participants). In out-of-school settings, a key factor to successful outcome was viewed as informal interaction.

4.2.6 Are important factors specific to intervention type?

This section addresses the factors influencing pupil effects by type of intervention. Figure 4.5 and Table 4.5 highlight the variation in important factors by type of intervention and subtle variations can be observed between the higher profile factors.

With artists' pedagogy, type of content and pupil factors showing up consistently across all three types, the main factors were fairly uniform across the types of intervention. Perhaps inevitably, continuity and progression were deemed very important in developmental interventions, associated with cohesion within or between phases and the links with both the wider artform curriculum or other subjects. Interestingly these features frequently caused negative experiences for pupils. Not all developmental interventions were viewed as a cohesive series of phases and this could explain the high reports of a lack of continuity between them. Similarly, in those interventions that were planned to advance learning in a developmental way, the continuity and progression would be particularly important and this factor has emerged as being of a higher profile than in one-off or series interventions.

Figure 4.5   Average sum of scores by type of intervention

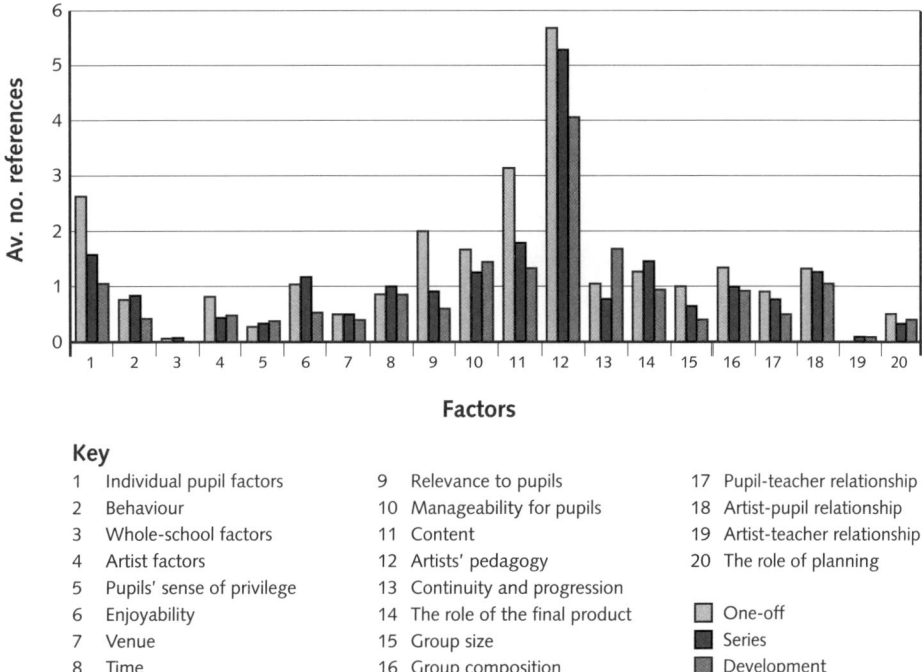

Key

1	Individual pupil factors	9	Relevance to pupils	17	Pupil-teacher relationship
2	Behaviour	10	Manageability for pupils	18	Artist-pupil relationship
3	Whole-school factors	11	Content	19	Artist-teacher relationship
4	Artist factors	12	Artists' pedagogy	20	The role of planning
5	Pupils' sense of privilege	13	Continuity and progression		
6	Enjoyability	14	The role of the final product	☐	One-off
7	Venue	15	Group size	■	Series
8	Time	16	Group composition	▨	Development

It is also interesting to note that the importance of the end product was ranked highly for one-off, but not for developmental or series interventions. This may suggest that the incremental learning dynamic in the latter types obviates, to some extent, the need for a substantial product at the end of the process.

Within artists' pedagogy, which again was ranked top in all types of interventions, some subtle variations occurred. For example, in one-off interventions the use of artform-specific resources was particularly important. However, this should be treated with some caution given the small number of one-off interventions and it is likely that this finding has emerged as a result of more intervention-specific factors. Allowing pupils ownership of the activity was more important within developmental interventions than in single series artform interventions. This is likely to have emerged with such importance as participants were involved for longer, there would be more time to develop skills and ideas and it could be easier for control or ownership to be passed onto the pupils without any detrimental effects. Interestingly, within the single artform series interventions, the types and clarity of explanation was given emphasis, specifically the use of demonstration. Where pupils were being exposed to new skills or content, it is unsurprising that the explanations given are important as they may be required more often.

Table 4.5   The five highest profile factors affecting outcomes by type of intervention

One-off	Series	Developmental
Artists' pedagogy	Artists' pedagogy	Artists' pedagogy
Type of content	Type of content	Continuity and progression
Pupil factors	Pupil factors	Manageability
Relevance	Role of end product	Type of content
Manageability	Manageability	Pupil factors

4.2.7 Are important factors specific to EAZ?

It may be worth bearing in mind that there were some minor differences between the range of interventions which occurred as the result of negotiations in schools in Bristol and Corby. No real differences emerged, however, in the important factors overall when analysed by EAZ. The most striking feature of the analysis was the degree of strength attached to the factors. Considerably more strength was attached to the factors in Bristol than in Corby. Given the much higher profile of the arts in Bristol, it seems possible that interviewees there could be more familiar with school-based arts interventions and consequently more practised in thinking and talking about them.

4.2.8 Factors and outcomes: what's the link?

In this final section, we turn to the important question of whether interviewees associated certain factors with any particular pupil outcomes, as depicted in Chapter 2. We also investigate whether pupils, teachers and artists highlighted the same associations and explore what might be the implications of any differences between the three sub-samples' views.

Table 4.6 relays a ranking of all explicit references made to the 11 broad pupil outcome types being linked to specific factors. Those factors highlighted in bold represent the most frequently mentioned link, italicised factors represent those noted by only one or two interviewees.

Table 4.6   What is the link? Pupil effects and their associated factors

Pupil effect	Factors linked by pupils	Factors linked by teachers	Factors linked by artists
Affective outcomes	• **Type of content** • Artists' pedagogy • Manageability • Enjoyability • Relevance • Role of end product • Artist–pupil relationship • Venue/space • Group size • Pupil behaviour/ response • Pupils' sense of privilege • Group composition • Pupil factors • *Pupil–teacher relationship*	• **Role of end product** • Manageability • Enjoyability • Relevance • Venue/space • Artists' pedagogy • *Time* • *Type of content* • *Group size* • *Group composition* • *Artist–teacher relationship* • *Artist factors* • *Pupils' sense of privilege*	• **Role of end product** • Relevance • Pupils' sense of privilege • Manageability • Type of content • Artists' pedagogy • Venue/space • Time • Continuity and progression • Artist–pupil relationship • *Enjoyability* • *Pupil–teacher relationship*
Artform knowledge, appreciation and skills	• **Type of content** • Artists' pedagogy • Pupils' sense of privilege • Enjoyability • Artist–pupil relationship • Manageability • Venue/space • Continuity and progression • *Group size* • *Group composition* • *Pupil–teacher relationship* • *Role of planning* • *Pupil factors* • *Artist factors* • *Time* • *Relevance*	• **Pupil Factors** • Type of content • *Continuity and progression* • *Pupils' sense of privilege*	• **Type of content** • Artists' pedagogy • Manageability • *Pupils' sense of privilege* • *Continuity and progression* • *Artist factors*
Social and cultural knowledge	• **Type of content** • *Artist–pupil relationship*	• *Artist factors* • *Type of content*	• **Type of content** • Venue/space

Figure 4.6   Continued

Pupil effect	Factors linked by pupils	Factors linked by teachers	Factors linked by artists
Knowledge, skills and appreciation beyond the arts	• Type of content • Venue/space		• *Continuity and progression*
Thinking skills	• **Artists' pedagogy** • *Relevance* • *Type of content* • *Role of end product* • *Group size*	• *Pupil factors* • *Artists' pedagogy* • *Continuity and progression*	• *Type of content* • *Artist–pupil relationship*
Developments in creativity	• **Artists' pedagogy** • Type of content	• Artists' pedagogy	• **Artists' pedagogy** • *Relevance* • *Manageability*
Communication and expressive skills	• **Type of content** • Artists' pedagogy • Group size • *Group composition*	• **Type of content** • *Pupils' sense of privilege* • *Artists' pedagogy* • *Continuity and progression* • *Group size* • *Group composition*	• **Artists' pedagogy** • Enjoyability • Type of content • Role of end product • *Group size*
Personal development	• **Manageability** • Role of end product • Artists' pedagogy • Type of content • Artist–pupil relationship • Pupils' sense of privilege • Group composition • Relevance • Group size • *Pupil–teacher relationship* • *Artist factors* • *Venue/space*	• **Role of end product** • Artists' pedagogy • Pupils' sense of privilege • Manageability • Group composition • Pupil • *Enjoyability* • *Venue/space* • *Group size* • *Pupil–teacher relationship*	• **Role of end product** • Artists' pedagogy • Pupil factors • Relevance • Artist–pupil relationship • Type of content • *Manageability* • *Group composition*
Changes in attitudes towards and involvement in the artform	• **Type of content** • Relevance • Artist–pupil relationship • Enjoyability • Artists' pedagogy • Pupils' sense of privilege • Manageability • Group size • *Role of end product* • *Group composition* • *Pupil behaviour/response* • *Venue/space*	• *Manageability* • *Role of planning*	• Enjoyability • Type of content • Artist–pupil relationship • *Artists' pedagogy* • *Role of end product* • *Artist–teacher relationship*

Figure 4.6   Continued

Pupil effect	Factors linked by pupils	Factors linked by teachers	Factors linked by artists
Social development	• **Group composition** • Group size • Type of content • Artist–pupil relationship • *Enjoyability* • *Venue/space* • *Manageability* • *Artists' pedagogy* • *Role of end product*	• **Group composition** • Artists' pedagogy • Role of end product • Group size • *Pupil–teacher relationship* • *Pupil behaviour/ response* • *Type of content*	• **Group composition** • Group size • Artists' pedagogy • Artist factors • *Venue/space* • *Artist–pupil relationship* • *Pupil behaviour/ response*
Transfer beyond the artform	• **Type of content** • Relevance • Manageability • Artists' pedagogy • Enjoyability • Artist–pupil relationship • Emphasis on the end product	• **Enjoyability** • Manageability • *Pupils' sense of privilege* • *Time*	• **Continuity and progression** • *Enjoyability* • *Manageability* • *Type of content* • *Group size* • *Role of planning*

Note: Those factors highlighted in bold represent the most frequently mentioned link, italicised factors represent those noted by only one or two interviewees.

Most strikingly, it is clear that pupils rated type of content as the main factor associated with seven different outcome categories in all. In contrast, artists specified its primacy as a factor for just two knowledge-related outcome categories (artform as well as social and cultural), while the teacher sub-sample only rated content as the main factor in relation to communication and expressive skills. Does this disparity suggest that teachers and artists might be under-estimating content? Would this fit with the low references to planning as a factor, assuming that a key component of planning would be the selection and design of the intervention's content? Alternatively, is it so obvious a connection, it remained unspoken by the professionals? Whichever interpretation, the voices of the pupils are surely cogently implying that an art intervention's substance and focus, rather than just its existence, makes a significant difference to the effects that can be achieved.

As we have seen earlier in the chapter, artists' pedagogy attracted the highest overall rating, yet it emerged relatively infrequently as the main factor for specific outcomes. This suggests that in general terms, participants believe artists' pedagogy to be important to interventions and to producing outcomes, but they find it harder to say which kinds of outcomes are linked to artist pedagogy. Artists' pedagogy also gets a much higher rating by pupils and artists, as a key factor across a number of outcomes, compared to teachers' accounts. In all, pupils associated this factor with nine outcomes types, compared to seven for artists (who top rated their pedagogy for creative and expressive skills) and only six for the teacher sub-sample, though notably with this interviewee type, it was never a top rated factor. No artist (and only an occasional teacher) saw artists' pedagogy as achieving thinking skills and yet, for pupils, this link was cited most. Similarly, pupils linked artists' pedagogy with transfer beyond the artform, whereas no teacher or artist made this connection. Changes in attitude to the artform are not attributed to artists' pedagogy by teachers either. The contribution of artists' pedagogy to developments in creativity, personal development and affective outcomes were noted similarly across all three sub-samples. Overall, do these findings suggest teachers are overlooking the significance of artists' pedagogy? Does it relate to a lack of involvement in the intervention? At the very least, the findings may point up how pupils' views on what makes outcomes happen for them is worth further consideration by practitioners and policy makers alike.

Other notable variations also are evident, some reflecting earlier findings. The role of the end product gets a high rating from artists and teachers as a key factor in relation to affective and personal development outcomes: pupils' references for this factor were lower. Yet, there were occasional unique links made by pupils between end product and such outcomes as thinking skills and changes in attitude to the artform (also picked up by a few artists, but no teacher). We can also see how teachers place pupil factors as having the most influence on artform knowledge and skills, while both artists and pupils cite content here. Manageability gets a number of only occasional references from artists, whereas its prominence as a factor is more evident among the views of pupils and teachers. Indeed, only one artist cited this factor in relation to personal development, though pupils gave it top-ranking for this outcome. Does this suggest artists may be underestimating the value of differentiation and task appropriateness compared to those who daily operate by such fundamental principles of effective learning?

Pupils, teachers and artists were all in accord over the high rating given to social development being determined most by group composition, but pupils and teachers saw this factor influencing personal development and affective outcomes more than did artists. Enjoyability featured more frequently as a factor influencing affective outcomes in the discourse of pupils and teachers and it is perhaps poignant that no teacher, nor artist, referenced the association between enjoyability and artform knowledge, though artists did rate this factor in achieving expressive skills and changes in attitude to the artform. Similarly, pupils' sense of privilege is linked to artform knowledge by pupils most. Again we can only speculate, but does this indicate how profoundly pupils associate pleasure and positive attention with effective learning and could practitioners and policy makers be more deliberate in their planning for the former so that the latter may follow?

Many other permutations and associations (or lack of) can be extracted from Table 4.6 and speculated upon. For instance, why do teachers so rarely mention artist–pupil relationship? Why does artist–teacher relationship emerge so rarely among either of these two sub-samples as affecting pupil outcomes? Why is group size given so little significance by the two adult sub-samples in particular?

Overall, the findings perhaps can begin to show where arts interventions might usefully focus more attention: would explicit cross-referencing better maximise pupil outcomes?

4.3 Summary

The chapter began by offering a framework of 20 broad categories of factors that are perceived to affect pupil outcomes of arts education.

According to the perceptions of the participants, the factors with the overall highest profile emerged as:

- Artists' pedagogy especially quality of explanation, feedback and demonstration; flexibility to pupils' needs and responses; providing opportunities for creativity; allowing pupils' ownership of the activity.

- Type of content especially giving the pupils hands-on experience, the development of technical skills and the historical/cultural context of the artform; offering engaging substantive content and making connections to 'real life'.

- Manageability in terms of conceptual and physical difficulty, as well as emotional vulnerability and centred on pitching the work or tasks at appropriate levels to avoid them becoming too easy or too demanding – though many pupils responded positively to high expectations of challenges.

- Emphasis on the end product – teachers and artists assigned considerable importance to the final product, be it a performance in dance or music intervention, or a work of art completed during a visual arts intervention. Pupils also cited it. Having a sense of progressing towards a final goal was seen as helpful to learning.

- Pupil factors including pupils' familiarity with the artform; pupils' familiarity with the teaching approach; SEN, learning or behavioural difficulties and gender.

- Relevance – here the notion of 'new' was repeatedly referred to across all interventions and older pupils in particular stressed the importance of relevance to current interests.

- Artist–pupil relationship including a sense of trust, rapport and mutual respect generated between artist and pupils (noted especially in series and developmental interventions); the artist's attitude to the relationship and to the differences perceived between the artist and the pupils' normal teacher. The importance of achieving the delicate balance between building trust and retaining control was emphasised.

- Continuity and progression, highlighted by some teachers, this focused on the design and sequencing of activities in longer-term interventions, as well as drawing out the intervention's links and continuities with the normal curriculum.

Other factors that were deemed to impart an important influence on pupil outcomes included: enjoyability, group size, group composition and issues relating to time and timing.

The factors adjudged to have the lowest impact on pupil outcomes were:

- artist–teacher relationship
- whole school
- role of planning
- artist
- pupils' sense of privilege.

Certain factors emerged as exerting a strong influence on pupil outcomes in all artforms (primarily, artists' pedagogy and type of content), though some variations were apparent across the artforms. For example, whereas end product, pupil factors and relevance were considered particularly influential in the visual arts, continuity and progression, artist–pupil relationship and manageability were rated highly in drama. Music, where pupil factors were ranked comparatively high, shared several affinities with art, except continuity and progression were ranked higher. Dance was distinctive in that manageability and group composition were ranked higher than many other factors for dance.

All but five of the factors influencing pupil outcomes were referenced more intensely in primary settings than those located in secondary or out of school. Type of content and continuity and progression were given relatively high ratings for strength as factors in primary schools. Manageability and pupil factors were ranked higher at secondary level than at primary or out-of-school settings. Artists' pedagogy remained the most important factor across all educational settings.

The main factors were fairly uniform across the three different types of intervention, with artists' pedagogy, type of content and pupil factors showing up consistently across all three types. Continuity and progression were deemed very important in developmental interventions, though the role of end product was not ranked as high in these type of interventions as in one-off or series interventions.

4.3.1 Specific links between pupil outcomes and perceived factors

An analysis of associations between perceived factors and specific pupil outcomes revealed several salient findings. Pupils rated type of content as the main factor associated with seven different pupil outcome categories. They also associated artists' pedagogy with nine outcome types, compared to seven for artists and six for the teacher sub-sample. The contribution of artists' pedagogy to developments in creativity, personal development and affective outcomes were noted similarly across all three sub-samples of interviewees. The role of the end product received a high rating from artists and teachers as a key factor in relation to affective and personal development outcomes. Pupils, teachers and artists were all in accord over the high rating given to social development being determined most by group composition.

5 Factors that affect the outcomes for teachers and artists

5.1 About this chapter

While the previous chapter considered factors associated with pupil outcomes, this chapter explores factors perceived to be instrumental in leading to teacher and artist outcomes.

5.1.1 Overview

What affects outcomes for teachers and artists? (5.2)

A typology of 14 different factors relating to the effects of interventions on teachers and artists is outlined, again followed by a focus on how often [frequency] and with what degree of emphasis [strength] these factors were mentioned. Illustrative discussion of those factors given particular emphasis follows, as well as an overview of any notable variation by location, type of setting, artform and type of intervention. Finally, this section also concludes with a discussion of how interviewees explicitly associated certain factors with particular teacher or artist outcomes and explores the implications of notable differences between perspectives.

The chapter concludes with a summary of the main findings (5.3).

5.2 What affects outcomes for teachers and artists?

In this section, we examine factors that were said to influence outcomes specifically for those teachers and artists involved in the AEI interventions. As in Chapter 4, we begin by presenting a typology of factors and then describe the frequency and strength with which these were perceived by teachers and artists. There then follows an illustrative discussion of those given particular emphasis.

5.2.1 A typology of factors contributing to teacher and artist effects

1 Artist–teacher relationship

This factor covers the working and personal relationship between the teacher and artist. References to the working relationship include the level and quality of communication systems between the teacher and artist. Personal relationship covers references to their level of rapport or shared values.

2 Aims-related factors

This encompasses a range of factors relating to aims of the interventions, including whether the aims were realised. Also included is whether the intervention complemented existing curriculum-specific aims or schemes of work and whether it involved the introduction of a new artform or genre. As well, the underpinning purpose of the intervention is covered here: if, for example, teachers viewed it as an opportunity for CPD or artists as an opportunity for experimentation.

3 Nature and extent of planning

This factor focuses upon the extent and nature of planning prior to and during the intervention. The provision of opportunity for mutual discussion and review at all stages of implementation and the nature and degree of planned follow-up activities could also be referred to here.

4 Opportunities for reflection

This embraces any reference to personal reflection by the artist and/or the teacher. Reflection could have been encouraged through being involved in the AEI study (e.g. being interviewed by researchers about aims and outcomes); through CPD opportunities; or through experimentation (with different age groups or methods for example).

5 Site context

Contextual factors such as the status of the artform in the school (or other host site) and the value attached to the intervention are captured here, including its perceived educational worth. Also covered are circumstances operating within the school or arts organisation extraneous to the intervention, such as staffing levels or institutional problems.

6   Teacher factors

This factor covers references to the teacher's experience of participating in arts (or other) interventions, to their familiarity with and involvement in teaching the artform and their general professional experience.

7   Timing

This factor includes issues such as the intervention's duration (length of sessions or phases) and how the intervention fitted in with the academic year, the school term or the artist's external commitments.

8   Content and process

The focus is on the nature of the content involved within each intervention and also its delivery. It includes issues of continuity and progression, both internally within the intervention and externally with regards to knowledge and skills in other curriculum areas. Delivery of content covers the use of grouping and of art-form specific resources.

9   Pupil factors

Factors relating to pupil response, behaviour, achievement, participation and familiarity with the artform are included here. The development of a relationship between artist and pupils may also be referred to, as is the pupils' sense of privilege at being included in the intervention and working alongside a professional artist. Pupil attributes such as age, gender and ethnicity are also incorporated.

10 Artist factors

References to the artist's personal and professional background, including their experience of pedagogy and classroom management and working with young people are included within this factor category. It also covers the artist's recognition of the teacher's specific professional expertise: for example, their behaviour management, teaching style, or their understanding of individual needs and abilities within their class.

11 Role of the teacher during the intervention

References to the influence of the teacher's role are incorporated here. Examples include the teacher as a participant and as a class manager. The teacher as an observer of artist style / skill, of particular pupils or as an observer of a pupil performance is included. Reassurance, support or help given to pupils or artists may also be referred to here.

12 Types of staff development during intervention

This encompasses factors such as the role of the teacher during staff development, the types of teaching involved, the presence of CPD sessions and the opportunity for teachers to contribute their own ideas. It also includes whether the emphasis lay in enhancing artform knowledge, as opposed to the teaching of the artform, or whether a balance was achieved.

13 Relevance

This addresses the relevance of the intervention to the teachers' and artists' personal and professional interests and to their career development.

14 Manageability

This factor refers to how manageable the teachers and artists found the intervention. It includes references to workload and time demands and whether these and the intervention itself, are congruent with the strengths and weaknesses of the teachers and artists.

5.2.2 Frequency and importance of factors perceived to be influencing teacher and artist effects

We can now examine which of these factors were perceived to be more or less influential in causing effects for teachers and artists. Which factors were more frequently identified? How important were these factors perceived to be? Were the same factors equally influential for both teachers and artists?

To address these questions, we consider the frequency with which each factor was reported across 33 AEI phases as causing or contributing to an effect. (The remaining phases were primarily concerned with teacher development and will be discussed separately.) The strength of the perceived importance of each factor is also considered.

Initially, we report the number of phases in which teachers and artists referenced any of the 14 factors outlined above. It is important to note that by and large only teachers commented on teacher effects and artists on artist effects, comparison can include both variation in nominated factors overall, as well as differences in the views of the two types of interviewee.

Figure 5.1 shows variation in the frequency of references to influential factors for teachers and artists. Overall, a high number of the typology factors were seen to be associated with teacher effects and across numerous phases. It is noteworthy that the variation in frequency of reference is much more pronounced for artists: indeed, factors influencing effects on artists showed quite some disparity, mentioned in as little as two to as many as 28 phases.

Figure 5.1   Number of phases in which each factor was perceived as influential over teacher and artist effects

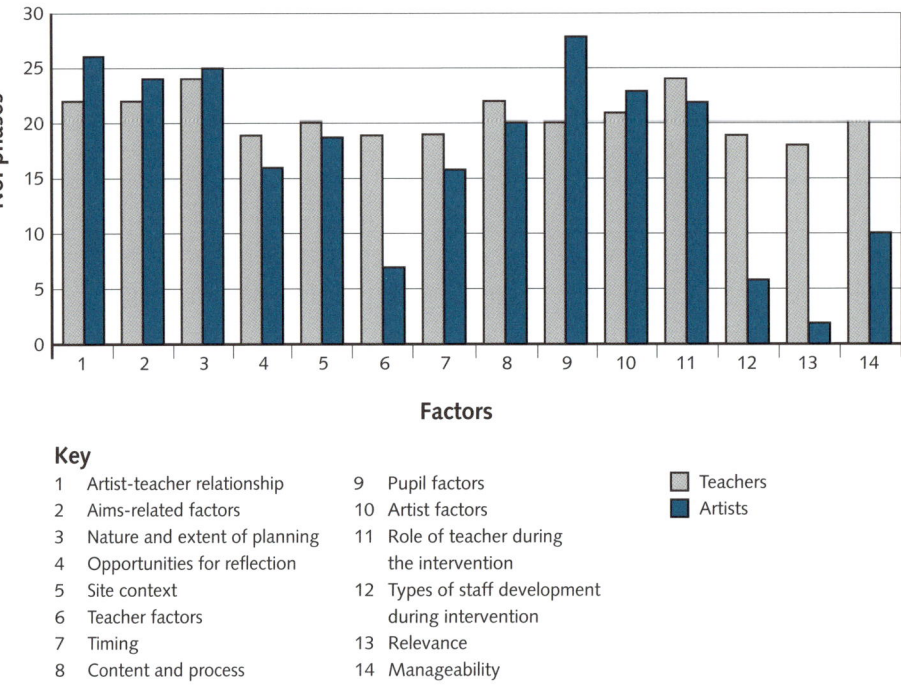

Key

1	Artist-teacher relationship	9	Pupil factors
2	Aims-related factors	10	Artist factors
3	Nature and extent of planning	11	Role of teacher during the intervention
4	Opportunities for reflection		
5	Site context	12	Types of staff development during intervention
6	Teacher factors		
7	Timing	13	Relevance
8	Content and process	14	Manageability

Teachers
Artists

The top five most frequently mentioned factors that affected teacher and artist outcomes are summarised in Table 5.1.

Table 5.1 indicates that it is the conceptual interchange and collaborative aspects between teacher and artist which begin to emerge as particularly well referenced factors affecting teacher and artist outcomes. Clearly, the nature and extent of planning, aims-related factors and artist–teacher relationship were frequently mentioned for achieving effects for both samples. Content and process and the role of the teacher during the intervention were frequently attributed to teacher effects and pupil and artist factors to the artist effects.

Table 5.1   Most frequently mentioned factors influencing teacher and artist outcomes

Factors influencing teacher outcomes	Number of phases	Factors influencing artist outcomes	Number of phases
Nature and extent of planning	24	Pupil factors	28
Role of teacher during intervention	24	Artist–teacher relationship	26
Aims-related factors	22	Nature and extent of planning	25
Artist–teacher relationship	22	Aims-related factors	24
Content and process	22	Artist factors	23

But how strong an influence were these most frequently mentioned factors? The rating system of how much emphasis was placed on each factor was undertaken. It emerged that some of the factors mentioned less often could be highlighted as particularly influential in the phases where they did operate and this is demonstrated in Table 5.2 and Figure 5.2.

Table 5.2   The factors perceived to have the strongest influence over teacher and artist effects

Influence on teacher effects	Influence on artist effects
Content and process	Pupil factors
Nature and extent of planning	Nature and extent of planning
Role of the teacher during the intervention	Role of the teacher during the intervention
Site context	Artist–teacher relationship
Artist–teacher relationship	Artist factors

By this 'intensity' rating system, variations between artists and teachers again can be observed in Figure 5.2. For example, the nature and extent of planning was perceived to be an important factor for both groups, but more so for artist outcomes than for teachers. Pupil factors were viewed as a decisive factor for artist effects, while conversely, content and process and site context were seen as more influential for achieving teacher outcomes than those for artists.

Figure 5.2   Relative strength of factors influencing effects on teachers and artists

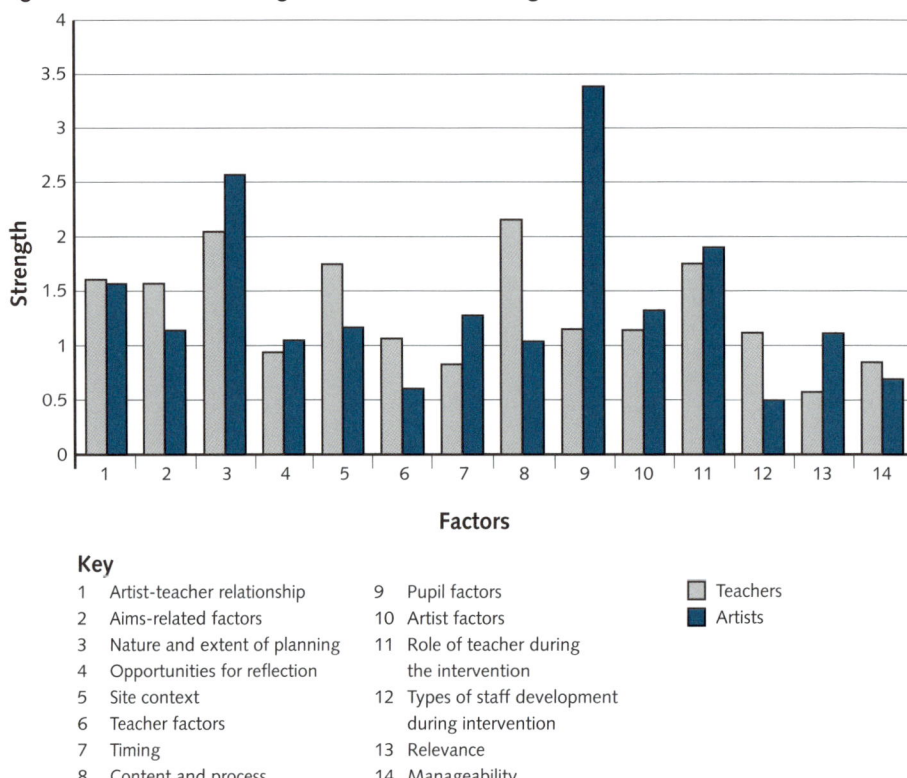

Key

1	Artist-teacher relationship	9	Pupil factors
2	Aims-related factors	10	Artist factors
3	Nature and extent of planning	11	Role of teacher during
4	Opportunities for reflection		the intervention
5	Site context	12	Types of staff development
6	Teacher factors		during intervention
7	Timing	13	Relevance
8	Content and process	14	Manageability

Teachers
Artists

Note: strength calculated on the basis of the average number of individual references to each factor made by those who made any reference to it.

This variation can be observed again in Table 5.2 which ranks the top five factors particularly emphasised by and about the two sub-samples.

Overall, content and process is the factor perceived to have the strongest influence for teacher effects and pupil factors for the artists. The role of the teacher during the intervention, nature and extent of planning and artist–teacher relationship were factors perceived as strongly influencing both teacher and artist outcomes.

Combining the factors most frequently and strongly identified allows us to determine overall the highest profile factors in causing teacher and artist effects.

For both teacher and artist outcomes, the high profile factors are:

• nature and extent of planning (factor 3)

• artist–teacher relationship (factor 1)

• the role of the teacher during the intervention (factor 11).

For teacher outcomes they also include:

- content and process (factor 8)
- site context (factor 5).

For artist outcomes, the emphasis is on:
- pupil factors (factor 9)
- artist factors (factor 10).

The factors with the lowest profile overall for teacher outcomes are:
- relevance (factor 13)
- timing (factor 7).

The factors with the lowest profile overall for artist outcomes are:
- teacher factors (factor 6)
- types of staff development during the intervention (factor 12).

5.2.3 Factors affecting teacher and artist outcomes: what do they comprise?

Nature and extent of planning (factor 3)

The nature and extent of planning emerged as the highest profile factor for achieving both artist and teacher effects. The extent of prior planning was most frequently mentioned, followed by the provision of opportunity for mutual discussion and review during the intervention. Where what might be termed 'responsive loose planning' was evident (using the group response and successes within the sessions to inform the next), this was also seen to be particularly influential.

Prior planning was evident in a variety of forms, ranging from brief telephone communication to lengthy or frequent face-to-face meetings where artists and their organisations could discuss their aims and intentions with the school or host institution. It ensured that sessions ran smoothly, established effective working relationships and allowed content to closely complement follow-up or previous work where appropriate. Prior planning's importance was also evident as the lack of such planning was occasionally cited as causing negative experiences, particularly for teachers. Problems perhaps inevitably arose when artists were unaware of constraints and priorities within school, when they had not met the class before, or had mis-information about the numbers, ages or abilities of pupils they would be working with. The lack of teacher time for prior planning was cited in a substantial number of phases.

Similarly, where opportunities for mutual discussion and review were not created, dissatisfaction and negative experiences were reported by both parties. This was commonly attributed to the lack of the teacher's non-contact time. Where this opportunity was created, both teachers and artists believed it had been a positive influence on them. Time was commonly created immediately before or after a session where discussions centred on 'how to move on', or around particular 'moods' of classes or individual pupils.

There were no negative experiences of 'responsive loose planning'. One teacher ensured that an overview was provided by the artist but stressed that this should not be too prescriptive, deliberately leaving plans open-ended, '…you can plan as much as you like and then they never quite work out, something always happens…' The artist welcomed this 'loose' approach as it provided an opportunity for sessions to be pupil led, allowing a flexibility to respond to the pupils and go along with their ideas.

Artist–teacher relationship

Like the nature and extent of planning, the relationship between the teacher and the artist emerged as high profile for both parties and was mentioned in a very high number of phases. The working relationship, such as the quality of communication, emerged as being more important than the establishment of good personal rapport. Where a good working relationship was secured, the artists felt as though staff were flexible and accommodating – 'it was a partnership' and that channels of communication 'were very clear and easy'. Teachers reported the ease with which they could interject in the proceedings at any point without damaging this relationship or undermining the artist and both parties were willing to accommodate the other. Indeed, one artist described a situation where teachers 'have been just as willing to drop everything and change what they're doing to fit in with me as I have with them'. Where the working relationship extended beyond the classroom to the wider school environment, artists felt particularly comfortable when other staff members and pupils knew who they were, why they were there and were willing to offer help.

Just under half of the responses citing this factor were from teachers and artists reporting negative experiences of their working relationship, usually due to poor channels of communication and a lack of teacher time. Where a poor working relationship was in evidence, teachers did not feel comfortable intervening in what they viewed as the artist's lesson, which could lead to feelings of discontent with the session and dissatisfaction if the teacher's aims were not met.

Very few negative experiences arose from personal relationships. Where this did occur, it was often closely associated with a poor working relationship, where a rapport had not been established and feelings became strained. Perhaps unsurprisingly, an effective working relationship was heavily associated with a positive personal relationship, but ultimately the quality of the former was seen as more important for determining the extent of both teacher and artist effects.

The role of the teacher during the intervention

Artists and teachers were affected by different elements of this factor. For teacher outcomes, the opportunity to observe the artist's style and skill had the greatest influence. It allowed them to see how an artist worked with young people and to observe their techniques, particularly instrumental in informing the development of their own resources for teaching the artform. The opportunity to observe individual pupils during sessions was also perceived as influential. Teachers valued the opportunity to watch individuals develop, mature and form new friendships. One teacher reported that seeing the pupils enjoying themselves increased her motivation to include drama in her lessons. Some teachers realised what their class were actually able to achieve when exposed to something different and could use it to effect subsequent pupil achievements. Artists also recognised the benefits accrued by teachers observing their classes.

The teacher's role in controlling pupils' behaviour was mentioned most frequently as having an effect upon artists' outcomes. Some artists felt it was not 'their place' to enforce ground rules and were happy for the teacher to intervene in an effective and undisruptive way. For example, where the teacher took responsibility for 'crowd control' this was greatly appreciated by the artist who felt that the pupils were more attentive when the teacher was present. However, some artists felt as though the teachers did not always use their power and experience to discipline children adequately or that the teacher's absence exacerbated behaviour problems. Teachers reported negative experiences if they exclusively controlled behaviour, detracting from their own level of engagement with the activities and content.

It was the teacher's role of offering reassurance, support or help that was seen as having the strongest influence on artists' effects. In one phase, where a good personal relationship had been established, the artist would look to the teacher for input in recognition of their understanding of the pupils. Artists spoke positively where teachers were there to '…keep me on the straight and narrow' and described team working and support from some teachers as 'excellent'. A few negative experiences of this factor were recorded. Occasionally artists did not feel supported by the teacher, specifically where they were not present in all workshops, or simply did not have the time to support the artists as much as they would have liked.

It is worth noting that when teachers participated in the sessions, their understanding of the pupils' needs and experiences was enhanced. The artists corroborated this; '…it's good for the teachers to join in too so that they can see that it's not as simple as it looks and that it must be hard for the kids too'.

Content and process

This factor was especially influential upon teachers, the delivery of content within the sessions and the use of a final display or performance being particularly mentioned. Where the delivery was influential, teachers benefited from seeing teaching approaches different to their own. One teacher described how seeing an actor deliver a session to her class had highlighted where she had 'gone wrong' previously, giving her heightened confidence to incorporate drama into her own lessons. Such exposure, then, is likely to contribute to the teacher's repertoire of techniques and inform their future practice.

The use of a final display or performance was also important for teacher outcomes. One teacher enjoyed seeing a musician cultivate her class and see the work 'come into fruition'. Watching the performance was pleasurable and increased her confidence in using a performance element in her own planning. Being able to see the pupils' growth in self-esteem and their huge sense of achievement following their performance in a special school was important to teachers, who again, planned to incorporate such opportunities into their class work. Finally, another artist testified to the effects amassed by teachers across the school as a result of a final display '…it'll be good for the staff to see what has been going on… they haven't got a feel for the whole project yet'.

Site context

Contextual factors also emerged as having a strong influence upon teachers, specifically the value attached to the intervention and external factors within the school. There were references to the positive effects of occasions where senior members of staff showed an interest and came to observe the sessions, or where other staff members had high regard for the activities. Where interventions were valued, teachers felt supported and sessions were felt to be generally successful.

However, just over half of the references to this factor were describing negative experiences and, in one secondary drama intervention, these references were particularly rife. The teacher blamed a lack of staffing for causing the collapse of one of the workshops, reporting that colleagues in the school were unaware of the importance of the intervention, that it had been 'at odds' with other school priorities and claimed it had 'been a slog to make to make it happen'. Frustrations arose where non-contact time was not protected and teachers were covering lessons whilst workshops were taking place, often supervised by members of staff outside of the department. In another instance, all members of staff were invited along to a workshop, yet no one reciprocated any interest by attending. It was felt that the senior management team had initially shown great enthusiasm for getting the project established, however 'once they got it, it dips off everybody's radar as important' allowing everyday pressures to overwhelm the intervention.

Other extraneous factors within the school could influence teacher outcomes, with references being made to negative experiences. For example, practical issues such as availability of rooms, staff sickness and security issues engendered stress. In one school, 'background problems' (including a serious pupil incident) were described as increasing teacher demands which encroached upon their involvement in the intervention. One teacher described the effects of external pressures: 'other factors within the school put pressure on you and the [project] becomes less and less important to you'. Importantly, it was the school organisation which was more commonly cited as a detrimental external factor than the actual school ethos.

Pupil factors

This factor was a very important influence upon artists. Its most prevalent element was the group response, followed closely by group behaviour. Just under half of the references described negative experiences for both aspects. Positive experiences of the group response included being 'pleasantly surprised' by the pupils' general attitude to the sessions. Some artists commented that the pupils worked very hard for them, or would pick up ideas quickly, inspiring them to work with young people again. In one secondary drama intervention, the artists commented that 'everybody responded really, really well and some people surprised us and impressed us'. Such a positive response on the part of pupils gave the artists new ideas and confidence. Similar experiences were reported with regards to pupil behaviour.

The negative experiences of this factor were very apparent in relation to pupil behaviour. Artists were frustrated where pupils were not concentrating or engaging with the sessions as they had hoped. One described how he 'gave up fighting against short attention spans and people running around' finding it easier to 'just accept it'. Teachers believed that some artists had not understood the reality of working with large groups of young people and had struggled with some of the responses and behaviours they faced. Artists involved in an inner city secondary school commented that the 'kids really tested us, pushed us' and describing them as 'the most challenging group I have ever worked with'. Behaviour in one primary intervention led the artist to question their role in the school and to seek training in motivating young people realising that she had 'expectations of pupils through rose tinted glasses' and had found the behaviour 'difficult', 'horrible' and 'unbearable'. Given this, the importance of the teacher contributing to behaviour management (as described previously) is unsurprising.

Artist factors

Experience of working within an educational context was a key factor in relation to artist effects. Where experience was lacking, some artists viewed the AEI as an invaluable developmental opportunity, enriching their capabilities as a practising artist and equipping them with expertise to offer subsequently to other schools. When artists did have prior experience of educational settings, they were better able to tailor their sessions appropriately and were better equipped to manage some of the pupil factors described above.

Where artists acknowledged the teacher's professional expertise in understanding the individual needs and abilities of pupils in their class, positive artist outcomes were achieved. For example, in one primary intervention, the artist 'respected' the teacher's knowledge of the children, involving her as joint facilitator in the session and this had positive effects upon her whole delivery and the success of the intervention. Equally, when artists acknowledged that (the teachers) know the kids and they know the system better than we do', this meant other factors such as the nature of planning and working relationships could be enhanced.

Throughout the interviews, it was thus apparent that numerous factors need to be considered if teachers and artists, as well as pupils, are to benefit from future arts interventions. By the same token, certain factors were not rated highly. Teacher factors, i.e. the relevance of the intervention to their personal/professional interests and career development was rarely mentioned as having an influence on outcomes. Furthermore, the length and timing of the intervention was a factor deemed relatively unimportant to artist effects, but even less so for teachers. This could be due to the tight time restriction teachers operate within, or is perhaps testimony to the suggestion that teachers are affected by arts interventions regardless of the length or timing within the academic year.

Artists were also reported as being relatively unaffected by teacher factors including the teacher's previous experience of arts interventions, of other interventions and of their familiarity with the artform.

5.2.4 Variations according to EAZ, educational setting, artform and type of intervention

The factors discussed thus far paint an overall picture of the perceived most and least influential factors for teacher and artist outcomes. In this section, we now examine how far there were notable differences according to variables such as EAZ, phase of schooling, artform and intervention type.

Variations by EAZ

It was noticeable that there was much consistency in the high pupil factors referenced by teachers in both EAZs and artists in Bristol. However, for artists involved in the AEI in Corby, two different factors emerged as being important: timing and opportunities for reflection. This is possibly because of the relative novelty of arts interventions in Corby when compared to Bristol. Were the artists less likely to have worked within the time restraints of schools? Would this consequently mean that timing issues might exert a greater effect upon any outcomes? Furthermore, the novelty of the experience may have prompted greater personal reflection in Corby, where the potential for further work was being recognised and future possibilities considered.

Variations by educational setting

Some subtle variations occur when the data was analysed according to the educational settings in which the interventions took place. In out-of-school settings, the development of a relationship between the artist and the young people and the high levels of their participation (pupil factors) were deemed specifically important, yet not so in primary and secondary school settings. Artists in out-of-school interventions expressed 'surprise' at participants giving up their free time over a number of sessions. Group behaviour (pupil factors) was deemed influential across all settings, but less so out of school, again the voluntary and informal nature of the setting may have been significant.

The influence of the teacher's role in the intervention also differed with intervention setting. The teacher exerting control over pupils was particularly important to artist effects across all settings, as was providing reassurance for pupils, though teacher participation was not given a high rating at secondary level.

Variations by artform

When the data was analysed according to artform, further subtleties were uncovered. As would be expected given its high profile for teacher effects, the content of the intervention was important to teachers across all four artforms. However, different elements of the content were emphasised within each. For example, the use of a final display or performance was deemed important in music and visual arts interventions more than in dance and even more so than in drama interventions. The artist's use of resources was only seen as important in visual arts interventions and the artist's use of groups only within music interventions. The types of explanations used by the artists were particularly influential for dance phases, yet were infrequently referenced in any other artform.

The role of the teacher was seen as important across all artforms. However, interestingly and possibly due to context-specific factors, within music interventions, teacher support for pupils and artist was less important and the teacher's role as participant was stressed instead. Teachers believed that their role in class control was particularly influential in dance interventions, more so than in any other artform. The opportunity to observe the artist's style and skill was particularly cited by teachers in art and drama interventions, which may suggest that in some interventions music and dance were seen as highly 'specialist' inputs, outside the teacher's skill-base.

Variations by type of intervention

The different types of intervention (one-off, series or developmental) had slightly different influential factors for both teachers and artists. For example, the artist–teacher relationship was particularly important for both parties during series interventions. This may be a consequence of the number of relationships that would have to have been established, either working or personal, due to the number of different artists involved overall. Types of staff development also emerged as an influential factor for teachers in series interventions, possibly a result of not only the number of different artists and associated skills, but also of the opportunity to explore one artform in a variety of ways.

The role of the teacher was particularly important in developmental interventions, much more so than in one-off or series interventions. Specifically, it was the opportunity to observe that was cited as important. Teachers here were able to observe an artist's skill or technique over a longer period of time. They also spoke of realising what the pupils were able to achieve and being able to observe individual pupils' progression and development as the intervention unfolded.

5.2.5 What factors affect outcomes for teachers in teacher development interventions?

This section considers the main factors contributing to effects of the three interventions (nine phases) focused primarily on providing CPD for teachers. Each phase took place within a primary school, two focused on dance and the other visual arts. The actual delivery of the nine phases varied considerably – four involved work solely between teachers and artists, the remaining five involved artists and teachers working together with pupils in different ways. The majority of responses from both teachers and artists were made with regard to the effects that the factors had on teachers, so it is worth considering that in this instance the artists' perceptions of influential factors for teachers have contributed heavily to the final results.

The most important factors affecting teacher outcomes across both types of teacher development interventions were content and process and site context. Interestingly, these were not followed by the nature and extent of planning, the artist–teacher relationship or the role of the teacher as would be expected given their high profile across the other interventions as a whole. Rather, these were replaced with the types of staff development in the intervention and then by artist and teacher factors, relevance and manageability – all of which were referred to as equally important. However, some variations occurred according to the delivery of the sessions which are shown in Table 5.3.

Table 5.3   Influential factors for teachers according to the CPD type

Teachers and artists only	Pupils, teachers and artists
Content and process	Content and process
Types of staff development	Site context
Site context	Relevance
Manageability	Nature and extent of planning
Teacher factors	Teacher factors
Artist factors	Artist factors

Phases exclusively involving artists and teachers

Table 5.3 clearly shows the most influential factors for teacher outcomes across both types of teacher development. The content of the intervention emerged as the most important factor in both types. Within the phases solely involving the artists and teachers, influential features of this factor included issues such as the historical background of the salsa dance, guidance on generic dance teaching skills, health and safety information, tools for teaching and planning and information or guidance on developing leadership skills. The type of explanation that the artist offered was also influential. For example, one artist used 'scaffolding'; starting simple and then building complexity into the sessions. Where the artist led the session as she would to pupils, flagging up teaching points throughout, introduced topics in a relaxed and calm manner and explained why she was developing the sessions as she was, the teachers reported reaping the benefits. The provision of opportunities for teachers' creativity was also deemed important in this type of teacher development. Where there was room for creative interpretation and creative task-based work, or the opportunity to find their own way of teaching, the teachers believed this was particularly influential.

The use of team teaching was seen to be a particularly influential element in one phase where teachers were provided with the opportunity to lead a pupil session to exercise all they had learnt. The teacher believed it was a good experience for two teachers and the artist to be modelling the dance to the pupils and that it had provided them with some leadership experience. Conversely however, in one phase, the teachers believed that it would have been more beneficial to have worked alongside their 'partner teacher', thus complementing their usual pedagogic practice and easing transfer into future classroom plans. Using advisory teacher style modelling or a 'holding hands' approach in the classroom, with diminishing levels of artist support, was also particularly influential. Teachers favoured this model and artists believed that it encouraged the teachers to take further steps into new roles, 'I will do progressively less and less and they will do more and more leading and directing'. Finally, in the discrete CPD sessions, one-to-one teaching, including teachers teaching each other was significant. One teacher worked quite closely with a colleague she was unfamiliar with prior to the intervention and another enjoyed teaching dance to and receiving feedback from a colleague.

The site context was also of importance, with emphasis attached to the status or value of the artform in school. In one intervention the school was aiming to raise the profile of dance and was very keen to get all teachers involved. As a result, the staff were 'generally keen to dance'. In another intervention, the head teacher supported the staff by speaking encouragingly of the teacher development and observing some of the sessions. Factors extraneous to the intervention were a salient influence within the site context factor. In one case several new members of staff felt they were in need of alternative staff development and different forms of training. Furthermore, LEA pressures to drive standards higher and government priorities on areas other than dance left some teachers with a negative attitude towards the training.

Within the broad category of manageability, a factor influential only in the artist to teacher form of CPD, the extent to which the intervention was congruent with the teacher's strengths and weaknesses was particularly influential. For example, negative experiences of this factor were expressed by teachers feeling ill-equipped to teach the pupils as part of the intervention. Some of them struggled to 'keep the beat whilst simultaneously giving instructions', felt as though they had been 'thrown into the deep end' or felt 'anxious' or 'daunted' by 'learning something new'. One artist reported that the teachers each had 'challenges as learners' and were initially very 'nervous' and required 'a lot of reassurance'. However, both teachers and artists believed this could be beneficial if they used their experience of learning as insight into how the children might feel.

Also within manageability, teachers spoke of workload and time demands as causing entirely negative experiences. One teacher reported feelings of anxiousness, feeling she lacked time to devote to the development in the light of other demands in the school. Another teacher resented the training for 'eating into' her non-contact time. In a different intervention, another teacher claimed that they had enjoyed working alongside the artist but thought 'it would be less hassle for me to just get on and teach dance myself'.

The influential teacher factors in artist to teacher development interventions were the teachers' familiarity with and experiences of teaching the specific artform. For example, learning salsa dancing was something completely new to the teachers and any prior information they had on it was deemed 'inaccurate' by the artist. They generally lacked skills in dance teaching and both teachers and artists agreed these would need considerable development. Conversely, where teachers did have experience of teaching dance, the intervention was viewed as more successful. Important artist factors included the artist's flexibility to adapt to the needs of their 'pupil(s)' and the artist's professional background. Indeed, one teacher was relieved that the artist was 'tuned in' to how the teachers felt and responded to this positively, adjusting the sessions accordingly to accommodate their progress.

Finally, the artist's experience of working in an educational context was also, unsurprisingly, very important. As highlighted in Section 3.2.2, artists with educational experience acting in the role of advisory teacher might be better placed to deliver teacher development of this kind, rather than artists with limited educational expertise, especially in the CPD field. This hypothesis is supported by the interviews with teachers who felt that artists with educational experience were 'tuned into language, pace and instruction' or 'very experienced', creating positive experiences for both teachers and artists. This could then be extended to pupils through the teachers' subsequent delivery of the artform.

Phases involving artists, teachers and pupils

It seems worth noting that this style of teacher development may more closely mirror the other interventions taking place across AEI and as such it is difficult to disentangle the factors solely influencing effects as a result of teacher development. However, once again, the content emerged as the most influential factor. The substantive content emerged as the most salient feature, including information on how to modify and transfer dance activities for different ages and how to encourage creativity in children. The artist's use of resources was also influential. Artists provided handouts, introduced new digital photography software and introduced teachers to kilns, textiles and modern styles of music. The provision of opportunity for creativity was also of importance.

Site context influenced teacher outcomes in these phases. The status or value of the artform in school was again a salient feature and the value attached to the intervention was also important. Teachers felt supported where other staff members valued the intervention and where senior management had encouraged all staff to take part.

Relevance contributed to teacher effects in teacher development phases involving artists, teachers and pupils, yet was much less important in phases where only teachers and artists were involved. Relevance to the teacher's personal/professional interests and to the development of skills was particularly apparent. Teachers were 'excited' by the opportunity to learn something that they could implement in the future; one teacher wanted to develop skills in digital photography on a personal level and to be able to disseminate this through the school. An artist commented that the teachers wanted to 'develop skills in an area they felt excited and passionate' about and this appears to have exerted a considerable influence. This could be due to the range of artforms covered in CPD interventions where teachers, artists and pupils were involved (dance, digital photography, ceramics and textiles as opposed to those solely including teachers and artists where only dance was covered).

As with all other phases of the AEI interventions, the nature and extent of planning emerged as an influential factor. As previous analysis would indicate, the salient features of this factor included opportunities for review and discussion during the intervention, the extent of planning prior to the intervention and the benefits of 'responsive loose planning'. As such, in these specific phases, this factor does not appear to operate in any different way to any other phase. However, in one instance, where planning prior to the intervention did not occur, the artist was unaware of the teachers' anxieties about teaching and doing dance. Therefore, it would seem to be particularly important for artists and teachers to liaise prior to a CPD session in order for such anxieties to be voiced and the artist to adjust the content, in advance, accordingly.

Teacher and artist factors also emerged as high profile in these teacher development interventions. Once again, the teacher's familiarity with the artform was particularly important, yet the experience of teaching the artform emerged as relatively unimportant in these interventions, perhaps due to the opportunity to be immediately and directly connected to pedagogy and pupil learning. The more influential artist factors differed slightly between the two types of teacher development; this appears to be a consequence of levels of pupil involvement. For example, the artist's recognition of the teacher's knowledge of individual abilities and needs within the class was particularly salient where pupils were involved in the teacher development.

5.2.6 Factors and outcomes: what's the link?

In this section, as in 4.2.8, we examine what particular factors are seen as having specific associations with certain teacher and artist outcomes. All references to such causality or association (in pupil-focused as well as teacher-focused interventions) were counted. Table 5.4 presents the top-ranking factors which interviewees linked to each outcome type. (These are highlighted in bold, while any single reference appears italicised). Once more, it is important to stress that it was teachers who almost exclusively commented on teacher outcomes and artists who almost always commented on artist outcomes.

Table 5.4 shows that content dominates teacher effects: unsurprisingly, what the intervention consisted of was felt to exert most influence on a range of outcomes, notably including motivation, affective outcomes, new awareness and value shifts, knowledge and skills and, ultimately, teachers' practice. Closely linked to this is the prevalence of role of the teacher: inevitably, how the teacher relates to (and can be involved in) the intervention was thought to affect outcomes.

In contrast, it is the category of pupil factors that was felt to be most influential for the artist: how pupils respond was seen to make a crucial difference to what an artist can take from the intervention. However, significantly, opportunities for reflection are cited as key to an artist's future practice. Neither party gave much emphasis to the specifics of planning, or the artist–teacher relationship, but teachers did, overall, give these a higher rating. Timing surfaced more often as a factor for artists (affective outcomes and increases in knowledge and skills being especially cited here), but this factor was thought to have a bearing on teachers' practice.

Table 5.4   What outcomes for teachers and artists are caused by specific factors?

Outcomes	Factors perceived as causing the effects for teachers	Factors perceived as causing the effects for artists
Career development	• *Nature of planning*	• **Pupil factors** • **Artist factors** • *Relevance* • *Manageability* • *Timing*
Material and provisionary		• **Content** • *Pupil factors*
Informational outcomes	• **Content** (artists use of resources)	• *Pupil factors*
Affective	• **Content** • Teacher factors • Role of teacher • Manageability • *Aims related* • *Artist–teacher relationship* • *Pupil factors* • *Artist factors* • *Types of staff development*	• **Pupil factors** • *Timing* • Artist factors • Content • Relevance • *Artist–teacher relationship* • *Aims related factors* • *Site context*
Motivational and attitudinal	• **Role of the teacher** • **Content** • Artist–teacher relationship • Pupil factors • Artist factors • *Types of staff development* • *Relevance*	• *Opportunities for reflection* • *Pupil factors*
New awareness and value shifts	• **Content** • **Role of teacher** • Aims related factors • Site context • Pupil factors • Type of staff development • Manageability • *Artist–teacher relationship*	• **Pupil factors** • Artist–teacher relationship • Nature of planning • Opportunities for reflection • Artist background • *Role of the teacher*
Knowledge and skills	• **Content** • Role of the teacher • Types of staff development during the intervention • Aims related factors • Artist factors • Artist teacher relationship • *Site context* • *Teacher factors* • *Pupil factors* • *Nature of planning*	• **Pupil factors** • Artist factors • Timing • Content • *Manageability* • *Artist–teacher relationship* • *Aims related factors* • *Opportunities for reflection*

Table 5.4   Continued

Outcomes	Factors perceived as causing the effects for teachers	Factors perceived as causing the effects for artists
Impacts on practice	• **Content** • Role of the teacher • Types of staff development • Pupil factors • Opportunities for reflection • *Timing* • *Manageability* • *Teacher factors* • *Artist factors*	• **Opportunities for reflection** • Pupil factors • Artist factors • *Aims related factors* • *Planning*
Institutional and strategic outcomes	• **Site context** • Content • *Pupil factors* • *Aims related factors* • *Planning*	• Context

Note: Those factors highlighted in bold represent the most frequently mentioned link, italicised factors represent those noted by only one or two interviewees.

What kind of messages for policy and practice are being signalled here? First and foremost, the inter-dependency of the three sub-samples emerges as a powerful finding. Artist outcomes are highly influenced by pupils; teachers learn from the substantive content and their own involvement in the intervention and (as 4.2.8 has shown), pupils also achieve most outcomes from the content and from the artist's pedagogy. However, it was also clear that the teacher's contribution to the process overall and in particular the receptiveness of their pupils, had not a little influence for artists. Additionally, it should be remembered that some teachers were also reporting learning from and about their pupils during an intervention. The prime message must be that an effective arts intervention actually consists of a Mutual Learning Triangle (MLT), a symbiosis from which outcomes can only be truly maximised when all three parties are operating in the role of both learner and teacher.

5.3 Summary

A framework of 14 broad categories of factors that are perceived to affect teacher and artist outcomes of arts education was outlined.

The conceptual interchange and collaborative aspects between teacher and artist were particularly well referenced factors affecting teacher and artist outcomes.

For both teacher and artist outcomes, the high profile factors (having combined 'frequency' and 'strength' and as perceived by participants) were:

- nature and extent of planning (especially the extent of prior planning, the provision of opportunity for mutual discussion, 'responsive loose planning' and review during the intervention)

- artist–teacher relationship (especially the working relationship, quality of communication) – though, significantly, just under half of the responses citing this factor were from teachers and artists reporting negative experiences of their working relationship, usually due to poor channels of communication and a lack of teacher time

- the role of the teacher during the intervention – for teacher outcomes, the opportunity to observe the artist's style and skill had the greatest influence; for artist outcomes, the teacher's role in controlling pupils' behaviour and in offering reassurance, support or help that was seen as influential.

For teacher outcomes they also included:

- content and process (especially the delivery of content within the sessions and the use of a final display or performance)

- site context (specifically the value attached to the intervention, school operational issues and especially the interest shown in it by senior and other staff) – though just over half of the references to this factor described negative experiences.

For artist outcomes, the emphasis was on:

- pupil factors (especially the pupil group response and group behaviour) – just under half of the references described negative experiences for both aspects

- artist factors (especially the existence of prior experience of educational settings).

The factors with the lowest profile overall for teacher outcomes were:

- relevance

- timing.

The factors with the lowest profile overall for artist outcomes were:

- teacher factors

- types of staff development in the intervention.

The role of the teacher as a determining factor on teacher and artist outcomes was particularly important in developmental interventions, much more so than in one-off or series interventions. The artist–teacher relationship was particularly important for both parties during series interventions.

Factors affecting outcomes for teachers in CPD interventions

The most important factors affecting teacher outcomes across both types of CPD interventions were content and process and site context. Within the content factor, knowledge about and skills in the artform, pedagogic skills in the artform, types of explanation, information on how to modify artform activities for learners of different ages, how to encourage creativity in children, the use of resources and opportunities for teachers' creativity were all considered to be valuable and instrumental. Within the site context, the status placed on the CPD and the artform was deemed to be crucial.

Other factors that were deemed to be influential were the types of staff development in the intervention, artist factors, teacher factors, relevance and manageability – all of which were referred to as equally important, though these varied according to the type of CPD provided.

Specific links between teacher and artist outcomes and perceived factors

An analysis of the specific associations between factors and effects for teachers and artists revealed that content as a factor dominates teacher effects: what the intervention consisted of was felt to exert most influence on a range of teacher outcomes, including motivation, affective outcomes, new awareness and value shifts, knowledge and skills and, ultimately, changes in teachers' practice. Closely linked to this was the prevalence of role of the teacher: how the teacher relates to (and can be involved in) the intervention was thought to have a substantial impact on outcomes.

In contrast, it was pupil factors that were felt to be most influential for the artist: how pupils respond was seen to make a crucial difference to what an artist can take from the intervention. However, significantly, opportunities for reflection were cited as key to an artist's development of future practice.

6 Effects and effective practices: an overview

6.1 About this chapter

This chapter presents a further and important level of analysis, looking overall at the effects of the AEI interventions studied and pinpointing the factors associated with those achieving the most and least outcomes. In doing so, it revisits certain factors which may have been under-represented in participants' accounts as outlined in Chapters 4 and 5.

6.1.1 Overview

Overall Ratings of effects (6.2)

A system for rating the impact of interventions is presented, drawing together effects on pupils, teachers and artists. The 15 interventions are given an overall 'effects-rating' and key findings from this exercise are outlined.

Features of interventions associated with overall ratings of effects (6.3)

In this section, the factors common to those interventions achieving highest and lowest ratings are revisited. The section focuses first on four factors not always given prevalence by interviewees, but which emerge as key to high-rated interventions. It then looks at those factors which interviewees did frequently refer to and summarises what the second-level analysis revealed about their contribution to overall effects.

Overall effects ratings and factors identified by interviewees (6.4)

The final section takes a last look at the degree of consensus between interviewees' perceptions of factors of effective AEIs and those emerging from the second-level analysis.

The chapter concludes with a summary of the main findings (6.5).

6.2 Overall ratings of effects

An overall rating system, based on the evidence from across the whole range of interventions and their phases, was first developed. Each phase was categorised by a low, mid or high rating according to the criteria given in Tables 6.1 (for pupil effects) and 6.2 (for teacher and artist effects).

6.2.1 Rating the effects on pupils

The key criteria for rating the effects on pupils were the range and 'strength' of effects perceived and evidenced by the various participants, as well as the extent to which impacts were (or were likely to be) sustained. Corroboration between sources was also considered where appropriate. Where pupils were perhaps too young to speak in detail about the impact of the interventions, more weight was given to significant others' perceptions. Table 6.1 shows the criteria applied when rating the effects on pupils in each phase.

Table 6.1   Criteria for rating effects on pupils

High-rating [3]	Mid-rating [2]	Low-rating [1]
• a broad range of effects evident	• a broad range of effects nominated with moderate or limited impact for most pupils in the group or, a narrower range of effects with mainly strong or moderate impact across the group	• the majority of categories nominated referred to as having had limited impact for the group or, effects evident for a smaller proportion of the group
• the majority of nominated effects perceived to be strong or moderate for the majority of pupils in the group		
• evidence of sustained nature of effects	• some sustained nature of effects evident or likely	• usually a smaller range of effects evident
• where possible, corroboration of perceptions between the various sources of data	• some corroboration of perceptions between the various sources of data	• effects least likely to be sustained

6.2.2 Rating the effects on teachers and artists

The criteria for an overall rating here also considered the range and strength of the perceived and evidenced effects, as well as the extent to which they were likely to be sustained. Indicators of the latter included teachers' and artists' conscious intentions to realise goals or effect change and their recognition of the measures needed to do so. In addition to the range of impacts achieved, the particular types of impact were also considered. Linking with other research, certain categories were prioritised as being the most indicative of the extent of impact (Kinder and Harland, 1991). These were:

- advances in knowledge and skills

- effects which indicated value shifts or congruence

- enhancements to practice

- effects that were evident 'far' from the site of application such as impacts on other colleagues or institutional outcomes.

According to Kinder and Harland (1991), such outcomes equated with the highest order or level of impact on teachers involved in CPD, more so than such effects as new awareness or informational outcomes and were the ones most likely to lead to changes in practice. Table 6.2 shows the criteria applied when rating the effects on teachers and artists.

Table 6.2   Criteria for rating effects on teachers and artists

High-rating [3]	Mid-rating [2]	Low-rating [1]
• a full range of impacts evident including the higher order types such as knowledge and skills, indications of value shifts and impacts on practice (individually and institutionally) • strength of impact indicating actual changes or evidence of intended change in practice • effects likely to be sustained	• a broad but not necessarily full range of effects, with some evidence (rather than strong evidence) of effects in the higher order types • includes some initial indications of enhancements to practice individually or within the institution	• impacts sporadic across the range or confined to a narrow arena • impacts mainly associated with new awareness and the affective domains and least likely to be sustained • strength of impact indicating some consideration of, or reflection on, possibilities raised but less likely to lead to changes in practice

When these overall ratings of impact of AEI interventions on the different participant groups are brought together, the variation between interventions is very apparent. Table 6.3 shows the ratings applied to each of the 15 interventions involved in AEI, according to the four different types of intervention: one-off, multi-artform series, single artform developmental and teacher development.

A number of key findings about overall effects emerge.

Table 6.3   **Ratings of effects in the 15 interventions**

	Intervention name	Artform	No. of phases	Effects ratings		
				Pupils	Teachers	Artists
One-off	Theatre-primary	Theatre	1	1	1	1
	College-art	Art	1	1	1	1
	Nursery-museum	–	1	2	3	1
	Dance-secondary	Dance	1	2	1	1
	Out-of-hours music	Music	1	2	–	1
Multi-artform series	Multi-artform out of school	Multi	3	2	3	1
	Multi-artform primary	Multi	3	2	1	2
	Multi-artform special	Multi	5	2	3	2
	Multi-artform secondary	Multi	6	2	1	1
Developmental, single artform	Primary development drama	Drama	3	3	3	3
	Secondary development drama	Drama	3	3	1	1
	Secondary development music	Music	5	1	1	1
Teacher development	Primary development art	Art	3	–	2	1
	Primary development dance	Dance	3	–	2	1
	Primary development dance	Dance	3	–	2	2

Note: No teachers were involved in out-of-hours music. Effects on pupils resulting from the teacher development interventions (for which there was limited supporting data) were not included in this analysis.

Very few interventions actually achieved high impact across the board for all participant types. The primary developmental drama and multi-artform special (although the latter to a slightly lesser extent) stand out as examples of universal high impact. However, one phase within another intervention (individual phases not shown in Table 6.3) also achieved reasonably high impact across the board (i.e. a rating of two or more for all of the participant groups): this was art in the multi-artform primary intervention.

The lowest impacts across the board were for the single-phase theatre-primary, college-art and secondary developmental music, as well as several phases within multi-artform series, at both secondary and primary level.

The effects ratings for pupils were highest in the developmental interventions (with one exception), whilst the lowest effects ratings for pupils occurred in several of the one-off interventions.

The highest effects ratings given for teachers were not in the teacher development interventions, but in three of the pupil-focused interventions: primary developmental drama, multi-artform special and multi-artform out of school. Each of these interventions resulted in some of the most notable impacts on the participant teachers and their colleagues and also included whole institution changes in practice with regard to the artform. This suggests that interventions focused primarily on providing professional development for teachers were not necessarily any more able to deliver outcomes for teachers than those where pupils were the central participants.

Interventions achieving higher impacts for teachers generally also had high impacts for pupils, though high pupil impacts were not always associated with high teacher impacts. The one-off nursery-museum intervention exemplifies this mutual teacher/pupil high impact, where the teacher – and also her institution – gained in ways beyond their normal practice and in so doing were able to develop and enhance what may otherwise have been short-term outcomes for the pupils.

Only in a few instances did artists achieve a higher effects rating than teachers. These included the multi-artform primary intervention overall, two separate art phases contained within multi-artform special and multi-artform secondary and a music phase in multi-artform secondary. The common characteristics in these particular examples included the potential for the artists to work in a new genre of their artform or in a new situation, e.g. with pupil types with whom they had not previously worked.

In sum and not surprisingly, the most common pattern in the effects ratings was a higher impact for pupils than for teachers, who in turn mostly received a higher impact rating than artists. Most interventions were focused on the pupils, with teachers mostly participating or observing and the artist viewed as the 'expert' and key provider of activities. Levels of impact may thus simply correlate with the opportunities taken or provided for different participants to learn and with the participants' openness to learning. Do certain teacher and artist roles adopted within these AEIs inevitably limit each one's opportunities for development?

6.3 Features of interventions associated with overall ratings of effects

This section presents our second-level analysis of the features that were associated with the interventions achieving the highest- and lowest-rating levels of impact, as defined earlier in the chapter. To do this, the researchers collated all the key details and information about the phases garnered from the interview data, observations and documents collected. The noted features of the phases were carefully grounded in the data, from interviewees' own descriptions or from researchers' observations. It included information about aims, plans, communication, changes to projects as they went along, comments about relationships with each other, content, pedagogy and so on. The researchers then examined whether there were any commonalities in the noted features of the phases that had the highest effects rating and any commonalities in the features of the phases with the lowest effects ratings. It become apparent, for example, that the recorded characteristic of collaborative planning was overwhelmingly present in all the top rated interventions and practically absent in the lowest rated interventions.

Consequently, our analysis here – unlike that of the previous chapters – is not about what factors teachers and artists felt had caused outcomes or successes, but is based on the more descriptive factors of what actually happened before, during and after the intervention, regardless of participants' perceptions of their causal significance. In the case of corporate planning, it is telling that, for some reason, interviewees did not often mention planning as an important factor contributing to pupil outcomes, or themselves make the link that a well planned intervention would have more successful pupil outcomes or contribute to certain types of outcomes. But in the second-level analysis described here, when we looked at the interventions that had the most successful pupil outcomes (in terms of an overall picture of range, strength, aims achieved, corroboration and so on), we noticed that in these interventions there were descriptions from teachers and artists of their planning and moreover of joint planning, clarity and good communication. Where there were less successful outcomes, we noticed that in these interventions, the teachers and artists described lack of planning and lack of joint planning and clarity of aims and communication between teachers and artists. Whilst teachers and artists may have linked planning to outcomes on themselves, they did not cite planning as often as features like artist pedagogy, as a factor in affecting pupil outcomes. It is perhaps significant that teachers and artists did not cite joint planning that often and this may indicate a need for greater awareness among teachers and artists of the extent to which their planning and the nature of their planning does make a difference to pupil outcomes.

As explained in Chapter 1, in cases where a finding is supported by one data type but not the other we do not suggest that either source should be given primacy. Rather than giving more weight to findings from one of the two data sources, it is more appropriate to ask why the particular finding may not be evident in both types. In most cases, this centres on inquiring why participants may or may not have perceived certain processes, factors or outcomes to be important.

The results of our second-level analysis focus initially on four key characteristics (shown in Table 6.4) which were not always articulated with any particular frequency or strength by participants in Chapters 4 and 5.

Table 6.4   Four characteristics common to interventions achieving the highest and lowest researcher ratings of effects, overall

Factor	Highest impact	Lowest impact
Type of intervention	Multiple-phase (either developmental or series) interventions	One-off interventions (or series interventions with no continuity or progression)
Planning	Emphasis on planning, communication and collaboration between teachers and artists prior to interventions, including shared aims	Limited evidence of planning or limited teacher–artist collaboration during planning
Artist–teacher relationships	Positive relationships between artists and teachers	Poor relationships between teachers and artists in some, but not all, cases*
Amount and spread of time	Longer amounts of time involved, but spread in a variety of different ways and with fitness for purpose[i]	Generally smaller amounts of time and particularly when spread over a long period

Note: *indicates that there was not a single variation of the factor which characterised interventions leading to either high or low ratings for overall effects.

6.3.1 Type of intervention

The classification of interventions into four broad 'designs': one-off; multi-artform series; single artform developmental and teacher development, was originally a construct of the research. The two interventions gaining the highest effects ratings overall were the primary developmental intervention and the special school series intervention – both involving multiple phases. Conversely, those attaining the lowest ratings for effects overall were generally one-off interventions, with only one exception – that of secondary developmental music, which involved five phases mounted more like a series of one-off projects – with little continuity and progression or cumulative effect evident between them. The importance of other factors in this particular case and each intervention's specific context or circumstances should also not be underestimated.

A key finding is that for all participant groups, series and developmental interventions generally produced higher overall ratings of effects. However, the association was particularly evident between type of intervention and effects for pupils; there were more exceptions to the relationship between intervention type and effects rating when applied to teachers and artists. This finding might be connected to how far the participant groups remained constant over different phases of the intervention. In most series and developmental interventions, the same pupils took part in all of the phases, whilst the multi-artform series interventions involved changing artists for each phase (as also did one of the developmental interventions in the same artform) and, in secondary schools, changing teachers for each phase.

Where there was continuity of teachers between phases, the level of impact on teachers and their institutions tended to be higher than those where different teachers took part in each of the phases. Similarly, the continuity of artists in successive phases of an intervention was associated with higher effects ratings for artists. However, there were exceptions to this trend for both groups. The key feature in the AEIs with higher effects ratings for artists (and to some extent also teachers) appeared to be their level of experience and potential for learning, coupled with their recognition of interventions as an opportunity for professional development.

6.3.2 Planning

One of the most notable aspects of the interventions with the highest effects ratings overall was the emphasis placed on planning prior to the whole intervention and each specific phase, though the specific nature of this planning varied. For example, whilst the theatre phase of the multi-artform intervention in the special school required organisation, little written detail was put in place. In contrast, for the first phase of the primary developmental drama intervention, the artists presented detailed plans to the school outlining the activities, topics and areas to be covered in each of the weekly sessions to be held throughout the term.

However, rather than focusing on the minutiae of the plans themselves, the aspect that appeared to be contributing to effective practices in the highest rated interventions was the collaborative nature of planning and, crucially, direct and effective communication between the teachers and artists. In these cases, most of the artists visited the school and where possible observed classes or met pupils.

They attached much importance to this element of their planning, feeling it provided them with necessary contextual awareness of both the particular school setting and the pupils, in turn facilitating the provision of appropriate activities and content. Interestingly, across the whole initiative, prior knowledge of the pupils was amongst the foremost 'wishes' of artists who had not gained it, for precisely the same reasons, with artists suggesting it may have increased outcomes for pupils, but also for themselves. This 'wish' was evident chiefly in the interventions with low effects ratings on pupils.

The involvement of teachers in the planning process, for example in negotiating the aims and content of interventions, was another key characteristic of highly rated interventions. The direct engagement of teachers and artists prior to the interventions (including any pre-intervention INSET activities) provided the opportunity for both teachers and artists to benefit and understand one another, as well as supporting outcomes for pupils. This facet was all the more important in view of the manifest fact that teachers and artists could have different discourses about arts education projects, their purposes and aims and different needs, values or starting points. This can be illustrated by a comparison of the aims identified by teachers and those by artists.

It was rare for any types of aims to be identified more so by teachers than by artists, although perhaps this was slightly the case for transfers to life in school. Where this did occur, it was for aims that were low profile anyway (i.e. only aimed for in a few phases). These included:

- artistic communication and expression

- attendance and behaviour during artform activities

- attitudes towards careers in the artform

- transfer to current life outside school.

For artists, there were certain types of aims that featured in their discourse more readily than in teachers' notions of aims. These were:

- general communication and expressive skills

- attitudes towards learning the artform

- artform confidence

- social development.

This latter category is particularly interesting. Whilst social developments did not quite feature in the top six types of aims (see Section 2.3.3), artists were over twice as likely as teachers to aim for developments in pupils' social skills – especially team working skills. Examples included: 'I think we also try to create a group dynamic' (artist, secondary drama);

To develop group understanding, cooperation and collaboration skills, to help with class room procedures such as finding partners, listening, speaking in front of each other. More specifically to explore concepts of what a good friend is, what a good classmate is, how we can help each other in difficult situations, what it is like to make a mistake and to explore similarities and differences between people.
(primary drama)

Artists were keen to encourage social skills, preparing the pupils to work together effectively.

Our analysis for this chapter demonstrated that investing in collaborative planning that included overcoming any tendency to speak from separate discourses and the negotiation of shared goals was associated with quality outcomes. In four phases, both the teacher and artist agreed strongly that the aims of the intervention had been met. They also believed they shared a high consensus over aims with the other party they were working alongside. Significantly, these four phases were all high-rating in terms of the effects on pupils. This consensus, both between aims and outcomes and between the teachers and artists, occurred in phases from both the primary and secondary developmental drama interventions, the highest rated interventions in terms of pupil outcomes. The nursery-museum intervention and a phase from the multi-artform secondary intervention were also notable for their degree of consensus and perceived success of aims; these interventions received a mid-rating for pupil effects.

In three further phases, the teacher and artist did not necessarily think all of their aims had been met, but they did share a consensus over what they were actually aiming for. Once more, these phases came from interventions receiving high- or mid-ratings in terms of the effects upon pupils: a phase from the secondary developmental drama intervention featured here again, receiving a high impact rating and phases from multi-artform primary and out-of-school interventions.

The findings underline the importance of communication, collaboration and engagement between the parties – not necessarily concrete plans or aims, but communicating and understanding each other's needs and ideas and sharing the evolution of aims. An example from one of the most highly rated interventions (in terms of outcomes achieved) reveals that the sharing of similar aims and values, even if actual aims had not yet been clarified or collaborated on between teachers and artists, was felt by participants to have positive ramifications: 'One of the reasons [X school] chose us to do this is because they knew we had a very similar approach and ethos towards education to themselves'.

When considered across all interventions and phases, the emphasis and nature of planning was undeniably associated with pupil effects ratings. Indeed, this factor was amongst the most strongly correlated of all identified qualities. The direct engagement of teachers and artists appeared to be the most influential aspect of the planning process on outcomes for teachers and artists themselves, though generally the influence of planning appeared less clear-cut than it was for effects on pupils.

6.3.3 Artist–teacher relationships

The interventions which achieved the highest ratings for effects overall were characterised by good relationships between artists and teachers. This was particularly evident within the two developmental interventions in which teachers and artists remained constant over a number of phases and had time to develop their working and personal relationships. In addition, the staff ethos of the special school addressed the challenging nature of the work by fostering supportive working relationships which were naturally extended to artists during interventions.

Looking at this issue across all phases individually, it emerged that good relationships between teacher and artist were often in evidence in phases where outcomes (particularly for pupils) were rated highly. However, the converse was not always the case, with other factors (such as the level of whole-school or senior management support, or the intervention's timing), sometimes appearing to override the benefits of a good artist–teacher relationship and inhibit the resulting outcomes.

Inevitably perhaps, several examples highlighted a connection between the artist–teacher relationship and the nature and extent of planning for the intervention that took place. As noted already, in the most effective examples, teachers and artists engaged in a highly collaborative process of planning, for which time was specifically set aside and during which their personal and professional relationship matured. For example, in the case of the primary developmental intervention, the extent of teacher–artist collaboration prior to each phase increased as the project progressed. For the first phase, the artists designed the project based on 'suggestions' and 'ideas' given to them by the teachers; but by the final phase the teacher–artist partnership was such that both were engaged in direct collaboration about the aims and activities, so much so that the teachers variously described the artists as working 'alongside us', as well as themselves working alongside the artists.

Conversely, there were some examples where artist–teacher relationships were more difficult: in one instance, it was noteworthy that the relationship had been soured by disagreement during the planning process and subsequent outcomes for all parties were more limited.

6.3.4 Amount and spread of time

One of the key variants particularly in the series and developmental interventions was the amount of time involved, from as little as 90 minutes in one instance, around six hours per phase in another to over 20 hours per phase in another. Not surprisingly, this impacted on the effects achieved by the participant groups. Indeed, the amount and the 'spread' of time was linked to the effects ratings, particularly on pupils, but also on teachers and artists. The primary developmental drama intervention (with the highest effects ratings across the board) was one that featured the highest inputs of time (over 20 hours per phase) as well as a variety of time-spread. It featured concentrated time (e.g. involving a two-week artist residency) and also regular project time (e.g. shorter workshops once a week for the whole term). A key element in almost all those phases achieving high effects ratings for pupils was the time involved, generally over ten hours and generally concentrated rather than spread thinly across the term.

However, also of consequence was the appropriateness of the amount and spread of time in context. For example, an important quality in the multi-artform special intervention was the reasonably short but concentrated amounts of time, such as several workshops on consecutive mornings, so as to maintain momentum for these pupils and allow skills to be built. In another example, secondary school pupils made considerable gains from two phases, one of which involved workshops of one hour 40 minutes once a week for several weeks and the other a concentrated block of four full days consecutively.

When tested against all the phases in all interventions, amount of time combined with spread of time was reasonably influential on effects ratings. The impact was more noticeable in the low-effects rated interventions, particularly those involving some of the least time overall (less than five hours and as little as 45 minutes). A tentative indication from the data concerned small amounts of time (i.e. less than ten hours total, in practice often around six hours) delivered in sessions of one hour each over a term or half-term period. In these cases, pupil, teacher and artist effects ratings tended to be lower than in interventions where similar amounts of time were more concentrated. Related to this is the issue of being 'off timetable', where this was possible and crucially, supported by the school, effects on pupils and to some extent on the teachers appeared to be enhanced.

Other aspects to do with time, such as timing within the school year, the normal length of lessons and so on were also recognised as influential in some cases. For example, art workshops involving secondary pupils were felt to be difficult to deliver within the constraints of the regular school timetable which allowed three sessions of only 45 minutes per week, though if the normal timetable had comprised longer or double lessons for art, this issue may not have arisen. Further, AEI phases occurring at the very end of a school year tended to result in lower effects ratings than other phases. Tiredness, as well as pupil excitability and teacher busyness at this time of year seemed influential in this regard, as well as disruption from other end of term activities. The overall status given to an intervention delivered at this point of conclusion in the 'learning calendar' may also be an issue.

This second-level analysis has highlighted four factors not greatly emphasised by participants. Looking at the features of interventions with overall high effects ratings uncovered a number of other factors that participants had referenced. These are now discussed.

6.3.5 The pupils

- High overall effect ratings for pupils were evident where content, including manageability and artists' pedagogy were 'matched' i.e. were appropriate and relevant to the pupils, given their background.

- Pupils' response to interventions, particularly demonstrated through their behaviour during the sessions, was linked to higher overall effect ratings. However, pupil behaviour, if not good, could correlate with higher artist effects ratings, where the artist learnt from the classroom management skills of the teacher.

6.3.6 The teachers

- Not surprisingly, if the teacher was present and participating in the AEI they gained more in terms of effects. More importantly, the second-level analysis showed that if the teacher was not present or not participating, the overall effectiveness rating for artist and the pupils were also lower.

- Teachers' relative inexperience in the artform often made for greater teacher effects, perhaps as a result of their greater potential for gain. However, teacher effects sometimes remained limited where teacher inexperience was coupled with a lack of enthusiasm for the artform or intervention, or a lack of willingness to 'have a go', 'take a risk' or try to develop.

- An experienced teacher involved in interventions could help to bring about greater effects for artists, particularly with reference to their development of classroom management techniques.

6.3.7 Site context

- If the whole school or department was supportive and the intervention had senior management team support, then it was more likely to have higher overall effects ratings impacts on teachers and, also, importantly on pupils.

6.3.8 The artist's experience, pedagogy and flexibility

- Artists gained most in the developmental interventions where they took part in multiple phases.

- Both of the highest scoring interventions overall were characterised by the involvement of highly experienced artists – particularly in terms of the artform, but also mostly in terms of the appropriateness of their pedagogy to the situation in which they were working.

- However, other factors could counteract an artist's experience, suggesting this in itself does not guarantee high-level outcomes for pupils. For example, two phases with low effects rating yet involving highly skilled and experienced artists also showed evidence of factors like: short amounts of time involved; pupils' mostly passive participation – watching essentially 'off the shelf' performances by the artist and limited planning for continuity and progression with other intervention activities or the regular artform curriculum.

- In the high-rating effects interventions, there was sometimes evidence of an artist's ability to adapt and be flexible if and when their pedagogy or the intervention content was not working or 'going haywire'. This capacity was generally what pulled them through and 'saved the day'.

- Where an artist had low experience of a pupil group but demonstrated a willingness and ability to learn and adapt as they went along (and, notably, had a supportive teacher), then high ratings for artist effects resulted.

- Closely linked with the artists' pedagogy and also sometimes their prior experience working with similar groups, the relationship between artists and pupils during interventions was associated with high levels of outcomes overall. Developmental AEIs, where the same artists and pupils worked together over multiple phases, enabling their relationship to deepen each time, also, perhaps inevitably, resulted in higher effects ratings.

- The relationship between artists and pupils was particularly associated with outcomes for pupils – where a phase was ranked highly for pupil outcomes, the artist–pupil relationship was almost invariably good, whilst the converse was similarly true.

6.3.9 Type of content

- High-rated effects were associated with interventions showing a combination of three areas: 'hands-on' participation including technical skills; the opportunity for the pupils to be creative and some sort of product, display or performance.

- Both of the interventions achieving the highest effects rating on pupils (in each case, developmental drama interventions) had a variety of opportunities for participation: hands-on, performing and being included as an audience themselves.

- The opportunity for pupils to be creative was a common feature of the phases where artists gained most (mid- or high-ratings). Interventions where pupils were primarily passive receptors of the artists' work rather than active contributors to the sessions resulted in far fewer outcomes for artists. Is it the case that artists do learn from the pupils' ideas, as well as facilitating the processes of experimenting, trial and error and improvements?

- There were a wide variety of types of product, performance or display in the AEIs, some associated with high effects ratings and some not so. One of the key qualities of effective product was that it was seen by pupils to be a 'professional endeavour' (the real thing, a real show, a real audience). Again, contexts varied; the 'real' audience could be the paying public, parents or classmates, but this had to be different from their classroom norm. Also, crucial here was that the pupils were supported by the artists and teachers and not put in positions of vulnerability.

- For pupils in particular, the 'real thing' also highlighted the concept of making something 'big' – particularly in those interventions involving display rather than performance, such as in the visual arts. Pupils of primary and lower secondary age who made something 'big' equated this notion with a wide range of effects from sense of achievement to gains in technical and social skills.

- Where end product was absent, or promised but not materialised, pupils did seem to achieve lower overall effects ratings. On the other hand, the end product was not a foregone conclusion of higher ratings: pupils feeling technically competent, combined with artist and teacher support and encouragement (even participation), were essential features.

- Interventions which provided the greatest level of outcomes for teachers and artists were those which were, to a degree, viewed as an opportunity for teachers' and artists' professional development and where this was in some way designed into the content delivered. In some cases this involved additional CPD sessions alongside artists' work with pupils, in others it was implicit in the way teachers and artists worked together either during the planning or delivery of the interventions.

6.3.10 Continuity and progression

- Various aspects of continuity and progression featured in the interventions and phases with highest researcher effects ratings: those AEIs with planned elements of continuity and progression, including incremental structure from session to session, as well as follow-up work, correlated with higher effects ratings for pupils.

- In some highly rated interventions, pupils also experienced continuity of the work in their normal classes through follow-up work with their teachers. Continuity might be promoted by teachers' references to the phases and their content, or by reminding pupils of what they had experienced and achieved, with links being made to the curriculum where appropriate.

- Serendipitous opportunity to follow-up or link with the AEI work tended to increase the chance of sustainability of effects. However, this was by no means as powerful an influence on effects ratings as the occasions (albeit rare) where continuity and progression was planned for within the intervention or across to the mainstream curriculum.

6.4 Overall effects ratings and factors identified by interviewees

This section compares the findings of the second-level analysis with interviewees' perceptions of the factors influencing outcomes for pupils, teachers and artists which were reported in Chapters 4 and 5.

As we have seen, a number of the factors which interviewees nominated to be 'high profile' in terms of influencing outcomes for pupils, teachers and artists were further substantiated by the overall effects-rating analysis. For example, the role of the artists' pedagogy and type of content within the intervention (including relevance, manageability and emphasis on an end product) were the highest profile factors perceived by interviewees as influential in determining pupil outcomes and corroborated by the secondary-level analysis as closely associated with outcomes for all participants. Similarly, those interviewees' perceptions of the importance of the nature and extent of planning and the artist–teacher relationship on outcomes for teachers and artists themselves were confirmed.

However, a number of areas revealed as influential by the secondary-level analysis were less frequently attested to by interviewees or less strong in their discourse. These arenas included:

- planning, as important for pupil outcomes (although it was also recognised as important to teacher and artist outcomes)

- type of intervention

- appropriateness and amount of time

- for teachers' and artists' outcomes, the extent to which the intervention was regarded as an opportunity for professional development and their own backgrounds and experiences.

These areas are discussed below.

When it came to pupil outcomes, both planning and the artist–teacher relationship were revealed by the secondary-level analysis as highly influential, though were not often foremost within interviewees' discourse. It seems plausible, however, that effective planning was understated in this way as a result of interviewees' focus on the influence of the artists' pedagogy and the content of interventions. The secondary-level analysis supports this assertion, revealing that artists' pedagogy and intervention content were more often deemed relevant and appropriate where teachers and artists had a close collaborative relationship, particularly during the planning stages.

The type of intervention (whether it was a one-off, multi-artform series, single artform developmental, or teacher development) was found to be influential in determining interventions' overall level of impact, particularly on pupils. However, this was not often described directly by interviewees, perhaps unsurprisingly, given that the type of intervention was a construct devised within the research for the purposes of classification and comparison and that the vast majority of interviewees only had experience of one intervention. Nevertheless, teachers and artists did provide accounts of what they felt would be the benefits of the opportunity to maintain work in the arts in the longer term and thus were perhaps implicitly commenting on 'type' of intervention.

The appropriateness of the amount and spread of time was identified by the secondary-level analysis as associated with outcomes for all of the participant groups, but particularly pupils. The artists interviewed appeared particularly sensitive to the influence of this factor on outcomes for pupils, though it was somewhat less prevalent in the teachers' and pupils' perspectives. Time and its association with outcomes for teachers was also not often referenced. It was one of the least frequent factors perceived by interviewees as associated with teacher effects and to some extent also artists'.

The extent to which the intervention was regarded as an opportunity for professional development also emerged as key to the level of effects achieved. The interventions which provided teachers and artists with the highest levels of outcomes were those where staff development was considered and incorporated in some way. Comparing this with interviewees' perceptions on opportunities for reflection and types of staff development, this area seemed under-recorded by most teachers and artists as a factor that would engender outcomes.

Teachers and artists also spoke infrequently about how factors relating to themselves (such as their own background, prior experience, motivations and attitudes) had influenced what they gained from interventions, although this, again, was revealed as influential. For example, outcomes for less experienced teachers could be enhanced by working with experienced artists and vice versa, where the parties were able and willing to learn from each other during the intervention.

In summary, perhaps the most important message revealed by the differences between interviewees' perceptions of the factors influencing outcomes and the features exposed by the second-level comparison of the characteristics of those resulting in the highest and lowest levels of outcomes, is the emphasis which needs to be placed on the relevance and appropriateness of an intervention to its context. Many of the factors perceived by interviewees as influential relayed the importance of interventions' 'fitness for purpose'. In addition, the secondary-level analysis revealed other 'fit for purpose' areas either overlooked or under-reported by interviewees, particularly the nature and extent of planning, the artist–teacher relationship and the design of the intervention in terms of type and time, as described in this chapter.

The second-level analysis and interviewees' perceptions suggest that 'intervention-context match' is key to the effectiveness of such arts education initiatives, with the acknowledgement that the context itself can be a key factor in shaping outcomes – for example, site or departmental context, children's and young people's abilities and predispositions and the particular experiences and motivations of the teachers and artists involved.

6.5 Summary

6.5.1 Ratings of effects

The chapter began by offering an overall rating system of the effects of arts interventions based on a second-level analysis drawing together the outcomes for pupils, teachers and artists (previously considered separately). According to the overall ratings:

- very few interventions achieved high impact across the board for all participants

- most commonly, there was a higher impact for pupils than for teachers, who in turn generally received a higher impact rating than artists

- the highest effects ratings for teachers were not necessarily in those focused on providing professional development for teachers.

6.5.2 Features of interventions

Four characteristics and their presence or limitations were identified as being particularly associated with those interventions achieving the highest or lowest effects ratings overall. These were:

- type of intervention – highest impacts in multiple-phase interventions, lowest impacts in one-off interventions

- nature and extent of planning – emphasising collaboration between teachers and artists prior to interventions with highest impact, but limited in those with lowest impacts. Teachers and artists may have different discourses about arts education projects, their purposes and aims, but where artists and teachers believed they shared similar aims and values, the highest outcome ratings were more likely to be achieved. The need for concrete plans and aims did not appear to be the most important aspect of collaboration between the parties. What seemed most important was the airing and sharing of aims and values as the project evolved, from its inception to its conclusion

- artist–teacher relationships – more positive in higher rated interventions

- amount and spread of time – generally larger amounts of time in higher rated interventions but spread 'fit for purpose' and smaller amounts of time in interventions with lower rated impacts.

In addition, the pupils' behaviours and responses, extent of teacher participation, supportive site, the artist's experience, pedagogy and flexibility, a content emphasising hands-on, creativity and 'professional endeavour' and opportunities for continuity and progression were all revealed as influential on levels of impact across the board.

6.5.3 Perceptions and second-level analysis

Interviewees' perceptions and the second-level analysis emphasised the importance of relevance and appropriateness of an intervention to its context. Many features identified by interviewees relayed 'fitness for purpose'. In addition, the second-level analysis highlighted a number of areas seemingly under-recognised by interviewees as important to outcomes. In particular, the nature and extent of planning as being important to pupil outcomes and the artist–teacher relationship as well as the design of the intervention in terms of the type and time as influential to outcomes for all participant groups.

Notes

i   This notion of a time spread with 'fitness for purpose' takes account of the context of the particular activities, the school and the pupils involved. For example, every morning for one week might be fit for the purpose of working with children with special needs; but two one-hour sessions two weeks apart might be inappropriate for producing a banner, where pupils didn't have time to finish their work because within each hour, time was needed to set up and put away, and where they would have preferred a two-hour block.

7 Conclusion

The main findings of the research have been summarised at the end of each chapter and in an opening Executive Summary. Rather than offer yet another summary here, we conclude instead by drawing together some of the research's main messages and implications for future policy and practice. We discuss these first by considering the study's contribution to the research literature (7.1), followed by some concluding thoughts on the wider implications of the study's findings for policy and practice (7.2).

7.1 Policy implications arising from the study's contribution to the research literature

There would seem to be good reasons for restricting the contextualisation of this study's findings to existing UK research and to research specifically concerned with arts interventions or, what was once referred to as, artist-in-school projects, rather than to 'arts education' in general. Comparisons with research in other countries present transferability problems due to differing educational and cultural environments, as well as contrasting backgrounds in the levels of experience of artists working in partnership with educators (e.g. see Winner's reference to differences in the types of pupils likely to take the arts in schools in the US and the UK in the Arts Council England, 2004, p. 10). Furthermore, relating the study to others that have specifically focused on arts interventions ensures that the evidence base and any policy implications emerging from it, is firmly grounded in analyses of this particular genus of arts education. Given the variety of methodological approaches employed, comparing the results of multiple investigations is complex enough, without confounding the comparisons still further by contrasting studies of arts interventions with those, say, of diverse forms of mainstream arts education provision[i].

Adopting this perspective then, the study can be seen as contributing to three particular fields of research literature:

- UK research into the impact of arts interventions or artist-in-school projects on children and young people

- UK research into the impact of arts interventions or artist-in-school projects on teachers, schools and artists

- UK research into the key characteristics of effective arts interventions or artist-in-school projects.

The research's contributions to each of these fields, along with any emerging policy implications, are summarised in turn.

7.1.1 UK research into the impact of arts interventions on children and young people

Three main UK sources present findings on the impact of arts interventions on children and young people: Sharp and Dust (1997), a revised and updated handbook for teachers and artists first published in 1990; Turner (1999), a report of seven Scottish case studies exploring 'quality in arts-education links' and Oddie and Allen (1998), a literature review of artists in schools projects from 'a practitioner's perspective'.

Oddie and Allen (1998) conclude their review with an upbeat assessment of the evidence to substantiate claims of positive impacts on pupils:

There is a growing body of evidence and testimony to indicate that the work of artists, in schools and colleges, enhances the quality of teaching and learning in the classroom ... there is evidence from heads, teachers, children and parents that working with artists can help to increase pupils' self-esteem and, through the encouragement of positive attitudes, enhance the learning of core literacy skills.
(p.76)

However, throughout their report, the 'research' evidence to support such a conclusion is highly elusive. The critical chapter is entitled 'a survey of *claims*' [our emphasis], in which the documenting of any research evidence (citations of Sharp and Dust, 1997 is virtually the only exception) is overshadowed by a series of references to pronouncements and assertions from writers who variously set out visions of what arts interventions/education might achieve (e.g. Robinson, 1982; Department of National Heritage, 1996; Arts Council of England, 1997 and National Curriculum documents). The description of seven projects, offered in a later chapter, does not include outcomes or impact as a reporting category and there are only sporadic isolated quotations as to the effects of the projects. Given that, in all other respects, this was a comprehensive review of the UK literature and that the authors were enthusiastic about artist in schools projects, we can only assume that they made every effort to identify research evidence on the impact on learners, but were largely unable to do so[ii], apart from Sharp and Dust (1997), to which we now turn.

Sharp and Dust (1997) and Turner (1999) are similar in that, although both sources outline impacts (the former refers to them as 'benefits', the latter as 'gains'), the amount of attention the topic receives is very small – less than a handful of pages in each report. This no doubt reflects the fact that both reports had priorities other than examining the effects of interventions. It is also true to say that the nature of the debate has changed since these earlier publications. There is greater emphasis on outcomes than was previously the case, particularly since the publication of the PAT 10 report in 1999 (DCMS, 1999), which argued for a stronger evidence base on the outcomes of the arts. It does mean, however, that the descriptions of the outcomes in these earlier works are lacking in many details: the status of the listed effects is not always clear (e.g. whether they were actually achieved or whether they are potential outcomes); little information on the empirical sources is given; perceptions are not triangulated; relative frequencies of the effects are rarely reported and the outcomes are not analysed in relation to different background variables (e.g. phase of schooling, artform). Briefly, the quality and transparency of the empirical evidence to support the listed 'benefits' and 'gains' appear fragile. But we stress again, documenting the effects of interventions was not the main purpose of either publication.

Sharp and Dust (1997) note the following benefits for pupils:

- insights into the professional arts world (e.g. artists' work and careers)
- understanding artistic processes
- trying new approaches (e.g. re-drafting in story writing)
- developing artistic skills
- enthusiasm, enjoyment and confidence-building
- role models (e.g. in terms of gender, ethnicity, disabilities)
- positive working relationships (e.g. being treated as a 'person')[iii].

Turner (1999) identifies the following gains:

- cognitive or intellectual gains relating to knowledge and understanding about a particular work of art

the arts–education interface: a mutual learning triangle?

- skill gains (e.g. voice control, collage technique)

- aesthetic understandings

- personal development

- affective aspects

- utilitarian outcomes (e.g. vocational skills, leisure time)

- expressive purposes[iv].

Clearly, our research endorses many of the outcomes for pupils cited in these two studies: notably, affective outcomes; artform knowledge, appreciation and skills and personal development (which may embrace much of Sharp and Dust's 'role models' and 'positive working relationships' benefits). However, by way of fulfilling one of the main reasons why the Arts Council funded the AEI research, it is contended that a salient contribution of this study is that it has brought robust and empirically sound evidence and analysis to bear on the way we understand these outcomes. For example, the outcomes are set out in a coherent schema; portrayals of effect types, including accounts of sub-types, are presented; relative frequencies and degrees of strength are provided; triangulation is offered; outcomes are examined against background variables and an analysis of incremental learning is included. In these ways, it is hoped that the research marks a significant step towards addressing the acknowledged gap in evidence on the outcomes of arts interventions for learners.

Moreover, in addition to corroborating effects noted by previous research, this study has identified several other outcome types not fully recognised as effects on learners in the existing literature:

- social and cultural knowledge

- knowledge, skills and appreciation beyond the arts

- thinking skills

- developments in creativity

- communication and expressive skills

- social development

- changes in attitudes towards and involvement in the artform

- transfer effects beyond the artform.

By doing so, the research offers powerful evidence to substantiate claims in certain of these areas (e.g. social development), as well as to promote a higher awareness of the kind of outcomes that pupils and young people can acquire from arts interventions, if they are appropriately targeted. Bearing in mind the finding that limited aims may have been instrumental in holding down the frequency levels of some of these outcome types, a key implication for policy and practice would seem to reside in giving greater consideration to initiatives that would broaden practitioners' ambitions and applications, when devising interventions.

The research extends the existing literature by presenting the results of various analyses of how outcomes for pupils varied according to key background variables. A number of these carried obvious implications for policy and practice. The finding, for example, that the prevailing pattern of effects of arts interventions corresponded fairly closely to the effects of mainstream arts education in secondary schools poses serious questions about what strategies need to be adopted in order to enhance the 'added value' of interventions over in-school provision. Similarly, the findings relating to variations in outcomes by artforms prompt the question as to whether greater differentiation by artform would increase the efficacy of arts intervention policies. Again, the research's confirmation of the suspected risks of negative effects associated with short-term interventions, compared to the manifest enriched impact on learning of certain types of sustained interventions carry clear messages about the most effective intervention models.

It is hoped that this study not only reinforces the empirical base of what is known about the outcomes of arts interventions, but extends existing knowledge to the benefit of evidence-based policy making.

7.1.2 UK research into the impact of arts interventions on teachers, schools and artists

Sharp and Dust (1997) provide an informative account of what can be seen as effects on teachers and schools, though from a research perspective the empirical base of their list shares many of the same shortcomings as their pupil effects. In particular, it is not always clear whether the effects have actually been evidenced or whether they represent potential outcomes – the verb 'can' is frequently used. Additionally, their list includes several 'process' experiences (e.g. contributions to the curriculum) rather than outcomes as consequential impacts, but this would seem to be a product of their focus on 'benefits' in comparison to our concern with outcomes and impact. However, their account identifies many positive outcomes for teachers and schools, notably:

- improved artform skills and teaching skills

- enhanced artform knowledge

- new vision of the artform

- increased confidence to teach artforms

- increased enthusiasm and interest in teaching the artform

- extended awareness of pupils' capacities

- closer relationship with pupils and teachers

- widened knowledge of links, contacts and networks

- raised status/profile of the arts in school

- extended positive image of the school.

There are several outcome types documented in the AEI which corroborate those identified by Sharp and Dust, in particular:

- informational

- affective

- motivational and attitudinal

- new awareness and value shifts

- knowledge and skills

- institutional and strategic outcomes.

Taken together, the two studies lend support to the view that many arts interventions afford important learning experiences for teachers and schools, even though, in the case of our research, most teachers in the AEI interventions did not construe them as explicit CPD opportunities.

In addition, the evidence base and analysis offered by the present study advances our understanding of the impacts on teachers and schools beyond that rendered by the existing literature. For example, it evidences other forms of impact on teachers (e.g. career development, material and provisionary outcomes), offers data on the relative frequencies with which outcomes were reported and, most crucially, opens up examination of the extent to which the various impacts on teachers and schools were translated into actual changes in their practice. It is this latter line of analysis which allows consideration of whether interventions involving pupil as well as teacher learning is more efficacious than those focusing entirely on teacher development. With salient implications for policy and practice, it is our contention that the emerging evidence-based proposition that interventions that allow for three-way learning (in the form of the mutual learning triangle) marks a significant contribution to the research literature.

A number of studies have observed that there are benefits, gains and learning for artists who involve themselves in arts interventions (Sharp and Dust, 1997; Turner, 1999; Pringle, 2002). With regard to the visual arts, the latter, for example, noted:

> *The artists engage with participants primarily through discussion and the exchanging of ideas and experiences. There is evidence of 'co-constructive' learning taking place, where shared knowledge is generated and the artist functions as co-learner, rather than knowledge being transmitted from the artist (positioned as infallible expert) to the participants.*
> (Pringle, 2002, p. 108)

However, none of these sources address the topic predominantly from an outcomes perspective or detail the impacts achieved in practice for artists and arts organisations. Apart from a reference to gaining satisfaction and a couple of examples of artists whose own creative work changed as a result of engagement with the educative process, Sharp and Dust focus more on motives and experiential aspects (e.g. financial benefits, access to facilities, reaching wider audiences). Similarly, Turner alludes to artists gaining inspiration from working with children and cites other writers on the question of whether artists really want to work at the arts and education interface.

Consequently, the presentation of the evidence on effects on artists and arts organisations in Section 3.3 represents an initial step towards redressing the lack of attention given to this topic from an outcomes perspective. Our findings were that:

- the effects on artists were generally less extensive than those on pupils and teachers

- the impact on educationally experienced artists and arts organisations was limited

- there were few long-term effects

- artists did not see interventions as offering CPD opportunities

- several artists expressed CPD learning needs (e.g. in classroom and behaviour management) and would have welcomed further training in this role.

These findings beg the question of whether more should be done to extend the practice adopted in some schemes and regions of constructing interventions as explicit, on-going and, for some, accredited, professional development experiences for artists. This issue takes on added significance for future policy development when seen in the light of the evidence that such factors as artist's pedagogical skills, the selection of content and artist–pupil relations were pivotal in determining the quality of learning outcomes for pupils.

7.1.3 UK research into the key characteristics of effective arts interventions

Sharp and Dust (1997) and Turner (1999) adumbrate what they see as the features of successful projects, but the empirical and methodological underpinnings of their lists are neither clear nor strong. Sharp and Dust, for example, state that 'from the findings of our research and our reading of the reports of other projects and schemes, we have identified the following features that characterise successful projects' (p.16). However, no definition of what counts as 'successful' is provided (e.g. successful for whom? successful in terms of its impact or its organisational efficiency? adjudged by whom? successful for all, most or some participants?), no explanation of the process of identifying factors is offered and no evidence is set out to substantiate the factors. Although Turner provides greater illumination of the identified factors through reference to data sources and also describes how the list she generated was developed through a consultation process with Arts Education Officers and schools that participated in the research, similar criticisms of the methodological basis to the identification of success-related features could be made.

From the outset of the AEI programme, it was important that the research adopted a methodologically robust and transparent approach to the identification of factors associated with effective interventions. This was done by exploring 'successful' projects through employing an outcomes-based methodology that allowed a systematic analysis of the frequency and strength of impacts and effects which in turn facilitated:

- the examination of triangulated participants' (i.e. those of pupils, teachers, artists) perceptions of general associations between outcomes and process factors

- the analysis of triangulated participants' (i.e. those of pupils, teachers, artists) perceptions of associations between process factors and specific outcomes

- the examination of how high and low outcome interventions (for three sets of participants) related to researcher observations of process characteristics. Thus permitting a form of analysis which could be used to cross-check the identification of process factors based solely on participants' perceptions.

As a result of these methods, it is contended that a major contribution of the study is that it brings a sound evidence-based methodology to bear upon the identification of features associated with successful or, more aptly, effective arts-education interventions. From this position, the research can offer evidence to lend support to some of the factors previously identified by Sharp and Dust (1997) and Turner (1999), challenge some and add some that do not appear to have been given the attention they deserve hitherto.

Essentially, ten features seem to be listed by Sharp and Dust (1997, p.16); a successful project:

1. addresses a school need

2. builds on the strengths of artists (e.g. artistic/technical knowledge and skills) and teachers (e.g. teaching skills)

3. is part of the ongoing work in the school

4. has teachers' and artists' commitment to the project and partnership

5. has ambitious yet achievable shared aims

6. has a budget to support joint planning and evaluation

7. is based on joint planning

8. is targeted at a specific group of pupils yet offers opportunities for others

9. is one in which the pupils are briefed about the project

10. has an evaluation.

Fourteen features are identified by Turner (1999, p. 57):

1. accountability – delivery as per agreement

2. clear objectives reached by negotiation

3. commitment (and enthusiasm) – by all concerned

4. cooperation/collaboration between artists and teachers

5. coordination – necessary in complex projects

6. evaluation – thought to be essential for improvement

7. extended contact – great if it can be managed

8. inclusivity – art for everyone

9. integrity – staying true to the values of the artform

10. planning and preparation – essential

11. practice – the ill-prepared artist may be worse than no artist

12. relevance (to curriculum and life of school)

13. responsiveness – to the need of pupils on the day

14. structure (of workshops)/variety of activity – pupils respond to a varied menu.

The AEI research endorsed a number of features highlighted in the above two sources: joint planning and shared aims in Sharp and Dust (1997) and clear objectives, extended contact (though shorter-term interventions could be effective in their own terms) and responsiveness to the needs of the pupils ('relevance' in our terminology) in Turner (1999). In so far as these factors have been identified by at least two studies, their significance for policy and practice is noteworthy.

On the other hand, many features proposed by these two sources were not evidenced by the AEI research as priority characteristics – neither through the perceptions of the three participant groups nor through the second-level researcher analysis. Echoing Turner's own observations on this topic, there was no research evidence to suggest that evaluation was a critical factor. Likewise, we could find no compelling evidence to indicate that inclusivity, accountability, artform integrity, briefing pupils, targeting specific groups while offering others opportunities, relevance to school needs and the curriculum or part of the on-going work were instrumental in driving the efficacy of interventions. To this extent, the current study raises questions about the veracity of the implicit recommendations of existing research surrounding these factors and suggests that their relevance to future policies and practices should be re-considered, though further research in a wider range of contexts is clearly required to explore these issues further.

Finally, perhaps the single most important and far-reaching contribution to the literature and evidence-based policy formation is to be found in the 'new' factors pinpointed by the AEI research. The majority of the most frequently and strongly identified characteristics in the AEI interventions were not highlighted by previous research. These comprised:

- artists' pedagogy

- type of content

- manageability

- emphasis on the end product

- pupil factors

- artist–pupil relationship

- continuity and progression.

The central nature of these factors is very different to those prioritised in earlier research. While the latter has tended to concentrate on organisational and managerial dimensions, the findings of the current study have accentuated features associated with the coalface reality of teaching and learning interactions – those adjoining the classroom or workshop experience. A pivotal message from the research and its three participant groups may be that, as key determinants of the quality of the learning outcomes, factors directly aligned to the teaching and learning interaction warrant closer scrutiny and deliberation. Whilst not detracting from the importance of the more removed managerial aspects (indeed our own analysis underscored the value of these) the study would suggest that such factors should not be accentuated at the expense of those that concern the immediacy of the teaching and learning experience.

If our findings are correct, and they certainly require corroboration, the implications for policy and practice development could be substantial and potentially transformative. It may well indicate that the success of educational programmes that involve artists and creative professionals could be enhanced by ensuring that the accompanying policies, management processes, advisory structures and supportive training events reflect the central importance of factors close to the teaching and learning experience. In short, the study prompts the question: are policies surrounding interventions at the arts-education interface as close to the action as this research suggests they should be?

7.2 Wider implications for policy and practice

Arguably, in recent years, the most influential document on arts education policy has been the Robinson Report (1999), which, to a certain extent, re-packaged 'arts education' as 'creative and cultural education'[v]. However, the sheer breadth and quality of pupil outcomes from arts interventions portrayed in Chapter 2 pose the question of whether aligning arts education initiatives too closely with the aims of creative and cultural education may be limiting and unsympathetic to the strengths and capacities of arts interventions. The results of the research clearly show that (a) the processes of arts education interventions provide more than creative and cultural outcomes and (b) that these two outcome types were not among the most frequently or strongly reported forms of impact of arts interventions. This would suggest that if policies on arts interventions are informed too heavily on an interpretation of the Robinson Report as emphasising the inter-changeability of arts education with creative and cultural education, there is a risk that many other powerful and, arguably, on the basis of this evidence, more immediately attainable effects associated with arts interventions could be eclipsed.

While it is certainly the case that the Robinson Report makes the case for a greater investment in creative and cultural education on the grounds that they can achieve similar outcomes to those identified in this research, the evidence described here offers little encouragement to a view that the reported effects flow from the creative and cultural development elements, processes and content of the interventions. If they did so, it could be expected that the frequency of high profile outcomes (e.g. developments in the personal domain, affective outcomes and increases in artform knowledge and skills) would correlate with that of creative and cultural developments. Given that, in this research, the latter were only mid- or low ranking outcomes respectively, this is clearly not the case. Furthermore, there was evidence that regardless of outcomes, pupils and young people rarely testified to the process traits associated with creative and cultural education. Indeed there were as many references from pupils to them not being able to use their own ideas in sessions, as there were to them being able to use their own ideas.

Additionally, our analyses of outcome routes and incremental learning revealed very few cases of creative and cultural developments leading to subsequent outcomes. Consequently, the research does not substantiate an interpretation of the Robinson Report that suggests that it is the elements of creative and cultural development which are especially important and instrumental in arts education as mediated through arts interventions. Other dimensions would seem to be as important, if not more important.

The high ranking of affective outcomes and the fact that so many young people found their involvement with AEI thoroughly engaging, stimulating and fulfilling, underlines the substantial contribution that arts interventions can make to meeting the Government's vision of ensuring that learning is an enjoyable experience. Nevertheless, a question mark might be posed about the sustainability of affective outcomes and how far they are used to generate learning outcomes beyond the (albeit powerful) sense of enjoyment. Arguably, over-reliance on the capacity of arts interventions to achieve enjoyment and other affective outcomes may detract attention away from the planning for other additional learning goals. Concerted efforts may be needed to avoid this happening.

For many pupils and young people, a new world of arts knowledge and skills was opened up through their encounter with professional artists. In a national and international policy context that frequently accentuates instrumental justifications for arts education and arts-education partnerships, the importance of learning the knowledge, skills and discipline associated with particular artforms should not go unnoticed. These may well constitute the foundation stones upon which all other learning outcomes need to be built. This would counsel against 'quick fix' solutions which assume that instrumental effects can be achieved without first establishing some solid foundations in artform knowledge and skills.

The array of outcomes in the personal domain suggest an important contribution for arts interventions in what many would see as the most fundamental aspect of young people's education: their emotional health. Those professionals who support the disengaged or disaffected (or seek to prevent such attitudes emerging) may perhaps see enormous potential in using arts interventions to address low self-esteem which often underpins these young people's anti-social activities and anti-learning stances. Findings from the questionnaires on declining self-esteem and self-image at school indicate just how much such experiences are needed. The AEI evidence also accentuates the case for longer-term commitments and strategies to tackle the problematic issues surrounding low self-esteem and disaffection from schooling.

Another area of major impact through AEI arts interventions was on young people's social development, including increased awareness and recognition that there is an equivalent centre of self in other people. The individual, familial and societal benefits of such developments in our young people are no doubt self-evident and it may be that the potential of arts interventions through artist-based partnerships in this arena requires more prominence and acclaim. Furthermore, in advancing the skills of teamwork, arts interventions would seem to offer a powerful and, in some respects, distinctive curriculum strategy for developing the social skills much required in the workplace.

Various evidence presented in Chapter 2 indicate that achieving other outcomes may need more concentrated and targeted endeavours to confront obstacles and prevailing orthodoxies that challenge the achievement of these effects. For example, it was felt that outcomes associated with increased knowledge and skills beyond the arts were difficult to achieve in the secondary phase largely because of heavily bounded and fragmented curriculum structures. The findings regarding the limited extensions to social and cultural knowledge raised the question of whether arts interventions, perhaps like normal arts education in schools, tend to accentuate form, skills and processes rather than content and meaning, in contrast to the adult world of arts which is redolent with social, moral and cultural issues. Could arts interventions offer an opportunity to redress this imbalance or would that compromise the hands-on appeal of arts interventions noted in Chapter 4?

The analysis of the relationship between outcomes and aims indicated that the limitations in the range of effects achieved may be the result of bounded ambitions rather than shortcomings in the design and implementation of arts interventions. The policy implications would be that if broader effects (e.g. the outcome types found to be less prevalent) are desirable, then encouraging teachers and artists to adopt a wider vision of the aims agenda would seem to be an appropriate strategy. However, with particular relevance to the Creative Partnership programme, it was significant that developing creativity was one notable exception in this regard: the design and delivery of AEI interventions did not generate this outcome to the level it was aimed for. Accordingly, this may be one outcome area which calls for more innovation in the prevailing approaches to the design and implementation of arts interventions.

The evidence also suggests that more attention should be paid to the issue of how highly engaging interventions will impact upon pupils' attitudes to the artform in the school. Arts interventions are likely to affect the way that pupils see and feel about their exposure to teachers' normal practice and curriculum provision. If an intervention is to avoid provoking critical reactions of the normal school diet, it would seem unwise for teachers not to get fully involved in designing, planning, helping execute, sustaining and learning from the intervention and the artist's input.

The factors identified in Chapters 4, 5 and 6 as the characteristics of arts interventions which frequently have a strong bearing on the nature and quality of learning outcomes provide much food for thought for policy-makers and practitioners alike. One emerging issue stems from the problem of how schools, other host institutions and brokers can access artists with the identified qualities. If the artist's pedagogy is a critical factor, what information is available to schools and other sites about individual or organisational capacities in this respect? To what extent can the growing number of artist databases and brokerage services of arts education agencies offer schools information on pedagogies and still more problematically, observations on the quality of artists' teaching repertoire? A related problem may be the limited awareness amongst teachers of these databases and services: hardly any teachers in the AEI research exhibited any knowledge of them. Another issue concerns training and professional development for artist, teachers and others in the management, design and execution of arts interventions: what forms of provision can best develop these professionals' awareness, knowledge and values surrounding the identified factors?

In addition to participants' perceptions of the key factors affecting the quality of learning outcomes, the analyses conducted by the research team elevated the significance of planning, the artist–teacher relationship and sustaining longer-term learning. Planning has a number of levels: logistics such as contracts, organising timing and venue and so on are a necessary but not sufficient component of high outcome rated interventions (e.g. through a series intervention, one host organisation learnt the need for logistical synchronisation). Planning in high-rated outcome interventions embraced more than these logistical matters, important though they were. In these cases, planning was about engaging in and committing to a collaborative process regarding the appropriate aims, design, content, context and pedagogies for the intervention, thus arriving at a creative and constructive 'chemistry' between artist and teacher and like all relationships, the good ones have to be worked at.

AEI demonstrated that quality outcomes come with quality interventions and these invariably have a cost implication, both in terms of straightforward finance and also time invested (before, during and after the intervention) by artist and teacher. Also, for teachers and artists in particular, investment can be costed in terms of the willingness to take risk and move beyond the familiar. Investment in the AEI by the host institution overall also tallies with quality outcomes. In other words, you only get out what you put in. In particular, AEI occasionally revealed a lack of investment by some teachers and schools in getting hold of an intervention and driving it forward, in seizing opportunities to sustain the learning initiated and especially in devising programmes of work that could facilitate longer-term incremental learning. Artists' lack of investment in the educational as opposed to the artistic dimensions of interventions was also apparent. Those viewing arts interventions as a low investment, an easy opportunity to provide a pleasant but essentially temporary diversion for young people will reap dividends (or lack of them) accordingly.

What does the AEI tell us about effective practices in arts interventions? What does it add to the debate about what works? Throughout the report, we have tried to address these questions by isolating the factors, both as perceived by the main participants (Chapters 4 and 5) and as analysed by the researchers (Chapter 6), that appear to be strongly and frequently associated with high levels of learning outcomes. The evidence from AEI would suggest that paying close attention to the highlighted factors in the conception, execution and aftermath of arts interventions would significantly boost their chances of engendering high quality outcomes.

But the reader may inquire whether there are any less atomistic and more general principles about effective practices to be extracted from AEI. While we would wish to respond positively to this common expectation, postulating generalisations about 'what works' is fraught with dangers, not least because what works in one context may not work in another. Indeed, there was ample evidence of this within AEI: the prevalence of such features as pupil, artist, teacher, school and site context factors all point to the importance of particularities as key determinants of outcomes – hence the need to see the design of arts interventions as essentially context-specific enterprises. However, by way of conclusion, we would like to reiterate the value of one general and overarching characteristic of effective practice alluded to in Section 5.2.5: the Mutual Learning Triangle (MLT).

We would suggest that, in broad terms, those interventions which came closest to approximating the MLT generated the highest quality outcomes; those that were some distance from it were often less successful. The MLT model underlines the substantial benefits to be gained by ensuring that all three of the main participant groups (namely, (i) pupils/young people/learners; (ii) teachers/schools or other host agents and (iii) artists/arts organisations) are fully engaged in and learn from the arts intervention and its legacy. The MLT offers the potential to add considerable value to bilateral learning approaches. By way of illustration, the evidence from AEI frequently testified to the consequences of omitting one side of the triangle:

- in comparing effects from AEI interventions with those from mainstream arts education in secondary schools, Chapter 2 presented clear evidence of the added value of incorporating artists into the teacher–pupil learning nexus

- within arts interventions, leaving artists out of the learning agenda (by focusing only on teachers' and pupils' learning) fails to maximise artists' scope for professional development that would be beneficial for future education-based work

- arts interventions with a CPD focus that left pupils out of the triangle were generally less effective in several respects than the advisory teacher styled approaches which allowed for the teacher to gain the artist's feedback and support in the context of teaching pupils. Indeed, the finding that high-level teacher outcomes accrued from pupil-focused interventions confirms that orthodox interventions involving pupils are an important CPD opportunity. Pupils need to be included even when there is a strong CPD objective

- the drawbacks associated with the lack of investment of teachers and schools in the MLT and its consequential reliance on a pupil–artist bilateral learning relationship have been well documented throughout the report (e.g. limited curriculum linkage, lack of valuing and support for the artist, lower levels of involvement in planning, reduced likelihood of positive pupil and artist outcomes, restricted professional development for teachers and above all, reduced capacity to sustain the learning beyond the life of the intervention).

Conversely, the analysis presented in Chapter 6 and the evidence on incremental learning, albeit limited to a small number of cases, endorses the message that full engagement by all three of the main parties in the MLT can bring substantial and high quality learning. We would not want to go as far as recommending that the triangles should always be equilateral ones, but, on the basis of the evidence discussed here, we would suggest that something approaching equivalence in MLTs would, in the majority of cases, raise the odds appreciably in favour of arts interventions generating successful outcomes.

Notes

i   In Section 2.4.2, we felt that it was valid and appropriate to compare the outcomes of secondary school AEI interventions with those from mainstream arts education programmes documented in Harland *et al*. (2000) because the data in both cases were collected from secondary schools, in similar contexts and by almost identical research methods.

ii It is pertinent that more recently the Arts Council England's (2004) report, *The Impact of the Arts* did not include sources of evidence on the effects of UK arts interventions on learners.

iii Since much that is described under the latter two headings read like process experiences, it is not clear exactly what the outcomes for pupils are.

iv It is noteworthy that these latter two gains (utilitarian and expressive) appeared to be drawn from other research rather than Turner's own data.

v   'By creative education we mean forms of education that develop young people's capacities for original ideas and action; by cultural education we mean forms of education that enable them to engage positively with the growing complexity and diversity of social values and ways of life.' (Robinson Report, 1999, p.6)

Appendix 1

AEI one-off interventions

Intervention name	Artform	Location	Host site	Client group	Artist	Content	Timing and duration	Venue	Cost
Out-of-hours – music	Music	Bristol	Large community/ concert hall	18 self-selected primary and secondary age boys and girls from various schools in area but not in EAZ	Artist works as freelance singer as well as with music organisation/ group. Accompanied by two assistant musicians	Gospel singing – vocal technique and learning of 3 songs (no music, all by ear) Third day dress rehearsal and evening performance as support act for touring arts group	Oct 2002: half term. 3 consecutive days – 3 mornings then evening performance on third day.	Large community/ concert hall	£3,601
Dance-secondary	Dance	Corby	Technology College	KS3 – 18 self-selected Y7 and Y9 girls from technology college	Arts organisation from outside Corby, one dancer and one trainee dancer	Watched performance, followed by discussions. Artist then in residency for 2 weeks working with one core group from each of the schools towards a performance of street dance on the theme 'acquaintances'. The 2 groups performed at each college in turn	June 2002: for 2 weeks 2 hr afternoon sessions; on 9th day rehearsal and performance in each of the two schools	Dance studio (actual performance took place in the gym)	£3,043
Nursery-museum	Art	Bristol	Nursery school	Nursery/foundation stage. 8 pupils	Young persons officer at local museum and art gallery	Half-day visit to gallery-museum. Theme: 'materials' (fitted in with term's work – so provided follow-up opportunity by teacher)	Nov 2001: half day visit to gallery-museum	Local gallery-museum	£0

AEI one-off interventions continued

Intervention name	Artform	Location	Host site	Client group	Artist	Content	Timing and duration	Venue	Cost
Theatre-primary	Drama	Corby	Primary	KS1 – Two Y1/2 mixed classes (performance and discussion), plus 2 reception classes (just saw performance)	Artist (and student from local college) from arts organisation based outside Corby – (booked by headteacher not ACE coordinator)	Performance from artist organisation. Theme related to teaching literacy. Short post-performance discussion on same day as performance	Spring 2002 – 1 day	School hall	£255
Secondary-art	Art	Corby	Community college	KS3–4. 40 Y10 pupils – 2 art GCSE groups	Freelance textile artist – part of voluntary-run arts organisation	Print making/printing methods and screen printing	April 2003: all normal art lessons for 4 weeks – 3 lessons per week	Normal art room	£4,895

AEI series interventions

Intervention name	Artform	Location	Host site	Client group	Artist	Content	Timing and duration	Venue	Cost
Multi-artform Special: phase 1	Theatre	Corby	Special school	Lower KS2 ability group; max 8 pupils at any one time; group changed slightly during school year 02/03	Small touring theatre company	3 performances of same show involving erection of show-specific venue in school. Theme of show 'the sea'; including range of sensory experiences	Oct 2001: 3 performances of same show; 40 mins each; within a single day	Show-specific venue within school	£736
Multi-artform Special: phase 2	Dance	Corby	Special school	Lower KS2 ability group; max 8 pupils at any one time; group changed slightly during school year 02/03	Two dancers from small arts organisation	Single INSET session for teachers preceded work with pupils; first day dancers met pupils and teachers then INSET after school; during other days worked with different group of pupils each morning and sample group every afternoon. Theme: different ways of moving body in space; need for and development of 'task' in partners, 'making shapes' with other people. Producing a final dance	May 2002: 6 full days residency	School hall	£3,600

the arts–education interface: a mutual learning triangle?

AEI series interventions continued

Intervention name	Artform	Location	Host site	Client group	Artist	Content	Timing and duration	Venue	Cost
Multi-artform Special: phase 3	Photo-graphy	Corby	Special school	Lower KS2 ability group; max 8 pupils at any one time; group changed slightly during school year 02/03	Photographer from small community arts organisation	4 visits to school by artist. First day spent with each: discussion on use of digital cameras (pupils each given camera to take home to practise). Day 2 – visit wildlife centre by bus to take photographs (sample pupils). 2 follow-up sessions mounting exhibition in each classroom from pupils' work. Work included INSET	Dec 2002: Two-week residency working with each class in the school for one full day and two half-day sessions	Classrooms and local wildlife centre	£2,920
Multi-artform Special: phase 4	Music	Corby	Special school	Lower KS2 ability group; max 8 pupils at any one time; group changed slightly during school year 02/03	2 specialists in African drumming from small music organisation	Artists worked with all classes at least once in the mornings and with sample group every afternoon. Sample group performance at end.	Jan 2003: 1-week residency	Classrooms and school hall	£2,100
Multi-artform Special: phase 5	Art	Corby	Special school	Lower KS2 ability group; max 8 pupils at any one time; group changed slightly during school year 02/03	Artist in paint and other media.	Artist worked with small groups of pupils – various activities in clay. Artist produced final piece from pupils' ideas for display in school	May 2003: weekly sessions over 1 month; working with different groups in the mornings and sample group in the afternoons	School art department	£2,600

AEI series interventions continued

Intervention name	Artform	Location	Host site	Client group	Artist	Content	Timing and duration	Venue	Cost
Multi-artform Secondary: phase 1	Drama	Bristol	Comprehensive	KS3 Y7–Y8; a class of 29 pupils	Small-scale local theatre company	Series of four drama workshops led by two members of theatre co. – one person the same each time, the other person different every time	Autumn 2001: weekly, 4 workshops each approx. 1 hour	School drama studio	£1,500
Multi-artform Secondary: phase 2	Art	Bristol	Comprehensive	KS3 Y7–Y8; a class of 29 pupils	Visual art freelance – 2 textile artists	2 textile artists worked with half the class each to produce felt and batik banners, including collage	Spring 2002: 1 and a half days	School art department	£811
Multi-artform Secondary: phase 3	Music	Bristol	Comprehensive	KS3 Y7–Y8; a class of 29 pupils	Musician known to head of music (from new organisation)	Composer worked with class to produce own musical – CD and performance at end of term	Summer 2002: 13 sessions during regular music lessons	School music department	£1,260
Multi-artform Secondary: phase 4	Dance	Bristol	Comprehensive	KS3 Y7–Y8; a dance class, all girls, containing some from original group, plus others not previously involved. Pupils split for PE	Freelance dancer based in Bristol	Dancer worked on street dance with 2 slightly different groups of girls. Some of the work was developed later and performed (i.e. teacher's input)	Autumn 2002: 2 sessions during consecutive dance lessons plus after-school session	School dance studio	£175

the arts–education interface: a mutual learning triangle?

AEI series interventions continued

Intervention name	Artform	Location	Host site	Client group	Artist	Content	Timing and duration	Venue	Cost
Multi-artform Secondary: phase 5	Poetry	Bristol	Comprehensive	KS3 Y7–Y8; an English class, containing some pupils from original group, plus others not previously involved. Pupils setted for English	Freelance poet from outside Bristol	Poet worked with pupils on writing and performing their own poems. Some performed at AEI celebrations with poet's support. Continued to develop work with a photographer – not part of intervention	March 2003 – During second half of term; 3 double English lessons	Normal English classroom	£5,189
Multi-artform Secondary: phase 6	Live Art	Bristol	Comprehensive	KS3 Y7–Y8; original class of pupils	2 live artists based in Bristol	Two 'live art' artists worked with pupils to produce a performance involving sounds and images of the school. An additional preliminary session during an art lesson as an introduction	June 2003: An introductory session followed by 3 days of workshops and performance (pupils off timetable)	School art department	£2,300
Multi-artform Out of school: phase 1	Turntablism	Corby	Youth centre	Young people aged 12 to 17 (selected for a specific phase only)	One artist and other workshop leaders from a voluntary media arts organisation	4 taster sessions and 5 day half term residency (turntablism skills and techniques) followed by performance and reward ceremony (including own CD)	Autumn 2001: 4 taster sessions, 5-day half term residency and performance and presentation	Local youth centre, media centre and arts venue	£6,400
Multi-artform Out of school: phase 2	Radio	Corby	Youth centre	Approx 8 young people aged 12 to 17 (selected for a specific phase only)	2 freelance artists	5 full day workshops over 3/4 weeks covering theory, practising skills, recording and airing a live show	Aug 2002: 5 full-day workshops over 3/4 weeks	Local youth centre and local FE College	£955

AEI series interventions continued

Intervention name	Artform	Location	Host site	Client group	Artist	Content	Timing and duration	Venue	Cost
Multi-artform Out of school: phase 3	Film	Corby	Youth centre	12 young people aged 12 to 17 (selected for a specific phase only)	2 artists from independent arts organisation	Filming, editing within Corby followed by performance	June 2003: weekend residency followed by sessions in Corby area and presentation	Residency at a centre outside Corby; filming around Corby	£5,900
Multi-artform Primary: phase 1	Music	Bristol	Primary school	KS2 – mixed Y3/4 class	Local gospel singer	Learnt songs and dances and created a performance	Autumn 2001: weekly sessions for approx 10 weeks	School hall	£725
Multi-artform Primary: phase 2	Visual art	Bristol	Primary school	KS2 – mixed Y3/4 class	Local workshop artist	Sculpture and different media. Fitted with curriculum topic on changing environments. Included trip to local sculpture park	Summer 2002: sessions twice a week for 4 weeks	Art room and trip to local sculpture park	£771
Multi-artform Primary: phase 3	Drama	Bristol	Primary school	KS2 – 28 Y4/5 pupils (research followed same sample of pupils from previous phases)	Artist from local street theatre company	Drama games, getting focused and concentration	Spring 2003: Tuesday afternoon sessions for 10 weeks.	Sometimes a classroom, sometimes the school hall	£1,438

the arts–education interface: a mutual learning triangle?

AEI developmental interventions

Intervention name	Artform	Location	Host site	Client group	Artist	Content	Timing and duration	Venue	Cost
Primary-developmental-drama: Phase 1	Drama	Bristol	Primary school	KS1 – All Y1 (2 classes) (approx 40 pupils)	Local arts co. based at the local theatre	Development of imagination, language and story telling. Artists' production fitted with current science topic 'ourselves'	Spring 2002: every Thursday for whole day broken into 2 sessions	School's junior hall and sometimes classrooms	£1,000
Primary-developmental-drama: Phase 2	Drama	Bristol	Primary school	KS1 – All Y1 (2 classes) (approx 40 pupils)	Local arts co. based at the local theatre	Develop skills knowledge and understanding in PSHE through practical dramatic activity. Visit to theatre	Autumn 2002: series of 1-hour sessions on Tuesday mornings and theatre visit	School's family learning room – withdrawal classroom that could be cleared of furniture; theatre	£1,957
Primary-developmental-drama: Phase 3	Drama	Bristol	Primary school	KS1 – All Y2s and some Y1s – approx 60 pupils in total	Local arts co. based at the local theatre	2-week residency to create an original piece of theatre for public performance (Storyline initiated by pupils around animals)	Summer 2003: 2-week residency – full days every day	Residency – both classes' classrooms, the art room and infants main hall. Final performance at local theatre	£3,480

AEI developmental interventions continued

Intervention name	Artform	Location	Host site	Client group	Artist	Content	Timing and duration	Venue	Cost
Secondary-developmental-drama: Phase 1	Drama	Corby	Secondary school	KS4 – Y10, 15 students selected from 2 GCSE drama groups	2 artists from small touring theatre co. based outside Corby	Physical theatre workshops comprising a range of activities to practise specific skills. Drama activities commanding space and gesture work	Autumn 2001: 2 full days	Drama studio	£426
Secondary-developmental-drama: Phase 2	Drama	Corby	Secondary school	KS4 – Y10 students (7 extra from the third GCSE drama group)	2 artists from small touring theatre co. based outside Corby	Creating a show as if they were a professional company. Based on ideas from students' responses to initial questionnaire on personal relationships. Presenting content through combination of dialogue and choreographed sequences	Summer 2002: 'Enterprise week' 4 consecutive days of the week where whole school engages in off-timetable activities	Drama studio	£390
Secondary-developmental-drama: Phase 3	Drama	Corby	Secondary school	KS4 – Y11, 15 pupils (same sample as in phase 1)	2 artists from small touring theatre co. based outside Corby	Physical theatre. Choreographic element. Developing more advanced dance skills to produce discrete small group sequence to perform to rest of group at end of the day	Spring 2003: 1 full day	Drama studio	£459
Secondary-developmental-music: Phase 1	Music	Bristol	Secondary school	KS3 – Y8 class in 01/02; same class in Y9 02/03	Freelance 'classical Indian musician' from outside Bristol	Related to music Scheme of Work. Watched musician perform and gave seminar. Some participation and discussion	Autumn 2001: 2 one-hour sessions	Normal music room	£470

the arts–education interface: a mutual learning triangle?

AEI developmental interventions continued

Intervention name	Artform	Location	Host site	Client group	Artist	Content	Timing and duration	Venue	Cost
Secondary-developmental-music: Phase 2	Music	Bristol	Secondary school	KS3 – Y8 class in 01/02; same class in Y9 02/03	Freelance community musician composer/jazz improviser	Related to music Scheme of Work. 'Recycling' Beatles songs music project. Involved a small group of pupils using guitars, as well as rest of class using keyboards. Individual performances to rest of class	Spring 2002: 6 one-hour lessons	Normal music room and practice rooms	£280
Secondary-developmental-music: Phase 3	Music	Bristol	Secondary school	KS3 – Y8 class in 01/02; same class in Y9 02/03	Freelance African drumming musician	Related to music Scheme of Work. African drumming – learning rhythms and piece of music – performance within class	Summer 2002: 5 one-hour sessions	Performing arts studio	£290
Secondary-developmental-music: Phase 4	Music	Bristol	Secondary school	KS3 – Y8 class in 01/02; same class in Y9 02/03; small group selected within the class to take part	Freelance Blues musician/ instrumental music teacher	Related to music Scheme of Work. Small group from class selected to work with musician on learning to play harmonica. Group performance to rest of class	Autumn 2002: 5/6 one-hour sessions	Normal music room and practice rooms	£362
Secondary-developmental-music: Phase 5	Music	Bristol	Secondary school	KS3 – Y8 class in 01/02; same class in Y9 02/03.; small group selected within the class to take part	Freelance steel pans musician and a musician helper	Related to music Scheme of Work. Small group selected to have steel pan lessons. Rest with normal music teacher doing 'Gamelan'. Performance at school awards evening	Summer 2003: 6 one-hour sessions including performance at school awards evening	Performing arts studio	£1,390

AEI teacher development interventions

Intervention name	Artform	Location	Host site	Client group	Artist	Content	Timing and duration	Venue	Cost
Primary-developmental: Phase 1	Dance	Bristol	Primary school	Class teachers of KS2 – Y4/5; targeted by intervention but all staff experienced workshops	Freelance dancer/dance education worker and dancer	INSET – all staff after-school dance workshop. Generic skills for teaching dance and relating dance to other curriculum areas. Rainforest theme	Autumn 2001: 1 after-school session. 1.5 hours (instead of staff meeting)	School hall	
Primary-developmental: Phase 2	Dance	Bristol	Primary school	Class teachers of KS2 – Y4/5; targeted by intervention but all staff experienced workshops	Contemporary dancer	INSET – all staff after-school dance workshop. Teaching a specific topic of dance – links between narrative and dance	Spring 2002: 1 after-school dance workshop. 1.5 hours (instead of staff meeting)	School hall	Total: £1,003
Primary-developmental: Phase 3	Dance	Bristol	Primary school	Class teachers of KS2 – Y4/5; targeted by intervention but all staff experienced workshops	Dancer from local dance agency	INSET – all staff after-school dance workshop. Techniques for teaching dance warm-ups, group work and relation to several themes suggested by teachers	Autumn 2002: 1 after-school workshop	School hall	
Primary-developmental-dance: Phase 1	Dance	Bristol	Primary school	1 senior teacher; 1 LSA	Local freelance dancer/dance education worker	INSET – learning new dance style – salsa	Autumn 2002 (4 sessions on a Thursday afternoon)	Local community centre	
Primary-developmental-dance: Phase 2	Dance	Bristol	Primary school	Teachers of KS2	Local freelance dancer/dance education worker	INSET – 2 teachers learning Latin American dance – 'holding hands' and diminishing levels of support from artist. Continuing and consolidating learning dance style in order to teach pupils and learning how to teach it	Spring 2003 (3 afternoon sessions)	Local community centre	Total: £877

AEI teacher development interventions continued

Intervention name	Artform	Location	Host site	Client group	Artist	Content	Timing and duration	Venue	Cost
Primary-developmental-dance: Phase 3	Dance	Bristol	Primary school	2 teachers and KS2 gifted and talented dance class	Local freelance dancer/dance education worker	Teachers gradually take over more teaching role of sessions and artists support diminishes. With pupils work towards performance at summer festival	Summer 2003: 4 afternoon sessions with pupils	School hall (plus one session in playground)	
Primary-developmental-visual art: Phase 1	Visual art	Corby	Primary school	Teacher development through co-teaching with artist and de-briefing after sessions. KS2 class (approx 28 pupils) and talented and gifted group	Artist from arts company outside Corby	Digital imagery – digital photography – pupils superimposing an image onto their own drawings	Autumn 2002: 4 workshops with talented and gifted class and 2 art afternoons with teacher's own class	Y4 classroom	£2,575
Primary-developmental-visual art: Phase 2	Visual art	Corby	Primary school	KS2 – Y4 class (approx 28) with pupils with special needs integrated into the group	Freelance ceramicist and ex-teacher from outside Corby	Ceramics – pottery based on some naïve art	Spring 2003: 2 workshops	Y4 classroom	£480
Primary-developmental- visual art: Phase 3	Visual art	Corby	Primary school	Teacher development through co-teaching with artist and de-briefing after sessions. KS2 class and talented and gifted group	Freelance artist from outside Corby	Textiles – produced 5 banners that incorporated screen printing, embroidery and tie dye	Summer 2003: 3 and a half days workshops	Y4 classroom	£1,120

Appendix 2

AEI Pupil Questionnaire (PRE-INTERVENTION)
School XYZ
Dance (or other art form)

◆ You are soon going to take part in a dance project. NFER is a research organisation and we have been asked to find out what you think about this dance project as you go through it. Before you start this project, we would be very grateful if you could answer the questions in this short questionnaire. We would like to know what you think about the things you do and learn about in your lessons.

◆ Your answers will be completely confidential and we will not tell anyone else. We ask you to write your name, but this is only for our own records.

◆ The questionnaire should take about fifteen minutes to fill in.

◆ The researcher with you today will explain how to complete the questionnaire. If you are not sure about any questions, please ask her for help.

◆ We are interested in YOUR opinions, so please don't discuss your answers with anyone else.

◆ It is **not** a test. There are no right or wrong answers, so just write what YOU think.

First, some questions about yourself.

1. Please could you write your full name in the box.

2. Are you male or female? *Please tick one box.*   Male ☐   Female ☐

3. What year are you in? *Please write in the box.*   Year ☐

4. We would like you to think about whether you would agree or disagree with the following statements. For each of these, look first at the words at the opposite end of each row, then circle **one** number which best matches which one you agree with.

A	I'm quite a confident person	1 2 3 4 5	I'm not very confident
B	I'm good at working with others in groups	1 2 3 4 5	I'm not good at working with others in groups
C	I'm doing well at school	1 2 3 4 5	I'm not doing well at school
D	most of my lessons are interesting	1 2 3 4 5	most of my lessons are boring
E	I find it easy to make new friends	1 2 3 4 5	I find it hard to make new friends
F	I look forward to coming to school	1 2 3 4 5	I don't look forward to coming to school
G	I'm good at lots of subjects	1 2 3 4 5	I'm not very good at many subjects
H	I feel good about myself and my future	1 2 3 4 5	I don't feel good about myself and my future
I	I find it easy to concentrate in lessons	1 2 3 4 5	I find it hard to concentrate in lessons
J	I'm good at cooperating with other people	1 2 3 4 5	I'm not good at cooperating with other people
K	think I understand myself and what I feel	1 2 3 4 5	I don't think I understand myself and what I feel
L	I'm good at understanding other people	1 2 3 4 5	I'm not good at understanding other people
M	I get on well with most grown-ups	1 2 3 4 5	I don't get on well with most grown-ups
N	I'm good at expressing myself	1 2 3 4 5	I'm not good at expressing myself
O	I behave well in lessons	1 2 3 4 5	I don't behave well in lessons
P	I'm good at creating things	1 2 3 4 5	I'm not good at creating things

DANCE OUTSIDE SCHOOL

The next set of questions are about dance outside school, at home or at dance clubs that are not held in school.

5. Are you involved in any dance clubs or dance activities that are **not** held in school?

    Please tick one box.

    Yes ☐   No ☐

    If Yes, what type of dancing do you do?

6. How often do you go to this dance club or take part in this dance activity?
    Please tick one box.

    Less than once a week ☐   Once a week ☐   Twice a week ☐   Three times a week or more ☐

7. How important is dance to you? *Please tick one box.*

Not at all		A bit		A lot	

8. Do your parents take part in any kind of dance activities? *Please tick one box.*

Not at all		A bit		A lot	

If Yes, what type of dancing do they do?

9. Would you say that dance is important to your parent(s)? *Please tick one box.*

Not at all		A bit		A lot	

DANCE AT SCHOOL

These next questions are about dance at school and we would like to know what you think about dance here.

10. Are you learning to dance at school? *Please tick one box.*   Yes | | No | |

If Yes, what type of dancing do you do?

11. What kind of things have you been doing in dance at school?

12. What are the best things about dance lessons at school?

13. What are the worst things about dance lessons at school?

[ ]

14. Do you want to take dance in Years 10 and 11 for GCSE? *Please tick one box.*

Yes [ ]   No [ ]   Not Sure [ ]

15. We know that there is a dance club held at school, do you take part in it? *Please tick one box.*

Yes [ ]   No [ ]

If Yes, what type of dancing do you do?

[ ]

16. We would like you to think about whether you would agree or disagree with the following statements. For each of these, look first at the words at the opposite end of each row, then circle **one** number which best matches which one you agree with.

dance is easy at school	1 2 3 4 5	dance is hard at school
I really enjoy dance at school	1 2 3 4 5	I really dislike dance at school
dance is important for job/career	1 2 3 4 5	dance is not needed for job/career
dance is important for adult life	1 2 3 4 5	dance is not important for adult life
we don't do enough dance at school	1 2 3 4 5	we do too much dance at school
I'm good at dance at school	1 2 3 4 5	I'm not good at dance at school
I learn a lot in dance at school	1 2 3 4 5	I don't learn much in dance at school

17. What do you think you have learnt or got out of taking dance so far at this school?

[ ]

18. Are there any particular things you would like to do in dance?

[ ]

THANK YOU VERY MUCH FOR YOUR HELP.

AEI Pupil Questionnaire (POST-INTERVENTION)
School XYZ
Dance (or other art form)

◆   Over the last few weeks you have taken part in a dance project. NFER has been asked to find out what you think about this dance project. To help us do this, we would be very grateful if you could answer the questions in this short questionnaire. We would like to know what you think about the things you did in the project and what you feel you may have got out of it.

◆   Your answers will be completely confidential and we will not tell anyone else. We ask you to write your name, but this is only for our own records.

◆   The questionnaire should take about fifteen minutes to fill in.

◆   The researcher with you today will explain how to complete the questionnaire. If you are not sure about any questions, please ask her for help.

◆   We are interested in YOUR opinions, so please don't discuss your answers with anyone else.

◆   It is **not** a test. There are no right or wrong answers, so just write what YOU think.

First, some questions about yourself.

1. Please could you write your
    full name in the box.

2. Are you male or female? *Please tick one box.*   Male [ ]   Female [ ]

3. What year are you in? *Please tick one box.*   Year [ ]

4. We would like you to think about whether you would agree or disagree with the following statements. For each of these, look first at the words at the opposite end of each row, then circle **one** number which best matches which one you agree with.

I'm quite a confident person	1 2 3 4 5	I'm not very confident
I'm good at working with others in groups	1 2 3 4 5	I'm not good at working with others in groups
I'm doing well at school	1 2 3 4 5	I'm not doing well at school
most of my lessons are interesting	1 2 3 4 5	most of my lessons are boring
I find it easy to make new friends	1 2 3 4 5	I find it hard to make new friends
I look forward to coming to school	1 2 3 4 5	I don't look forward to coming to school
I'm good at lots of subjects	1 2 3 4 5	I'm not very good at many subjects
I feel good about myself and my future	1 2 3 4 5	I don't feel good about myself and my future
I find it easy to concentrate in lessons	1 2 3 4 5	I find it hard to concentrate in lessons
I'm good at cooperating with other people	1 2 3 4 5	I'm not good at cooperating with other people
I think I understand myself and what I feel	1 2 3 4 5	I don't think I understand myself and what I feel
I'm good at understanding other people	1 2 3 4 5	I'm not good at understanding other people
I get on well with most grown-ups	1 2 3 4 5	I don't get on well with most grown-ups
I'm good at expressing myself	1 2 3 4 5	I'm not good at expressing myself
I behave well in lessons	1 2 3 4 5	I don't behave well in lessons
I'm good at creating things	1 2 3 4 5	I'm not good at creating things

Doing the dance project

5. Did you enjoy taking part in the dance project? *Please tick one box.*

Not at all		A bit		A lot	

6. Could you tell us three things about the dance project that you **particularly** liked?

> 1.
>
> 2.
>
> 3.

7. Could you tell us three things about the dance project that you did **not** like?

> 1.
>
> 2.
>
> 3.

8. Was the dance project different from your normal dance lessons? *Please tick one box.*

Yes ☐   No ☐

If Yes, what was different about it?

```
[                                                                    ]
[                                                                    ]
[                                                                    ]
[                                                                    ]
[                                                                    ]
```

What you got out of the dance project

9. Do you think you learnt anything or got anything out of the dance project? *Please tick one box.*

Yes ☐   No ☐

If **Yes**, what did you learn through it? If **No**, why do you think you didn't learn anything?

```
[                                                                    ]
[                                                                    ]
[                                                                    ]
[                                                                    ]
[                                                                    ]
[                                                                    ]
[                                                                    ]
```

10. What do you feel that you may have got out of taking part in the dance project? *Please tick **one** box for each of the following possible effects.*

I think that the dance project has ...	No	A little	A lot	Not Sure
1. taught me particular dance skills and techniques				
2. given me self-confidence socially and helped me to get on with people				
3. helped me to feel good about myself				
4. helped me to learn in other subjects				
5. helped me to think and solve problems				
6. helped me to understand my own and other people's feelings and emotions				
7. helped me think about a future job or career				
8. made me want to work harder in dance at school				
9. taught me to think more critically about dance so that I feel more able to decide what I think is good dance and what is not				
10. made me want to work harder at school generally				
11. made me want to do more dance out of school				

	No	A little	A lot	Not Sure
12. given me knowledge about dance and appreciation of people's dance				
13. helped me to express myself better				
14. made me more able to work as part of a team				
15. given me a sense of pleasure, enjoyment and satisfaction				
16. helped me to realise that I am capable of more things than I thought				
17. helped me to understand and know the type of person I am				
18. helped me learn more about social issues and problems				
19. made me more aware of the things around me				
20. made me more aware of other people's cultures, their traditions and how they see the world				
21. helped me to be more creative and imaginative				

11. We would like you to think about whether you would agree or disagree with the following statements. *For each of these, look first at the words at the opposite end of each row, then circle **one** number which best matches which one you agree with.*

dance is easy at school	1 2 3 4 5	dance is hard at school
I really enjoy dance at school	1 2 3 4 5	I really dislike dance at school
dance is important for job/career	1 2 3 4 5	dance is not needed for job/career
dance is important for adult life	1 2 3 4 5	dance is not important for adult life
we don't do enough dance at school	1 2 3 4 5	we do too much dance at school
I'm good at dance at school	1 2 3 4 5	I'm not good at dance at school
I learn a lot in dance at school	1 2 3 4 5	I don't learn much in dance at school

12. Is there anything else you would like to tell us about the dance project?

THANK YOU VERY MUCH FOR YOUR HELP.

Appendix 3

Follow-up schedule: pupils (secondary master)

Note to interviewer: Don't forget to follow up anything you did not ask at intervention, especially if it is not asked as a follow-up here. Please also prepare in advance which items you will need to ask from this schedule – depending on the nature of your intervention. Tick or asterisk the ones you will be asking.

Preamble: [put into your own words as appropriate]

- Thank you very much for coming to be interviewed.

- This interview is to help us find out what kinds of longer-term impact there might have been from the [initiative/project … name it if possible] that you and your class were involved with [last year/last term …].

- The interview will take about 40 minutes, 'is that okay?' [NB – if part of a series or development this could be shorter, e.g. 30 mins, but then make the final one fuller].

- The interview will be completely confidential. Your teachers, friends and parents will not be told anything you say, so please feel free to say exactly what you think.

- Remember, this is not a test. There are no right or wrong answers and if there are any questions you don't understand just ask me to explain. It is your views that we are interested in and anything you can tell us will be important to the research.

- Confirm okay to record – 'it helps me to be able to listen really carefully to the things that you have to say'.

Introduction

Just to start with, please could I get some brief bits of information about you on the tape, so we know who the interview is with when we listen to it.

Get name, age and year group on the tape.

1 Pupil introduction

1.1 Is there anything you really like about school at the moment?

What do you like about it and why?

1.2 Is there anything you don't really like about school at the moment?

What don't you like about it and why?

1.3 Do you think you have changed in any ways since I first started coming to interview you?

Probe:

- In what ways?
- Why do you think that is?

Probe hobbies:

- Any new hobbies?
- Have you stopped being involved in any of the things you used to do in your spare time?
- Any hobbies you would like to take up?
- Reasons

Probe school activities:

- Any new activities at school out of lesson time?
- Any that you have stopped doing?
- Any activities you would like to be involved in?
- Reasons

1.4 Could I just check

a. Have there been any changes in whether you tend to join in any activities at school such as sports and social events?

b. Have there been any changes in your behaviour at school?

c. Have there been any changes in how well you think you are getting on at school?

d. Have there been any changes in your attendance?

Reasons

1.5 Which subjects do you learn best at school now?

Why do you think you learn those best?

Has that changed since I first started coming to interview you?

2 Views on learning about arts/artform

2.1 Can you remember what you thought about learning [arts/artform] at the beginning of last term/last year, when I first started coming to talk to you?

How important did you think it was?

How interested were you in it?

How much did you enjoy it?

2.2 Do you think your views have changed since then? In what ways?

Probe: importance, interest, enjoyment

2.3 Why do you think your views on learning [arts/artform] have changed?

For example:

- different teachers?
- different topics/content?
- different way of learning?
- a particular topic/activity/project that you've done?
- developed more understanding, improved knowledge or improved skills?

If in same year group as at start of initiative

2.4 How do you feel about the amount of time you spend on [arts/artform] in year [x]?

If changed year group since baseline (and if not already known)

2.5 Now that you are in year [x] what arts subjects are you taught?

2.6 How many lessons do you have a week in those subjects?

2.7 Is that different to the number of lessons you had last year?

How do you feel about those differences?

If followed through key stage 4

2.8 Are you pleased with the subjects you are doing for GCSE? Why? Why not?

Are there any subjects you are particularly pleased that you are doing?

Are there any you are not pleased that you are doing?

Are there any subjects you wish you were doing instead?

Reasons

If pupils are about to make their options for GCSE

2.9 Which subjects are you planning to take for GCSE? Why?

3 Follow-up content and process of interventions (with links to effects and outcomes on the pupil)

Note to interviewer: If this is at the end of a whole series/developmental initiative you will need to briefly clarify the length of each term's intervention and the organisations/artists worked with and artforms. Then for each content question and each process question you could ask for comparisons between the various projects.

I would like to follow up with you some things about the initiative/project [name it if possible] that you and your class were involved with, with [artist(s)/organisation], last term/last year … [as appropriate].

3.1 Firstly, just to check:

a. it was [… artist(s)/organisation] you worked with?

b. and it was in [music, art, dance, drama, other?]

c. and it was last term/last year …?

d. and how many session were there altogether?

e. where did the project take place?

3.2 Did you attend all the sessions/the whole project?

If no: How many did you miss?

Why did you miss them?

3.3 What do you think the aims were for the project?

Prompt: what do you think it was the artist and your teacher wanted you to get out of the project?

I'd like to ask you a few questions about **what** you were doing and learning about and then some on **how** you were doing and learning things.

3.4 So, firstly, can you remember what you were doing and learning about on the project?

Probe:

- What types of [music, art, dance, drama] did it involve?

- Was it based on any themes?

- Could you describe what it was about? – Details/examples

- Resources – equipment, tools, materials, instruments, spaces

3.5 Very briefly, what did you think about the content?

For example, enjoyable, helpful, appropriate?

Now I've got some questions about how you were doing and learning things.

3.6 Can you remember anything about how you were doing and learning things on the project?

Note to interviewer: Probe differences/similarities with the norm and what they thought of certain ways of working e.g. helpful, enjoyable?

a. How was the artist(s) working with you? What did you think about that?

b. What was teacher doing during the project when the artist(s) was there? What did you think that?

c. How was your class grouped? What did you think about that?

d. Could you choose who you worked with? What did you think about that?

3.7 a. How much practical activity did *you* get to do?

What did you think about that?

b. How much watching or listening to that artist(s) did *you* do?

What did you think about that?

3.8 Whose ideas were used in the project?

Probe:

- the artist(s)', the pupils', your own, the teacher's?
- What did you think about that?
- Who chose the topic or theme?
- What contribution could you and your class make to the project?

3.9 Were there times when the artist(s) or your teacher let you know how you were getting on and gave you some feedback?

Probe:

- How did they do that? [establish whether teacher or artist feedback]
- Was it helpful? Reasons

3.10 Was there a final performance or display as part of the project?

- What did you do for that?
- How did you feel when you performed the work?
- How did you feel when your work was displayed?

3.11 Was there any evaluation or assessment of the whole project?

For example, evaluation form, class test, class discussion

Probe:

- When did this take place?
- Who was involved in this evaluation?
- Was it helpful? Reasons.

4 Effects and outcomes

Effects on pupils

4.1 a. What are the main things you have got out of working on this project?

b. What do you think it was that has made that happen/made you feel like that?

- was it the way you were learning things?
- the things you were doing?
- the whole project?
- a specific activity?
- the performance or display?
- something else?

c. Could you give any examples of when this has happened …

4.2 a. Has the project made a difference to you in any way?

Probe:

- Has it made a difference to your attitudes or views on anything?
- Do you do anything differently?

b. What do you think made that difference?

- was it the way you were learning things?
- the things you were doing?
- the whole project?
- a specific activity?
- the performance or display?
- something else?

c. Could you give any examples of when this has happened …

I've got some questions now about some things that people sometimes say have happened to them because of doing [the arts/music/dance/drama/art], things that they have got better at, or things that have improved and I just wanted to check these with you. I'll also ask you for some examples if you feel this has happened to you.

Note to interviewer: these grey boxes contain previous 'definitions' of effects. Please use the example words as prompts only. You do not need to probe each of these words.

4.3 Enjoyment, for example, excitement, buzz, fun, happiness, sense of achievement or satisfaction, fulfilment

4.3 So, first of all, has the project made any difference to your enjoyment of [arts/artform]?

If yes: In what ways? Could you describe the type of enjoyment you have felt?

What do you think it was that has made that difference?

Examples within the intervention

If no: Why not?

4.4 Understanding, knowledge and appreciation of artform, for example, understanding and knowledge of processes, tools, techniques, materials and products, historical context. Ability to decode works of art. Appreciation or more positive attitudes towards works of art/processes/products.

4.4 Has it made any difference to your understanding and knowledge of [arts/artform]? [probe appreciation]

If yes: In what ways? Could you describe some of the things you understand more or have a better knowledge of now?

What do you think it was that has made that difference?

Examples within the intervention

If no: Why not?

4.5 Skills in the artform, for example, developing technical skills, practical approaches, methods, specific skills and tools of the trade.

4.5 Has the project made a difference to your skills in [arts/artform]?

If yes: In what ways? Could you describe some of the skills you have gained or improved on?

What do you think it was that has made that difference?

Examples within the intervention

If no: Why not?

> **4.6 Creativity, for example, imagination, experimentation, innovation, being inventive, developing ideas.**

4.6 Has it made any difference to your creative skills or creativity?

If yes: In what ways have you been creative because of the project?

What do you think it was that has made that difference?

Examples within the intervention

If no: Why not?

> **4.7 Thinking and problem-solving skills, for example, thinking more clearly, working around problems, challenging/ questioning ideas, thinking 'on the spot'.**

4.7 Has it made any difference to your thinking or problem-solving skills?

If yes: In what ways? Could you describe the types of thinking you have got better at because of the project?

What do you think it was that has made that difference?

Examples within the intervention

If no: Why not?

4.8 Communication skills, for example, development of use of language, communication with others, expressing opinions, views or feelings.

4.8 Has it made any difference to your communication skills?

If yes: In what ways? Could you describe the types of communication that have improved because of the project?

What do you think it was that has made that difference?

Examples within the intervention

If no: Why not?

4.9 Awareness of social, cultural and moral issues, for example, awareness of equal opportunities, racism, sexism etc. Cultural traditions, cultural diversity, multiculturalism

4.9 Has it made any difference to your knowledge and understanding of social (society) or cultural issues?

Probe: awareness of social and moral issues

If yes: In what ways? Could you describe the types of knowledge or understanding you gained of?

What do you think it was that has made that difference?

Examples within the intervention

If no: Why not?

4.10 Personal development, for example, sense of self, under-standing self better, self-esteem, self-confidence, belief in own abilities, coping with new situations.

4.10 Has it made any difference to your personal development?

If yes: In what ways? Could you describe the ways you have developed as a person.

What do you think it was that has made that difference?

Examples within the intervention

If no: Why not?

4.11 Social development, for example, abilities in teamworking, group work, cooperating and getting on with others, understanding others' point of view.

4.11 Has it made any difference to your social skills or social development?

If yes: In what ways? Could you describe the ways you have developed socially?

What do you think it was that has made that difference?

Examples within the intervention

If no: Why not?

4.12 Therapeutic outcomes and physical fitness/wellbeing, for example, relaxation, calming, release of tension/stress, escapism – particularly from other lessons, physical fitness

4.12 Do you think the project has had any effect on you in a relaxing way or on your wellbeing?

If yes: In what ways?

What do you think it was that has made that difference?

Examples within the intervention

If no: Why not?

If series/developmental ask 4.13

4.13 Thinking about all these effects that we have just talked about, would you say that any of these have built on the effects that happened to you from the previous project [with …]?

In what ways?

Examples

4.14 Do you think the project has made any difference to how interested you are in learning [artform]?

In what ways?

What do you think it was that has made that difference?

- was it the way you were learning things?
- the things you were doing?
- the whole project?
- a specific activity?
- the performance or display?
- something else?
- examples?

4.15 Do you think that the project has made any difference:

- to how interested you are in other subjects [including other artforms]?
- to the way you learn in other subjects [including other artforms]?
- to how much you understand in other subjects [including other artforms]?

In what ways?

What do you think it was that has made that difference?

- was it the way you were learning things?
- the things you were doing?
- the whole project?
- a specific activity?
- the performance or display?
- something else?
- examples?

4.16 Do you think that the project has made any difference:

- to how you feel about school in general?
- to how you behave in school?
- to your attendance in school?
- to any of the activities you take part in outside school? (might already be covered)

In what ways?

What do you think it was that has made that difference?

- was it the way you were learning things?
- the things you were doing?
- the whole project?
- a specific activity?
- the performance or display?

- something else?

- examples?

4.17 Do you think that the project has made any difference to what you might want to do for a career or job?

In what ways?

What do you think it was that has made that difference?

- was it the way you were learning things?

- the things you were doing?

- the whole project?

- a specific activity?

- the performance or display?

- something else?

- examples?

Effects on teachers

4.18 Do you think the project has made any difference to your [arts/artform] teacher(s)?

In what ways?

What do you think it was that has made that difference?

- was it the way you were learning things?

- the things you were doing?

- the whole project?

- a specific activity?

- the performance or display?

- something else?

- examples?

Effects on artist(s)

4.19 **Do you think the project has made any difference to the artist(s) who was involved?**

In what ways?

What do you think it was that has made that difference?

- was it the way you were learning things?
- the things you were doing?
- the whole project?
- a specific activity?
- the performance or display?
- something else?
- examples?

Effects on school

4.20 **Do you think the project has made any difference to your school?**

In what ways?

What do you think it was that has made that difference?

- was it the way you were learning things?
- the things you were doing?
- the whole project?
- a specific activity?
- the performance or display?
- something else?
- examples?

Effects on community and family

4.21 Do you think the project has made any difference to your family?

In what ways?

What do you think it was that has made that difference?

- was it the way you were learning things?
- the things you were doing?
- the whole project?
- a specific activity?
- the performance or display?
- something else?
- examples?

4.22 Do you think it has made a difference to other families or parents?

In what ways?

What do you think it was that has made that difference?

- was it the way you were learning things?
- the things you were doing?
- the whole project?
- a specific activity?
- the performance or display?
- something else?
- examples?

4.23 Has it made a difference to the community around the school?

In what ways?

What do you think it was that has made that difference?

- was it the way you were learning things?
- the things you were doing?

- the whole project?
- a specific activity?
- the performance or display?
- something else?
- examples?

Art as an outcome

4.24 How important would you say the final product or what you were making/doing was to you?

Probes:

- Did you see that as an outcome of the project?
- Was it essential to have made that product?
- Could the process have been worthwhile without it?

General

4.25 Out of all the effects we've just talked about, which has been the most important effect for you from this project and why?

5 Final evaluation of the initiative

5.1 Since finishing the project, has any work at school followed on or carried on from the project in any way?

- What work has followed on?
- In which subjects?
- How has it followed on?

5.2 Since finishing the project, what have you been doing and learning about in your [arts/artform] lessons?

a. Have you had any good [art/dance/drama/music] lessons since finishing the project? What made them good?

b. Since finishing the project, have you had any [art/dance/drama/music] lessons that were not so good? What made them not that good?

5.3 Just in your [artform] lessons, have you used any of the types of resources [such as .... refer to q. 3.4] since the project finished?

Examples

5.4 Has what you were doing and learning about on the project linked with any other subjects? In what ways?

5.5 Thinking of all the effects we talked about, that you felt had happened because of the project, have you noticed any of those effects in your [artform/arts] lessons since finishing the project?

Examples

5.6 Are you working with, or have you worked with, any artist(s)/organisations since the project I came to look at?

Probe:

- same artist(s)
- different artist(s)
- what were/are you doing?
- what did you/are you getting out of it?

5.7 Looking back at the project, do you think it was relevant and appropriate (suitable) as a project for you and your class?

Why/why not?

If series/developmental ask 5.8

5.8 Did you feel that what you were doing in each project built on the last project?

In what ways?/Why not?

5.9 Did you feel you knew enough about the project as it was taking place?

5.10 If you could make any changes to the project, what would those be?

5.11 Are there ways you would like the work you did on the project to continue in the future?

Anything else you would like to say? Thank you very much indeed for all your comments.

References

ARTS COUNCIL ENGLAND (2004). *The Impact of the Arts: Some Research Evidence*. London: Arts Council England.

ARTS COUNCIL OF ENGLAND (1997). *Leading Through Learning*. London: Arts Council of England.

BRISTOL ARTS PLAN (2001). *The Arts and Education Interface: Arts Plan*. Bristol: Bristol Education Action Zone.

BRISTOL EDUCATION ACTION ZONE (2001). *Bristol Education Action Zone: Review*. Bristol: Bristol Education Action Zone.

CASTLE, K., ASHWORTH, M. and LORD, P. (2002). *Aims in Motion: Dance Companies and Their Education Programmes*. Slough: NFER.

CHALLENGE FOR CORBY (1999). *Challenge for Corby*. Corby: Corby Education Action Zone.

DEPARTMENT FOR EDUCATION AND SKILLS (2003). *Excellence and Enjoyment: a Strategy for Primary Schools*. London: DfES.

DEPARTMENT FOR CULTURE, MEDIA AND SPORT. POLICY ACTION TEAM 10 (1999). *Arts & Sport: a Report to the Social Exclusion Unit*. London: Department for Culture, Media and Sport.

DEPARTMENT OF NATIONAL HERITAGE (1996). *Setting the Scene: the Arts and Young People*. London: DNH.

DOHERTY, P. and HARLAND, J. (2001). *Partnerships for Creativity: an Evaluation of Implementation*. Slough: NFER.

DOWNING, D. (1996). *Artists in Leeds Schools: a Review of Leeds City Council's Artists in Schools Programme*. Leeds: Leeds City Council, Department of Education.

DOWNING, D., ASHWORTH, M. and STOTT, A. (2002). *Acting with Intent: Theatre Companies and Their Education Programmes*. Slough: NFER.

DOWNING, D. and WATSON, R. (2004). *School Art: What's in it? Exploring Visual Arts in Secondary Schools*. Slough: NFER.

EISNER, E. (1998). 'Does experience in the arts boost academic achievement?' *Art Education*, **51**, 1, 7–15.

GARDNER, H. (1993). *Multiple Intelligences: the Theory in Practice*. New York, NY: Basic Books.

GODFREY, F. (2002). *Editorial. Opt for Art 1995–2000*. Engage*plus*. London: Engage.

GREAT BRITAIN. STATUTES (1999). *Protection of Children Act 1999. Chapter 14*. London: The Stationery Office.

HARLAND, J., KINDER, K., LORD, P., STOTT, A., SCHAGEN, I., HAYNES, J., CUSWORTH, L., WHITE, R. and PAOLA, R. (2000). *Arts Education in Secondary Schools: Effects and Effectiveness*. Slough: NFER.

HARLAND, J., MOOR, H., KINDER, K. and ASHWORTH, M. (2002). *Is the Curriculum Working? The Key Stage 3 Phase of the Northern Ireland Curriculum Cohort Study*. Slough: NFER.

INGS, R. (2002). 'The arts included.' Report of the First National Conference on the Role of the Arts in Pupil Referral Units and Learning Support Units, Gulbenkian Foundation and The Arts Council of England, Birmingham, 29 October.

JOYCE, B. and SHOWERS, B. (1982). 'The coaching of teaching', *Educational Leadership*, **40**, 1, 4–8.

KINDER, K. and HARLAND, J. (1991). *The Impact of INSET: the Case of Primary Science*. Slough: NFER.

LORD, P. (2003). *Pupils' Experiences and Perspectives of the National Curriculum: Updating the Research Review 2002–2003* [online]. Available: http://www.qca.org.uk/254_1956.html [15 February, 2005].

MOGA, E., BURGER, K., HETLAND, L. and WINNER, E. (2000) 'Does studying the arts engender creative thinking? Evidence for near but not far transfer', *The Journal of Aesthetic Education*, **34**, 304, 91–104.

ODDIE, D. and ALLEN, G. (1998). *Artists in Schools: a Review*. London: The Stationery Office.

PRINGLE, E. (2002). '*We Did Stir Things Up*'. *The Role of Artists in Sites for Learning*. London: Arts Council of England.

ROBINSON, K. (Ed) (1982). *The Arts in Schools: Principles, Practice and Provision*. London: Gulbenkian Foundation.

ROBINSON REPORT. DEPARTMENT FOR EDUCATION AND EMPLOYMENT. DEPARTMENT FOR CULTURE, MEDIA AND SPORT. NATIONAL ADVISORY COMMITTEE ON CREATIVE AND CULTURAL EDUCATION (1999). *All Our Futures: Creativity, Culture & Education*. London: DfEE.

SHARP, C. and DUST, K. (1997). *Artists in Schools: a Handbook for Teachers and Artists*. Slough: NFER.

TAMBLING, P. and HARLAND, J. (1998). *Orchestral Education Programmes: Intents and Purposes*. London: Arts Council of England.

TURNER, E. (1999). *Building Quality Links: Research on the Arts–Education Interface*. Stirling: University of Stirling, Institute of Education.

WINNER, E. and HETLAND, L. (2000). 'The arts and academic improvement: what the evidence shows', *Journal of Aesthetic Education*, **34**, 304, (whole issue).

Index

social and cultural knowledge
20, 36–7, 54, 55, 57, 63,
89, 155
social development 22–3, 34–5,
57, 63, 89, 157, 221
thinking skills 20–1, 37, 55, 57,
63, 89
transfer beyond the artform 24,
40–1, 50, 55, 57, 63, 89,
157
corroboration of 42–3
developmental learning 16, 75–88,
91
educational settings 62–9, 150–2
emotional health xiv, 220
factors affecting pupil outcomes
127–61
artist factors 128, 146, 200–1
artist–pupil relationship 131,
141–2
artist–teacher relationship 131,
144–5
artist's pedagogy 130, 136–7
behaviour 128
content 129, 137–8
continuity and progression 130,
142, 202–3
educational settings 129
enjoyability 129
frequency and importance of
131–6
group composition 130–1
group size 130
high profile factors 136–44,
159–60, 199–200
low profile factors 144–7,
160–1, 199–200

manageability for pupils 129,
138–9
pupil factors 128, 140
pupil–teacher relationship 131
pupils' sense of privilege 129,
147
relevance to pupils 129, 141
role of planning 131, 145–6
role of the final product 130,
139–40
site context 200
timing and time allocation 129
whole-school factors 128, 145
frequency, strength and nature 16,
17–43
and in-school arts teaching 67–9,
91
and intervention aims 16, 44–55,
90, 221
and interventions xi–xiii, 44–55,
70–5, 91, 188, 199–200, 204
mapping the outcomes 17–25
negative effects 41–2
self-esteem viii, ix, 22, 28–9,
33–4, 54–5, 60, 62, 69, 70,
77, 78, 83, 85–6, 89–90, 147,
172, 209, 220
variation by artform 55–62
variation by cost 69–70
variation by EAZ 70, 154
variation by educational setting
62–9
variation by type of intervention
70–5, 91

Robinson Report (1999) xiii–xiv,
219–20